THE BATTLE OF BONG SON

Operation *Masher/White Wing*, 1966

KENNETH P. WHITE

CASEMATE
Pennsylvania & Yorkshire

AN AUSA BOOK
Association of the United States Army
2425 Wilson Boulevard, Arlington, Virginia, 22201, USA

Published in the United States of America and Great Britain in 2024 by
CASEMATE PUBLISHERS
1950 Lawrence Road, Havertown, PA 19083, USA
and
47 Church Street, Barnsley, S70 2AS, UK

Copyright © 2024 Kenneth P. White

Hardcover Edition: ISBN 978-1-63624-401-3
Digital Edition: ISBN 978-1-63624-402-0

A CIP record for this book is available from the British Library

All rights reserved. No part of this book may be reproduced or transmitted in any form or by any means, electronic or mechanical including photocopying, recording or by any information storage and retrieval system, without permission from the publisher in writing.

Printed and bound in the United Kingdom by CPI Group (UK) Ltd, Croydon, CR0 4YY
Typeset in India by DiTech Publishing Services

For a complete list of Casemate titles, please contact:

CASEMATE PUBLISHERS (US)
Telephone (610) 853-9131
Fax (610) 853-9146
Email: casemate@casematepublishers.com
www.casematepublishers.com

CASEMATE PUBLISHERS (UK)
Telephone (0)1226 734350
Email: casemate@casemateuk.com
www.casemateuk.com

Cover image: Troops sweep area north of Phu Cat in Deception Phase. (National Archives)

Contents

Maps		vii
Prologue		xi
1.	Preparing for Battle	1
2.	Tragedy Strikes	17
3.	Attack	31
4.	Breakout from the Cemetery	43
5.	A Pincer Action	59
6.	Closing Out Phase I	75
7.	Into the An Lao Valley	83
8.	The Eagle's Claw	95
9.	Yelling Like Madmen	111
10.	Death in a Narrow Place	125
11.	The Iron Triangle	143
12.	No Rest for the Weary	155
13.	The Go Chai Mountains	167
14.	Black Horse	177
15.	Conclusion	187

Appendix I: Book of Honor, Operation Masher/White Wing, *January 24–March 5, 1966, in the Republic of Vietnam*	191
Appendix II: Memorandum Requesting Name Change	204
Appendix III: Citations	205
Glossary	209
Bibliography	213
Index	217

Maps

1.	South Vietnam	viii
2.	II Corps Tactical Zone	ix
3.	Binh Dinh Province	x
4.	Bong Son Area	15
5.	7th Cavalry Attacks the North Vietnamese at Phung Du, January 28, 1966	30
6.	Reinforcements Arrive, the Fighting Moves North, January 29–30, 1966	58
7.	Heavy Fighting Continues North and Northwest of Phung Du, January 31–February 1, 1966	74
8.	Attack into the Kim Son Valley, February 11, 1966	94
9.	7th Cavalry Attacks the Viet Cong in the Suoi Run Valley, February 15, 1966	123
10.	5th Cavalry Attacks Viet Cong Heavy Weapons Battalion, February 16–17, 1966	141
11.	Attack into the Iron Triangle, February 18–21, 1966	142
12.	1st Cav Base Camp at An Khe, February 19, 1966	166

Map 1. South Vietnam

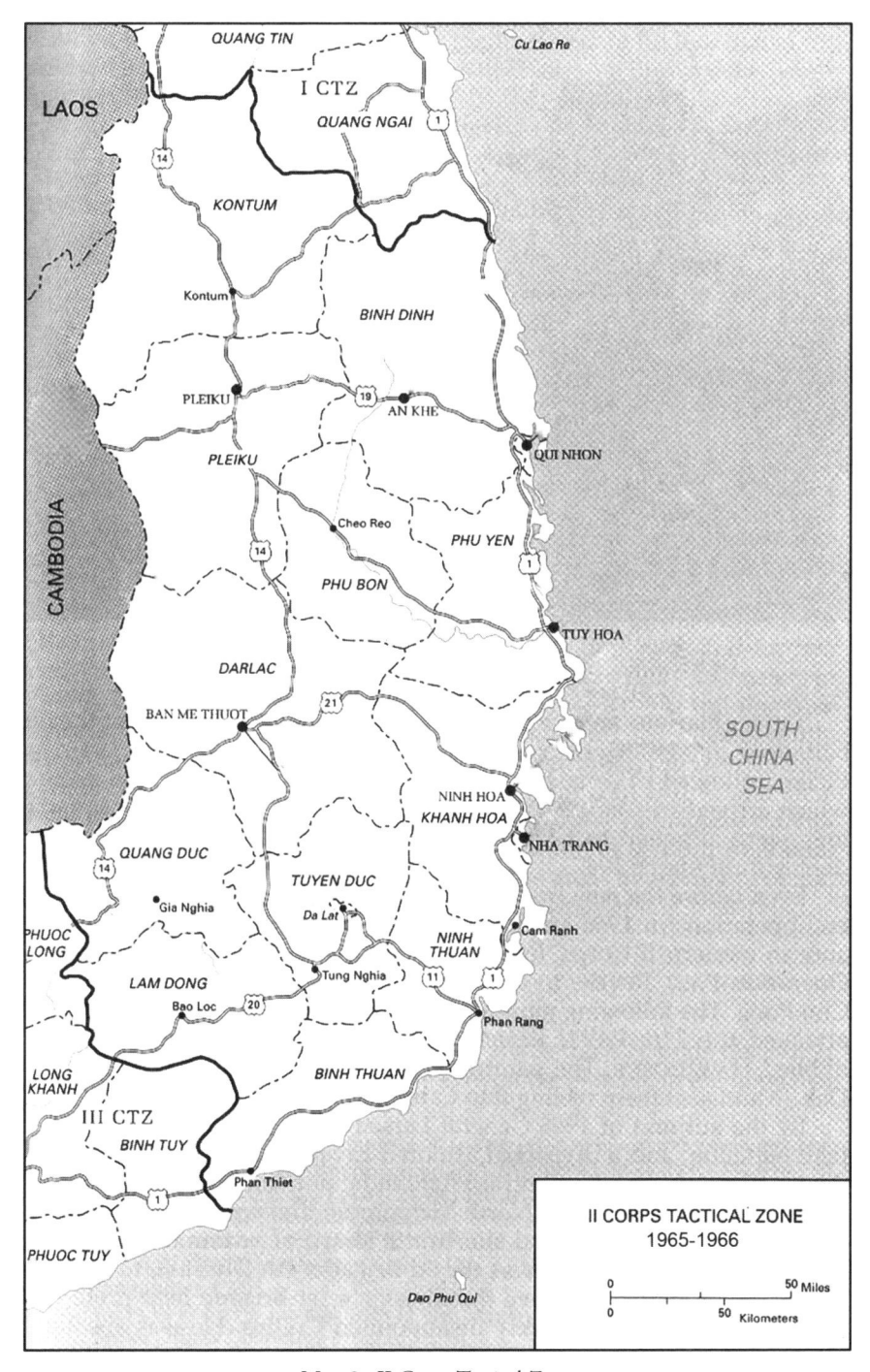

Map 2. II Corps Tactical Zone

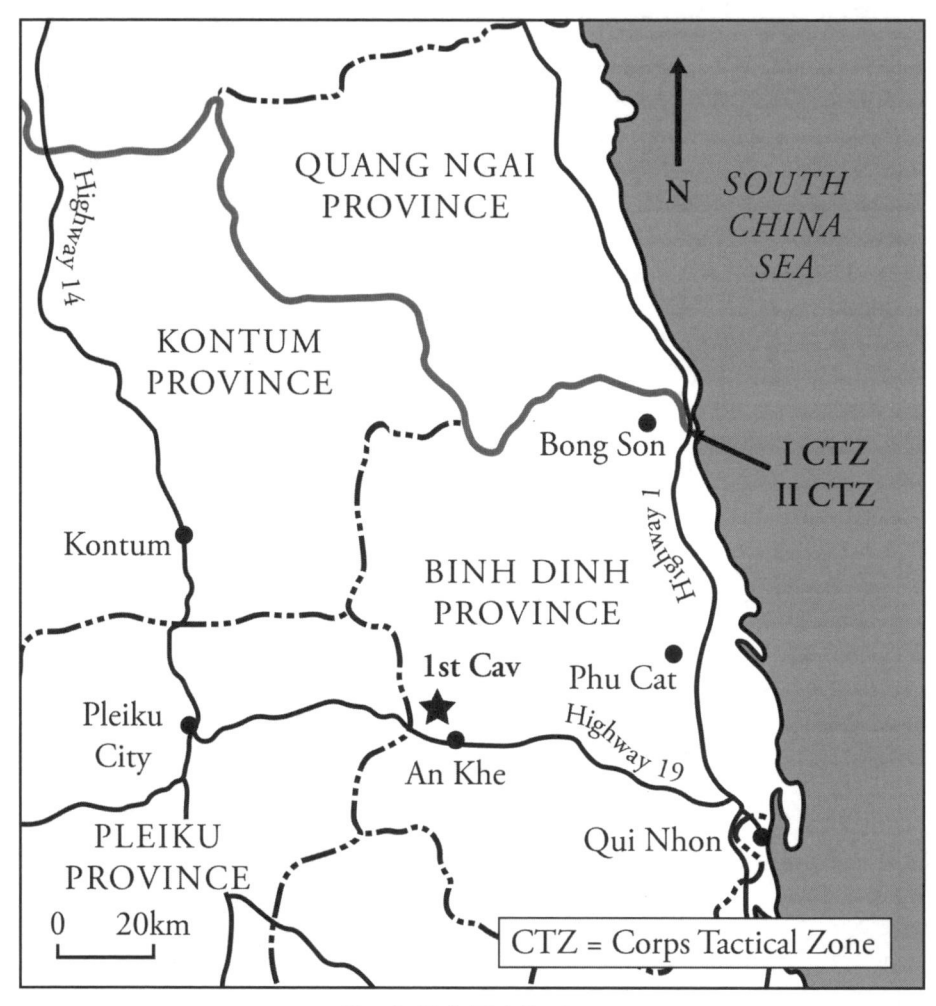

Map 3. Binh Dinh Province

Prologue

By the start of 1965, South Vietnam was in imminent danger of collapse.[1] The Communist Viet Cong had greatly increased the size of its fighting force in 1964 with the aggressive recruiting of local guerilla fighters, and had stepped up its attacks on the South Vietnamese government. Its master, the Communist North Vietnamese, had been sending conventional army units south since the summer of 1964 to support the Viet Cong in its guerilla war and to put pressure on the South Vietnamese military.[2] Senior U.S. military leaders at the Military Assistance Command, Vietnam (MACV), the joint-services command responsible for controlling the American war effort in Vietnam, estimated that the Viet Cong's fighting force had increased in size by nearly 50 percent in 1964, from 32 battalions at the beginning of the year to 46 battalions at the year's end—an increase of 14 battalions or the equivalent of roughly five regiments—and that the North Vietnamese had been sending entire regiments south for assignment to Viet Cong and North Vietnamese Army (NVA) divisions.[3] Senior U.S. military leaders also estimated that nearly three quarters of the country was under the control of the

---

[1] In a memorandum to President Lyndon B. Johnson in December 1964, Assistant Secretary of State William P. Bundy, together with National Security Advisor McGeorge Bundy and Secretary of Defense Robert McNamara, concluded that South Vietnam was in imminent danger of collapse. President Johnson declined to approve the Joint Chiefs of Staff proposed mission of attacks against North Vietnam in Operation *Flaming Dart*, and instead ordered McGeorge Bundy to travel to Saigon with a team of military and civilian experts to assess the situation there. William Conrad Gibbons, *U.S. Government and the Vietnam War, Executive and Legislative Roles and Relationships*, Part IV (Princeton, NJ: Princeton University Press, 1995), 13–14.

[2] A document identified the specific North Vietnamese Army regiments that were in South Vietnam in 1964 and the dates when they had arrived. Global Security, "North Vietnamese Army and Viet Cong Infantry/Artillery Regiments," www.globalsecurity.org.

[3] John M. Carland, *Combat Operations, Stemming the Tide, May 1965 to October 1966* (Washington, D.C.: Center of Military History, United States Army, 2000), 12.

Viet Cong and that its control was increasing.[4] Many of the roads between the cities and towns were blocked by the Viet Cong closing them to civilian travel, causing isolation and economic chaos in the rural areas. Furthermore, the unabated flow of Communist troops into the south reduced the role of the Army of the Republic of Vietnam (ARVN) to providing security for the provincial capitals and district headquarters, and the refugee camps that had grown up around them. General William C. Westmoreland, commander of the MACV, warned: "We are headed toward a Communist takeover ... sooner or later, if we continue down the present road at the present level of effort."[5]

Following a fact-finding trip to South Vietnam by President Lyndon B. Johnson's national security advisor, McGeorge Bundy, and a team of military and civilian experts, President Johnson approved a request from the Joint Chiefs of Staff and General Westmoreland to send ground troops to South Vietnam to buy time for the South Vietnamese government to complete a planned military buildup. President Johnson authorized four U.S. Marine battalions, totaling 3,800 men, to deploy to northern South Vietnam to defend the airbase at Da Nang, the Republic of Vietnam Air Force (VNAF) facility that was being used jointly by the VNAF and U.S. Air Force (USAF), to conduct bombing operations over North Vietnam.[6] A month later, President Johnson authorized three U.S. Army combat brigades, totaling 10,000 men, to deploy to central and southern South Vietnam to defend the airbases at Bien Hoa and Vung Tau that were also being used jointly by the VNAF and USAF to conduct bombing operations over North Vietnam, as well as to port facilities on the central South Vietnam coast to establish and maintain defenses

---

[4] The Communists were believed to control nearly three-quarters of South Vietnam. Ken Burns and Lynn Novick, *Vietnam War, An Intimate History*, based on documentary film by Burns and Novick (New York: Alfred A. Knopf, 2017), 147.

[5] General William C. Westmoreland, COMUSMACV (Commander, U.S. Military Assistance Command, Vietnam), "Military Estimate of the Situation in Vietnam. 5–12 March 1965," 5.

[6] General Westmoreland requested that 3,500 U.S. Marines be sent to northern South Vietnam to defend the airbase at Da Nang against Viet Cong forces, and that three U.S. Army combat brigades, totaling 10,000 men, be sent to central and southern South Vietnam to defend the port facilities under construction along the central coast, and to the airbases at Bien Hoa and Vung Tau that were being used to conduct bombing operations over North Vietnam. John M. Carland, *Combat Operations, Stemming the Tide, May 1965 to October 1966* (Washington, D.C.: Center of Military History, United States Army, 2000), 15; Stanley Karnow, *Vietnam: A History* (New York: Penguin Books, 1983), 431–33; Phillip B. Davidson, *Vietnam at War: The History, 1945–1975* (Novato, CA: Presidio Press, 1988), 343–44.

for supply facilities under construction there.⁷ Soon afterwards, President Johnson approved a proposal from the Joint Chiefs of Staff and General Westmoreland requesting a U.S. Army division, the 1st Cavalry Division (Airmobile),⁸ and a South Korean division, if obtainable, to deploy to South Vietnam to counter the continuing Viet Cong and North Vietnamese aggression.⁹ The 1st Cav would go to the Central Highlands and the Korean division to locations in the vicinity of Qui Nhon on the central South Vietnam coast. The divisions would assume ground combat roles and would allow General Westmoreland to begin offensive operations against the Viet Cong and North Vietnamese, something that he had been unable to do to date in the war.

The 1st Cav was a 16,000-man-strong force that had been testing the concept of fielding large formations of infantry transported and almost totally supported by helicopters. It had been testing the concept at Fort Benning, Georgia, for two years on the chance that it would be called on for duty in South Vietnam. The South Koreans responded to President Johnson's request by sending elements of the Republic of Korea (ROK) Capital "Tiger" Mechanized Infantry Division to South Vietnam, with the 3rd Battalion of the 1st Regiment arriving in September.

The 1st Cav arrived at the port of Qui Nhon in mid-August and set about constructing a base camp deep in the Central Highlands. It selected a site for the camp that was located along the boundary of Binh Dinh and Pleiku provinces, next to the U.S. Special Forces Camp at An Tuc/An Khe, along Highway 19, the main east–west road through the highlands.¹⁰ It was 65 kilometers west of Qui Nhon on

---

7   President Johnson conducted his "Why We Are in Vietnam" press conference to the nation on July 28, 1965. In it, he stated that America was in Vietnam "to fulfill one of the most solemn pledges of the American Nation—to help defend this small and valiant nation, and today I have ordered the Airmobile Division to South Vietnam." President Lyndon B. Johnson, "Why We Are in Vietnam" press conference, July 28, 1965, Part 2 of 3. https://www.historyonthenet.com/authentichistory/1961–1974/4-vietnam/1-overview/4–1964–1968/19650728_LBJ_Why_We_Are_In_Vietnam.html.

8   1st Cavalry Division (Airmobile) deployed to South Vietnam in stages, starting in early August 1965. 1st Cavalry Division Association, *The 1st Air Cavalry Division, Vietnam, August 1965–December 1969* (Paducah, Kentucky: Turner Publishing Company, 1995), 20–27.

9   Pentagon Papers (Gravel Edition), "National Security Action Memorandum 328, 6 April 65."

10 The advance party of the 1st Cavalry Division (Airmobile), together with the 70th Engineer Combat Battalion, started work clearing the area for a base camp at An Khe in August 1965. Major General T.J. Hayes III, "The Military Engineer: TME Looks Back: Vietnam, Army Engineers in Vietnam," USA, January–February 1966 issue.

the coast and 65 kilometers east of Pleiku City, the capital of Pleiku Province. From it, the 1st Cav could dominate the region by launching operations to the mountains and coastal lowlands to the east and to the high plateaus of the western Central Highlands and Cambodia to the west. The camp would also serve as a deterrent to the Viet Cong and North Vietnamese if they were to succeed in seizing control of the highlands and then attempt to split South Vietnam in half along the Pleiku City–Qui Nhon axis using Highway 19 as their main avenue of attack.[11]

By the start of October, the 1st Cav was ready for operations against the Viet Cong and North Vietnamese. Intelligence reports from the district police in Binh Dinh Province indicated that Viet Cong main force battalions were operating in the area directly east of the 1st Cav's base camp and in the mountains to the northeast of it. However, operations in Binh Dinh Province would have to wait. The division-sized B-3 Front of the North Vietnamese Army had launched its Tay Nguyen (Western Highlands) Campaign attacking the U.S. Special Forces Camp at Plei Me, 40 kilometers south of Pleiku City.[12] The camp was located on Provincial Route 5, a one-lane dirt road that veered off to the southwest from Highway 14, the main north–south road through the western Central Highlands, toward the camp and toward the eastern entrance to the Ia Drang Valley. The North Vietnamese had surrounded the camp with two regiments of infantry and had set an ambush north of it along Route 5 for any ARVN relief force from Pleiku City that might attempt to relieve the camp.

At the request of the South Vietnamese commander of the ARVN units operating in the Central Highlands, General Westmoreland directed Major General Kinnard, commander of the 1st Cav, to send a battalion-sized task force to Pleiku City to assume the security role from the ARVN unit that would be relieving the camp. The task force arrived at Pleiku City the next morning. As destiny would have it, the 1st Cav spent the next five weeks battling the regiments of the B-3 Front in the Ia Drang Valley. It soundly defeated them in a series of hard-fought battles and virtually destroyed them as an effective fighting force. By the end of November, the B-3 Front had had enough of the 1st Cav and fled the Ia Drang Valley into

---

[11] A document provided a detailed list of the early operations of the 1st Cav, from October 3–19, 1965, which included Operation *Shiny Bayonet* and Operation *Happy Valley*. Stephane Moutin-Luyat, *Vietnam Combat Operations, A Chronology of Allied Combat Operations in Vietnam, 1965* (Military Assistance Command, Vietnam (MACV), 2009).

[12] For "a detailed description of the siege at the U.S. Special Forces Camp at Plei Me in October 1965," see Captain Melvin F. Porter, "Siege of the U.S. Special Forces Camp at Plei Me, October 20–23, 1965." "Project CHECO Southeast Asia Report, The Siege of Plei Me, Report #160, 19–29 October 1965." USAF SE Asia Team, Project CHECO, 24 February 1966, 1–4.

neighboring Cambodia, where it took refuge in the jungle sanctuaries.[13] Shortly afterwards, the 1st Cav units were extracted from the Ia Drang Valley and returned to their base camp at An Khe for rest and refit.

This story is about the start of large-scale search-and-destroy operations against the Viet Cong and North Vietnamese. It is about ground troops from the U.S. Army's 1st Cavalry Division (Airmobile), supported by troop-carrying helicopters, helicopter gunships, and aerial- and ground-based artillery, searching for the Viet Cong and North Vietnamese in their jungle sanctuaries and attacking and destroying them when found. General Westmoreland believed that the best way to defeat the Communist troops was to use a search-and-destroy strategy to find them, together with the application of maximum American firepower on them when found. He believed that this strategy would eventually wear down the Communist troops to the point where the leaders in North Vietnam would be willing to negotiate an end to the war, with South Vietnam still relatively intact. Once this point was reached, pacification and political programs could be put in place by the ARVN to defeat the Viet Cong guerilla forces in the rural areas to help win the allegiance of the local populace to the South Vietnamese government.

This story is about air mobility being used to transport ground troops over great distances to strike at the enemy, often delivering troops to positions under intense enemy fire, resulting in pilots and crew members, as well as infantry passengers, being hit with automatic weapons and small-arms fire. It is about air mobility being used to extend the range of artillery guns to better support the attacking infantry troops by transporting the guns in sling load to locations on mountaintops and ridges that otherwise would not have been accessible to them because of the lack of roads.

This story is about South Vietnamese soldiers from the ARVN 22nd Infantry Division, the ARVN Airborne Brigade, and the ARVN 3rd Troop, 3rd Armored Cavalry Squadron, who supported the 1st Cav troops in the fighting and paid a heavy price for their participation in it.

This story is about weather—tropical weather that is dictated by a monsoon climate. In the Central Highlands, the monsoon delivered torrential downpours in the late afternoons and evenings, and drizzle with heavy ground fog in the early mornings, for much of the year. Frequently, the start of an operation would be delayed because of the weather, and the helicopters would be limited to flying in extreme combat emergencies only, and at extremely low altitudes and reduced air speeds, thereby increasing their vulnerability to enemy ground fire. Where possible, operations were planned taking into account the effect of the weather on target areas and enemy movements. This story is about weather that often interfered with the

---

[13] A description of the North Vietnamese Army division-sized B3 Front can be found in "Flames of Fire. B3 Front in Vietnam—Flames of War." https://fliphtml5.com/miqg/vmeh.

flow of battle. Rain and fog would move into an area, limiting visibility, resulting in a weather-hold keeping the supporting aircraft on the ground, forcing the attacking troops to halt their attack and pull back to a defendable position. Roving squads of enemy soldiers led by Viet Cong scouts familiar with the terrain then searched the battlefield in the rain and fog looking for any 1st Cav troopers who might have become separated from the main body of troops, or who might have been too badly wounded to link up with the main body, and execute them.

Finally, this story is about refugees—mostly women, children, and old men—who were either unable to flee the fighting before it started or were afraid to do so, fearing that if they did, the Viet Cong, when it returned, would give their hootches (huts) and small plots of land "to those more deserving." This story is about the failure of the South Vietnamese government to respond to the humanitarian needs of these people and to protect them from the Viet Cong and North Vietnamese.

CHAPTER ONE

Preparing for Battle

General Westmoreland considered the Central Highlands of South Vietnam to be strategically important to the American war effort. He understood that if the North Vietnamese were to succeed in seizing control of the highlands, they could attack to the east along the Pleiku City–Qui Nhon axis using Highway 19, the main east–west road through the highlands, as their main avenue of attack and possibly split South Vietnam in two. He also considered Binh Dinh Province, which was located along the central coast and bordered Pleiku Province on its west, to be key to the war effort in the highlands. Not only was it where Highway 19 emerged from the highlands onto the coastal plains and intersected with Highway 1, forming the main gateway to the highlands, but it was also where the U.S. Army's growing support complex at the port of Qui Nhon was located.

Binh Dinh Province consisted of narrow tropical lowlands, or plains, along the immediate coast and rugged jungle-covered mountains to the west. The plains were heavily cultivated and consisted of flat rice paddy fields, flooded with ankle- to knee-deep water, and small sandy, dry-crop islands covered with palm groves, bamboo thickets, and thatched-roof hootches in which the farmers and peasants who worked the rice paddy fields lived. Dikes partitioned the rice paddy fields into individual rice paddies and helped to control water levels. Where the plains were not cultivated, they consisted of tangled vegetation, fallen trees, and razor-sharp elephant grass. The mountains ranged in elevation from zero meters at the point where they met the rice paddies to 1,200 meters or more in the western sections of the province that bordered Pleiku Province. They were covered in double- and triple-canopy jungle that reached heights of 60 feet or more. The overgrown vegetation at ground level made moving through the mountains nearly impossible without the use of a machete. Heavily cultivated valleys cut through the mountains, extending the rice paddies beyond the immediate coastal area into the otherwise mountainous interior of the province. The plains were a major source of rice, as were the valleys.

In terms of land area, Binh Dinh Province was one of the largest provinces in South Vietnam and was also one of the most populous, with 800,000 or more inhabitants. Most of the people in the province lived in the port city of Qui Nhon in the Con River Basin in the southeast corner of the province, or else in the coastal plains and valleys north of Qui Nhon in the Phu Cat, Phu My, or An Lao areas, or in the town of Bong Son. The areas to the west and northwest of Qui Nhon were relatively sparsely populated.

The North Vietnamese had a longstanding stranglehold on the people in Binh Dinh Province and on rice production there, dating back to the period following World War II when the Communist Viet Minh (Ho Chi Minh's resistance army) wrestled control of the province away from the French colonial forces. Their hold on the people tightened over the years with the creation of the National Liberation Front in 1960 and with North Vietnamese Army regulars pouring into the province from North Vietnam via the Ho Chi Minh Trail in 1964 and 1965. Between the North Vietnamese and Viet Cong, Binh Dinh Province had become as complete an enemy stronghold as one could imagine. The influence of the South Vietnamese government there was almost non-existent, except for a government outpost and district headquarters at the U.S. Special Forces Camp at Bong Son. A small contingent of South Vietnamese soldiers from the ARVN's 22nd Infantry Division provided security for the camp and district headquarters. The soldiers, however, were reluctant to venture too far from the camp for fear of being ambushed by the North Vietnamese and Viet Cong. The camp was manned by a 12-man Special Forces A-team, Detachment A-321, and some 200 or so Montagnard tribesmen forming two Civilian Irregular Defense Group (CIDG) companies, along with their families who lived outside the camp. The camp was surrounded by a security fence and had a dirt airstrip next to it capable of accommodating USAF C-123 Provider and C-130 Hercules aircraft that served as the camp's main supply line.

The North Vietnamese considered Binh Dinh Province to be "liberated" territory, so much so that they constructed a barrier across Highway 1 at the southern end of Bong Son, a few hundred meters north of where Route 514 veered off from Highway 1 westward toward the Special Forces camp and An Lao Valley. It was proudly manned by a Viet Cong guard element that openly dared anyone to intervene. According to the American advisors at the Special Forces camp, no one went near it until the troops of the 1st Cav later arrived in the Bong Son area and drove the Viet Cong from the position.

When the 1st Cav arrived at Qui Nhon it immediately began constructing a base camp in the Central Highlands at a location previously selected by an advanced party from the division. From the camp, on the boundary between the provinces of Binh Dinh and Pleiku, the 1st Cav could dominate the mountains and coastal plains to the east and the western Central Highlands and Cambodia to the west. It was also hoped the camp would deter the Viet Cong and North Vietnamese from attempting to attack targets to the east using Highway 19 as a main avenue of advance.

By October 1965, construction of the camp was complete and the 1st Cav was ready for operations. However, while the 1st Cav had been busy with its base camp, the division-sized B-3 Front of the North Vietnamese Army laid siege to the U.S. Special Forces Camp at Plei Me, 40 kilometers south of Pleiku City at the eastern entrance to the Ia Drang Valley. At the request of the South Vietnamese commander of II Corps, the combat tactical zone for South Vietnamese military units operating in the Central Highland, General Westmoreland directed the 1st Cav to send a battalion-sized task force to Pleiku City to assume a security role from the ARVN unit that would be relieving the Special Forces camp. However, the 1st Cav spent the next five weeks battling the B-3 Front in the Ia Drang Valley, soundly defeating it in a number of hard-fought battles and virtually destroying it as an effective fighting force. At the end of November, the B-3 Front fled the Ia Drang Valley and took refuge in neighboring Cambodia, where it was safe from attack by the 1st Cav. President Johnson insisted that American forces honor the neutrality of Cambodia in spite of the fact that the North Vietnamese built large base complexes there from which they launched attacks into South Vietnam. With the immediate threat to the Special Forces camp over, General Westmoreland ordered the 1st Cav to return to its base camp at An Khe for rest and refit, and then to initiate search-and-destroy operations against the Viet Cong and North Vietnamese forces in the mountains and coastal plains of Binh Dinh Province to the east.

The Pleiku Campaign, as it was called, resulted in more than 1,450 enemy soldiers killed and 177 captured. The 1st Cav suffered 305 killed on the battlefield and more than 525 soldiers wounded. (The Pleiku Campaign is well documented in the books *We Were Soldiers Once … And Young*, by Lt. Gen. Harold G. Moore (Ret.) and Joseph L. Galloway, and *Pleiku, The Dawn of Helicopter Warfare in Vietnam*, by J. D. Coleman).

By mid-January 1966, intelligence reports from the district police of Hoai Nhon and Hoai An districts in northeast Binh Dinh Province indicated that the North Vietnamese Army's Sao Vang (Yellow Star) Division was operating in the province, and that two of its three regiments were in the Bong Son area. The Quyet Thang Regiment (18th NVA Regiment) was bivouacked in the vicinity of Dam Tra O-Lake, a large freshwater lake 16 kilometers southeast of Bong Son between Highway 1 and the South China Sea. The regiment was recovering from its brief, yet violent, encounter with the troops of the 1st Cav in the Soui Ca Valley, 25 kilometers southwest of Bong Son, in mid-December, when it suffered 137 soldiers killed in what the 1st Cav called Operation *Clean House*. In mid-January, the regiment was preparing to celebrate the Vietnamese New Year, Tết Nguyên Đán—or Tet for short—which started on January 21 and lasted until January 24.

The Quyet Tam Regiment (22nd NVA Regiment), the second regiment of the Sao Vang Division, was operating on the coastal plain north of Bong Son, also known as the Bong Son Plain, in the village of Phung Du, 11 kilometers north of the town. It was reported to be operating rice distribution and recruiting centers there. The 22nd NVA Regiment was a relatively new unit to South Vietnam that had infiltrated from North Vietnam in late 1965. It had returned only weeks earlier from southern Quang Ngai Province, where it completed its initial indoctrination to operations in the South.

The location of the Sao Vang Division's third regiment, the Quyet Chein Regiment (2nd Viet Cong Regiment), was unknown. It was reported to have recently left Binh Dinh Province for action in southern Quang Ngai Province, and in the absence of any hard intelligence to the contrary, was believed to still be there. The 2nd Viet Cong Regiment was one of the original Viet Cong main force regiments formed by the National Liberation Front (the political organization formed in the South in 1960 by the Communist North Vietnamese to overthrow the South Vietnamese government) and had been battling government forces in the northern provinces since that time. The regiment had been assigned to the Sao Vang Division in September 1965, as the third of the division's three regiments when the division was formed to reinforce the Viet Cong in its guerilla war against the South Vietnamese government.

The Viet Cong political organization in the area, the D21 Local Force Company, was also known to be operating in both the Bong Son area and in the An Lao Valley to the west.

The intelligence reports in mid-January also indicated that three unidentified and unconfirmed NVA/Viet Cong battalions with an estimated total strength of 2,000 were on the Bong Son Plain, indicating that some type of redistribution of forces was being undertaken by the North Vietnamese command in the province.

The operation against the North Vietnamese and Viet Cong in Binh Dinh Province would be known as Operation *Masher* and would be led by Major General Harry W. O. Kinnard and the 1st Cav. It would be the start of large-scale search-and-destroy operations against the Viet Cong and NVA in South Vietnam and would be the largest offensive operation undertaken by the MACV since it was formed in 1962. It would also be a test of General Westmoreland's search-and-destroy strategy where the troops of the 1st Cav—supported by troop-carrying helicopters, helicopter gunships, and aerial- and ground-based artillery—would search for the Viet Cong and North Vietnamese in their jungle sanctuaries and attack and destroy them when found.

Major General Kinnard was known as the paratroop officer of the 101st Airborne Division in World War II who suggested the famously defiant answer "Nuts" to a German demand for the 101st to surrender in Bastogne during the Battle of the Bulge in December 1944. Kinnard lived a life of service to his country, which included battling the Japanese in the Pacific as well as the Germans in Europe. Shortly after graduating from the U.S. Military Academy at West Point, he was assigned to Pearl Harbor, where on the morning of December 7, 1941, he manned a machine-gun position defending the base against the attacking Japanese. In the early hours of D-Day, June 6, 1944, as part of Operation *Overlord*, he parachuted into the flooded plains surrounding the town of Sainte-Mère-Église to secure the exits that the American troops would need later that morning to get off Utah and Omaha beaches. In September 1944, during Operation *Market Garden*, he participated in the Allies' airborne attack against German forces in the Netherlands, for which he was awarded the Distinguished Service Cross, the nation's second-highest medal for heroism in combat.

In the late 1950s and early 1960s, Kinnard was instrumental in the development of the airmobile concept. As a brigadier general, he commanded the 11th Air Assault Division (Test) at Fort Benning, Georgia, where for two years it tested the concept of transporting and almost totally supporting infantry troops by helicopter. In July 1965, when President Johnson announced that he was sending the "airmobile division" to Vietnam to counter the increasing North Vietnamese aggression, the Pentagon stated that the colors of the 11th Air Assault Division (Test) were being cased and retired, and that the division was being redesignated the 1st Cavalry Division (Airmobile), with Kinnard as commander.

Kinnard would lead his troops through Operation *Masher*, which would target the heavily populated and agriculturally rich area of Bong Son in the coastal region in northeast Binh Dinh Province, 85 kilometers north of Qui Nhon and 450 kilometers northeast of Saigon. The operation would consist of two phases, preceded by deception operations intended to disguise the 1st Cav's main area of interest and allow the division to move its troops from its base camp in the highlands to the coastal plains and into positions close enough to Bong Son from which they could attack the enemy. The deception operations would be conducted along the immediate coast south of Bong Son; they would start on January 24 and end on January 27.

Phase I would start immediately after the deception operations ended. It would target the North Vietnamese units known to be operating regimental recruiting and rice distribution centers in the hamlet of Phung Du on the Bong Son Plain. It would run from January 28 to February 4. Phase II would start immediately after Phase I ended, with the 1st Cav shifting its direction from the Bong Son Plain west to the An Lao Valley, known to be a major north-to-south logistical and communications route for North Vietnamese and Viet Cong units moving through the area. It would target the NVA units operating there, and would also search for the headquarters of the Sao Vang Division believed to be located on the high ground north of the An Lao Valley, and if found, attack and destroy it. Phase II would run from February 4 to March 6. In total, the deception operations and the two phases were expected to last six weeks.

The timing of Operation *Masher* was such that the 1st Cav would be able to move its troops to the Bong Son area and position them to attack the North Vietnamese on the morning of January 28 without disrupting the Tet holiday. Tet was the biggest and most popular Vietnamese holiday of the year. It symbolized the solidarity of the Vietnamese people, and senior American commanders in South Vietnam understood the importance that the South Vietnamese people placed on Tet and were careful to honor it. Attacks or major operations by the Americans during the holiday period would, it was felt, be deeply resented by the South Vietnamese people and would likely only hurt the American cause.

The 3rd Brigade of the 1st Cav, commanded by newly promoted Colonel Harold ("Hal") G. Moore, would lead Phase I. Units from the 1st and 2nd Brigades of the 1st Cav would be prepared to reinforce the 3rd Brigade if the size of the enemy forces located and engaged warranted additional infantry support. The 2nd Brigade, led by Colonel William R. Lynch, Jr., would join Moore and the 3rd Brigade for Phase II.

Colonel Hal Moore was a self-made warrior. He expected nothing less than the best, both from himself and from the troopers in his command. At the age of 17, he dropped out of St. Joseph Preparatory School in Bardstown, Kentucky, before finishing high school and moved to Washington, D.C., because he felt that his chances of getting an appointment to West Point were better if he was living in a big city. There, he got a job working during the daytime in the U.S. Senate book warehouse in the Senate Office Building and finished high school at night, graduating from St. Joseph Preparatory School with his class of 1940, at the age of 18. Shortly afterward, while still working days at the U.S. Senate book warehouse and now attending evening classes at George Washington University, he received an appointment to West Point after first turning down one to the U.S. Naval Academy.

During the Korean War, Moore commanded a mortar company and then a rifle company in the 7th Infantry Division. In the late 1950s and early 1960s, he was involved in the development of the airmobile concept at Fort Benning along with then-Brigadier General Harry Kinnard. As a lieutenant colonel, he was instrumental in the development of the airmobile concept setting the standards for airmobile training and testing. In July 1965, when the Pentagon announced that the 11th Air Assault Division (Test) would become the 1st Cavalry Division (Airmobile), Moore's 2/23rd Infantry battalion was redesignated the 1st Battalion, 7th Cavalry Regiment (1/7th Cav). This was the same unit that Lieutenant Colonel George Armstrong Custer commanded nearly a century earlier at the battle of the Little Bighorn. At the battle of LZ X-Ray in the Ia Drang Valley, in November 1965, Moore's determination paid off when the 1/7th Cav found itself fighting for its very survival against a North Vietnamese force that greatly outnumbered it. Moore's leadership was credited with the unit's survival, and he was awarded the Distinguished Service Cross for his actions. After the battle, he was promoted to colonel and commanded the 3rd Brigade. Two years later, he was promoted to brigadier general, making him the first of his West Point class of 1945 to reach the general officer ranks.

After the battle at LZ X-Ray, the troops of the 1/7th Cav nicknamed Moore "Old Yellow Hair," after Custer. Moore, like Custer, had light-colored hair and a light complexion, but unlike Custer, Moore was able to defeat the enemy.

The 3rd Brigade consisted of the 1st and 2nd Battalions, 7th Cavalry Regiment; the 1st Battalion (Airborne) and 2nd Battalion, 12th Cavalry Regiment; and the 1st Squadron, 9th Cavalry Regiment—a battalion-sized reconnaissance squadron of observation helicopters and gunships, and aero- and ground-based rifle platoons. It included aerial- and ground-based artillery batteries, aviation units, engineering companies, and other support units, and totaled nearly 5,700 men. For Phase II, the 1st and 2nd Battalions, 5th Cavalry Regiment, along with additional artillery, aviation, engineering, and support units from the division, would join the operation.

Although the 3rd Brigade got the assignment to lead the operation, the brigade, as well as the division as a whole, was suffering from combat fatigue as a result of the battles in the Ia Drang Valley two months earlier.[1] The 3rd Brigade had suffered 237 killed in action, 258 wounded, and four missing. The division overall had suffered 305 killed in action, more than 525 wounded, and nine missing. Many of the units in the brigade, as well as in the division, were operating at less than 80 percent of their authorized strength, with large numbers of their troopers being replacements who had only arrived in country in mid-December or early January. Consequently, the units were still not fully reconstituted after the fights in the Ia Drang Valley. Of equal concern was the condition of the division's helicopters. In mid-January, 108 of its 478 helicopters were not flyable due to damage received in the fighting in the Ia Drang Valley, and were sitting on the helipad at the division's base camp at An Khe awaiting new parts in order to resume operations.

The division was also dealing with the drain on manpower caused by malaria.[2] In the first three months that the 1st Cav had been in country, nearly 3,000 of its troopers had contracted malaria. Sick with high fevers, uncontrollable shaking, and chills, they had to be pulled out of the field and transported to the 15th Med aid station back at An Khe, where doctors and medics worked to get their fevers down. The troopers almost always recovered from the disease and returned to their units in the field after 10 days or so, but the high rate of infection in some units—especially in the infantry units—created turmoil in the ranks and severely hindered a unit's strength and combat effectiveness.

In 1965, the U.S. Army had well-established procedures for dealing with malaria based upon its experiences in previous wars, such as during World War II in the South Pacific. The troops in Vietnam were provided with anti-malaria pills (chloroquine-primaquine-phosphate), mosquito netting, and insect repellent, but they quickly learned just how difficult it was to take advantage of these measures under battlefield conditions. There were two types of anti-malaria pills: a big orange one that was to be taken by mouth once a week, on the same day of the week if possible, and a little white one that was to be taken daily except on the day that you took the big orange one. Both were intended to be taken with food. Failure to follow these rules could result in an upset stomach, or worse, diarrhea. The troops

---

[1] John M. Carand, *Combat Operations, Stemming The Tide, May 1965 to October 1966* (Washington, D.C.: Center of Military History, United States Army, 2000), 201–03.

[2] Personnel statistics showed the extent to which malaria and other infectious diseases affected division manpower in January 1966. 1st Cavalry Division (Airmobile), "Quarterly Command Report for Second Fiscal Quarter, FY 1966, 1 Oct–31 Dec 65," 5.

quickly learned how important it was whenever possible to avoid places where mosquitoes bred, such as standing water, and to protect themselves by keeping their fatigue sleeves rolled down, in spite of the heat, and using mosquito nets and repellent agents.

The only silver lining to the malaria problem was that the North Vietnamese and Viet Cong suffered from the disease as much as did the Americans, if not more.[3] The following passage from a captured Viet Cong document, *Medical Section of Viet Cong Group 81*, described the malaria situation for the Viet Cong in South Vietnam in 1966:

> Malaria is now the primary cause which impairs our health, decreases our strength, and hinders our activities. In many areas, the rate of malaria cases increased from 40 percent to 50 percent in 1966. In some units, the malaria rate has been recorded as high as 80 percent and has caused units to discontinue combat operations for periods as long as one month. An analysis of 3,505 current Viet Cong/North Vietnamese Army hospital records reveals that approximately 67.4 percent of the medical admissions were hospitalized due to malaria.
>
> Malaria rates vary from two percent to 100 percent of the strength of individual units. The malaria incidence rate is highest during the months of March through June in Kontum and Pleiku Provinces, while in other areas, the rainy season (May through August) produces the highest incident rate of malaria. The overall malaria rate for VC/NVA forces in South Vietnam during 1966 was 155 per 1,000 personnel per month. A sharp increase in the malaria rate is experienced when the troops travel through Laos and Cambodia and enter Kontum and Pleiku Provinces.

Colonel Moore's plan for the operation called for the troops of the 3rd Brigade to move to the Bong Son area in stages, starting on January 24. The 1/12th Cav would move by helicopter to an area immediately north of Phu Cat on the coastal plains, 45 kilometers south of Bong Son. The 1/7th Cav would move to the area by convoy. The area was designated Landing Zone (LZ) Hammond and would serve as an aircraft laager area and forward support base for the division.

On January 25, the 1/7th Cavalry would move northward by convoy 35 kilometers to the southern portion of the Cay Gap Mountains, 10 kilometers south of Bong Son, and initiate reconnaissance-in-force operations toward the coast. The 1/9th Cav would support the 1/7th Cav in its reconnaissance operations as well as conduct aerial and ground reconnaissance in the LZ Hammond area. Lieutenant Colonel Robert McDade and his 2nd Battalion, 7th Cavalry would move by USAF C-123 Provider and U.S. Army CV-2 Caribou aircraft from the division's base camp at An Khe to the Special Forces Camp at Bong Son. There, they would occupy positions to secure the camp for the brigade's forward command post and be prepared to act as a ready reaction force for the units conducting deception operations to the south.

---

[3] Captain Robert E. Wright, ADA Adjutant, "4th PSYOP Group Special Report—Effect of Malaria on Combat Effectiveness of Viet Cong and North Vietnamese Army Forces (U)" (Carlisle, PA: U.S. Army Military History Institute, Army War College, March 3, 1969), 1–10. Translation of captured Viet Cong document.

After what happened in the Ia Drang Valley two months earlier, Colonel Moore wanted to keep the battalions well within mutual supporting distance of each other in the event that one of them encountered trouble and required reinforcement. At LZ X-Ray in the Ia Drang Valley, the 1/7th Cav found itself fighting for its very survival some 25 kilometers and a 30-minute round-trip helicopter flight from the nearest force capable of reinforcing it. Colonel Moore wanted to make sure that at no time in this operation would a battalion be more than a 10–15-minute round-trip helicopter flight away from reinforcements.

Lieutenant Colonel McDade was one of only a few officers to have served in an infantry unit in each of three wars. In World War II, he commanded a rifle platoon in the South Pacific; in the Korean War, he commanded a rifle company; and in the Vietnam War, he commanded the 2nd Battalion, 7th Cav. He was awarded several medals for his actions in combat and was wounded four times. History, however, would remember him as the commander of the American unit that suffered the largest number of casualties in a single battle in the Vietnam War—the 2/7th Cav, at LZ Albany in the Ia Drang Valley, on November 17, 1965. In that battle, the 2/7th Cav suffered 155 KIA, 124 WIA, and four MIA. The enemy—the 8th Battalion, 66th NVA Regiment; the 1st Battalion, 33rd NVA Regiment; and the headquarters element of the 3rd Battalion, 33rd NVA Regiment—also suffered heavy casualties in the battle, leaving 403 bodies on the battlefield. Historians and military experts alike have written numerous articles about what happened at LZ Albany, making it one of the most analyzed battles of the entire Vietnam War.

On January 26 and 27, the 1/7th Cav would intensify its deception operations by continuing to sweep northward along the coast toward Bong Son, while the 1/9th Cav would continue to support the 1/7th Cav in its reconnaissance operations. The 2/7th Cav would air assault from the Special Forces camp northward to a position 5 kilometers north of Bong Son, on the high ground, adjacent to Highway 1, designated Position Dog. It would secure the position for the 3rd Brigade's forward command post. Dog would serve as the jumping-off point for the 7th Cav's attack into the Bong Son Plain on January 28. The 2nd Battalion, 12th Cavalry, would move by USAF C-123 and CV-2 aircraft from the division's base camp in the highlands to the Special Forces Camp at Bong Son and remain there on stand-by ready to reinforce the troops of 7th Cav, as needed. Phase I would begin on the morning of January 28.[4]

Operation *Masher* would be supported by the ARVN 22nd Infantry Division, an ARVN Airborne Brigade from Saigon's general reserve, and the 3rd Battalion, 1st Regiment of the Republic of Korea (ROK), Capital "Tiger" Mechanized Infantry Division. The Korean battalion had only arrived in South Vietnam in late September

---

[4] Description of coastal plain north of Bong Son based on topographic maps of Vietnam, Binh Dinh Province, Hoai Nhon District, Map sheet 6837-IV, and author's recollection. http://www.rjsmith.com/topo_map.html. Ray's Map Room. Vietnam Areas of Operation.

1965, and in mid-January 1966 was still preparing for combat operations. The U.S. III Marine Amphibious Force, Task Force Delta, a multi-battalion-sized task force, would carry out a complementary operation to Operation *Masher* in neighboring Quang Ngai Province to the north of Binh Dinh Province. The III Marine Amphibious Force had been released of its passive defensive mission at the Da Nang airbase by President Johnson and authorized to move out and engage Viet Cong and North Vietnamese forces in combat.

In Operation *Thang Phong II*, the South Vietnamese companion operation to Operation *Masher*, the 40th (Mechanized) Regiment of the ARVN 22nd Infantry Division would secure the area immediately south of Bong Son, to include Route 514 and the areas around the Special Forces camp, the district headquarters, and the refugee center next to the camp. The 41st Regiment of the ARVN 22nd Infantry Division would secure Highway 1 from south of Bong Son to the vicinity of LZ Hammond, a distance of 45 kilometers, and the ARVN Airborne Brigade would secure Highway 1 in the area directly east of the Bong Son Plain.

In Operation *Flying Tiger*, the Korean companion operation to *Masher*, the 3rd Battalion, 1st Regiment, of the ROK Capital Infantry Division would secure Highway 1 from the point where it intersected with Highway 19 to LZ Hammond, a distance of 25 kilometers. The Korean battalion would also secure Highway 19 from where it intersected with Highway 1 west to the An Khe Pass. Security of the pass and Highway 19 west to the 1st Cav's base camp would be handled by the 1st Cav as part of its routine base camp security.

Security of Highways 19 and 1 by the Koreans and ARVN would ensure that the 1st Cav had a secure ground supply line by road from its base camp in the highlands to Bong Son, a distance of 120 kilometers. It would also ensure that the two roads were open to civilian travel between An Khe and Qui Nhon, and Qui Nhon and Bong Son.

Finally, in Operation *Double Eagle*, the U.S. Marines would sweep from the coast southward across Quang Ngai Province toward the provincial boundary with Binh Dinh Province and the northern portion of the An Lao Valley, destroying any North Vietnamese forces they encountered and preventing any enemy forces from fleeing northward into the province to escape the attacking 1st Cav. It would also include U.S. Navy destroyers offshore that would provide naval gunfire in support of 1st Cav operations.

Timed to coincide with the end of the deception operations and planning phase of Operation *Masher*, reconnaissance activities would be initiated on the evening of January 27 and would continue for a period of five days in parallel to the 3rd Brigade's operations on the Bong Son Plain. Special Forces Detachment B-52, also known as Project Delta, would conduct surveillance activities west of the Bong Son Plain in the An Lao Valley, while the 1st Cav was busy battling the North Vietnamese at Phung Du. Project Delta was an elite American/South Vietnamese long-range reconnaissance unit that had been in existence since 1964. It had caught the attention of General Westmoreland and his commanders at the MACV for its ability to operate in enemy territory and provide first-hand intelligence on enemy positions and movements.

The detachment was headed by Major Charles Beckwith, also known as "Chargin' Charlie," who was instrumental in the activities leading up to the battles in the Ia Drang Valley two months earlier. As the commander of Project Delta, Major Beckwith organized a reinforcing and ready-reaction force consisting of several American advisors and two companies of South Vietnamese Rangers, totaling about 175 men, and led the force through enemy lines to get into the Special Forces camp at Plei Me[5] while it was under siege from the B-3 Front's 32nd and 33rd Regiments at the start of the Pleiku Campaign.[6] Once inside the camp, Major Beckwith, as the senior officer present, took charge. He immediately reorganized the defenses and launched a breakout against the enemy soldiers who laid siege to the camp. The breakout, however, was short-lived. The Rangers had barely cleared the gate when a battalion from the 33rd Regiment opened fire on them from well-dug-in positions. The Rangers immediately started to take casualties and were forced to retreat back into the camp in chaos, but not before 14 men had been killed, including one of the American advisors to the Ranger companies.

For the reconnaissance activities in the An Lao Valley, three long-range reconnaissance teams would be inserted into the valley for the purpose of confirming the presence of large North Vietnamese forces there. It was reported by the MACV Binh Dinh Sector Advisor at the Special Forces camp that one of the three battalions of the 22nd NVA Regiment, possibly the 8th Battalion, was garrisoned at the district headquarters in An Lao village. It was believed that the headquarters of the Sao Vang Division was located on the high ground north of the valley, along the Binh Dinh–Quang Ngai provincial boundary. The teams would be inserted just before dark on the evening of January 27, and if they found the enemy, the 1st Cav would respond with a reaction force prepared to engage and destroy them, according to

---

[5] A document provides a description of the reaction force at the Plei Me Special Forces Camp in October 1965. Captain Melvin F. Porter, "Project CHECO the Southeast Asia Report: The Siege of Plei Me, Report #160, 19–29 October 1965," USAF SE Asia Team, Project CHECO, February 24, 1966, 3–4.

[6] A document from Ray Davidson describes the U.S. Special Forces Project Delta, commanded by Major Charles Beckwith. Project Delta was selected to reconnoiter the northern end of the An Lao Valley in search of the headquarters of the Sao Vang Division in parallel to the 3rd Brigade's attack into Phung Du. Intelligence gathered by the Project Delta teams would be used by the 1st Cav in Phase II of Operation *Masher*. Ray Davidson, "A Man is Not Dead Until He is Forgotten, The Story of Frank N. Badolati," http://www.projectdelta.net.

the plan that Colonel Moore and his 3rd Brigade commanders developed with Major Beckwith.

The hamlet of Phung Du, where the North Vietnamese were known to be located, was a large, sandy, dry-crop island that was surrounded by flooded rice paddies and ringed with palm groves with tall palm trees, bamboo thickets, hedgerows, and elephant grass. Hootches, where the farmers and peasants who worked the rice paddies lived, were scattered among the palm groves. The hootches were typically arranged in clusters of four or five, with small corn fields, potato patches, and fenced-in areas for chickens, pigs, and other livestock located next to them. Some of the clusters had small burial areas, or graveyards, located nearby, with burial mounds dotting the surface. The dead were buried on top of the ground and covered with mounds of dirt. Many of the hootches had shelters or holes nearby that were dug into the ground, where the villagers could take cover in the event of nearby fighting. They also had wells where they could get fresh ground water for drinking. The hamlet had an estimated population of several hundred or more inhabitants. It was similar to the other rice-growing hamlets on the Bong Son Plain, except that its location was significant: at the geographical center of the southern portion of the plain at the intersection of a network of heavily traveled trails—some dirt, some partially asphalt—that allowed the villagers to travel between the hamlets and Highway 1 to the east, where Bong Son to the southeast and Tam Quan to the northeast were located. The trails were wide enough to allow handcarts to be used to bring rice to the markets at harvest time, and they provided access to the neighboring hamlets that otherwise may not have been accessible without splashing through flooded rice paddies.

The provincial boundary between Binh Dinh and Quang Ngai provinces not only divided the two provinces, but also divided I Corps (pronounced "Eye Core") and II Corps ("Two Core") Tactical Zones. During the war, South Vietnam was divided into four corps, or military regions, by the American and South Vietnamese militaries for purposes of tactical operations. Each corps was an administrative and command area. I Corps was located in the northernmost portion of South Vietnam and extended from the southern boundary of the demilitarized zone (DMZ) separating North and South Vietnam to the southern boundary of Quang Ngai Province, just north of the Bong Son Plain. It consisted of five provinces and included the cities of Quang Tri, Dong Ha, Hue, Da Nang, and Chu Lai. American military units operating in I Corps were under the administrative control of the U.S. III Marine Amphibious Force, while South Vietnamese units were under the control of the South Vietnamese I Corps.

II Corps was located immediately south of I Corps and extended southward to the northern boundary of III Corps, north of the Saigon/Long Binh area. It consisted of the provinces of South Vietnam's Central Highlands, including Binh Dinh, Pleiku, and Kontum provinces. U.S. military units operating there were under the administrative control of the U.S. Army's I Field Force (pronounced "First" Field Force); South Vietnamese units there were under the control of the South Vietnamese II Corps.

Administrative and command areas were such that tactical, or maneuver, units were not supposed to go beyond their assigned command boundaries. Thus, the U.S. Marines would be restricted from maneuvering southward across the provincial boundary into Binh Dinh Province to engage any North Vietnamese forces attempting to escape the attacking 1st Cav. Likewise, the 1st Cav, the ARVN Airborne Brigade, and the regiments of the ARVN 22nd Infantry Division would be unable to pursue fleeing enemy forces northward from Binh Dinh Province across the provincial boundary into southern Quang Ngai Province.

A great deal of discussion among General Westmoreland and his planners at I Field Force Vietnam was devoted to the tactic of the hammer-and-anvil at the operational level. With it, one force—in this case, the U.S. Marines—would create a solid barrier against which an attacking force—the 1st Cav—would drive the enemy, thereby shattering it. But the hamlet of Phung Du was a day's march from the provincial boundary, and much of the terrain between it and the provincial boundary was open rice paddy fields and rolling hills. It would be difficult for enemy soldiers to move across this area and hide from pursuing observation helicopters, gunships, and aero rifle platoons. The enemy soldiers might instead try to flee westward to the Da Dan Mountains and An Lao Valley.

While the troops of the 7th Cav and 12th Cav would be busy battling the North Vietnamese on the Bong Son Plain, combat engineers from the 1st Cav's 8th Engineer Battalion, Alpha Company, would construct a LZ at Position Dog that would support a helicopter laager area and a 2,100-foot-long airstrip capable of landing CV-2 and C-123 aircraft. The laager area was needed for the helicopters supporting the infantry operations in the area. The airstrip was needed primarily for use in the event that the Sao Vang Division closed Highway 1 as a ground supply line and attempted to isolate the cavalry units on the coastal plain. Once completed, the position would be renamed LZ English, in honor of SP5 Carver J. English, Jr., from Kenner, Louisiana. SP5 English, who served in Headquarters Company, 8th Engineer Battalion, died in the mid-air explosion of a CH-54 Flying Crane helicopter on January 5 while completing an ammo resupply mission for a 1st Cav artillery unit.[7] The helicopter was believed to have been hit by enemy ground fire in the Highway 19 area, west of the Mang Yang Pass, between Pleiku City and the 1st Cav's base camp at An Khe. It exploded in mid-air and came crashing down to the ground. A Huey helicopter that was operating close by in support of a battalion from the 2nd Brigade got to the crash site in an attempt to rescue any survivors, but

---

[7] Both English and Hammond served in Alpha Company, 8th Engineer Battalion. "Coffelt Database of Vietnam casualties," http://www.coffeltdatabase.org.

the helicopter was fully engulfed in flames, preventing any type of rescue attempt. Once the fire died out, the bodies of the three crewmembers and two passengers onboard were recovered.[8]

In parallel with the construction of an LZ at Position Dog, division engineers would also build LZ Hammond, which would include a laager area for helicopters and a 3,200-foot-long airstrip capable of handling CV-2 and C-123 aircraft. The airstrip would also support the larger C-130 aircraft and would be capable of accommodating eight parked C-130s. The LZ was named in honor of SFC Russell E. Hammond, a demolition specialist with Alpha Company, 8th Engineer Battalion, from Pittsburgh, Pennsylvania. SFC Hammond was killed in action on November 5 in the Ia Drang Valley. He was a passenger in a truck that was returning from a search-and-destroy mission when the truck ran over a land mine in the road and exploded, killing him. Construction of LZ Hammond was also expected to take two to three weeks.

The deception operations would begin on January 24 and end on January 27.

---

[8] Obituary of Carver J. English, Alpha Company, 8th Engineer Battalion. "Obituary of SP5 Carver J. English, Jr., from Kenner, Louisiana," *Pacific Stars & Stripes*, Friday, January 7, 1966.

PREPARING FOR BATTLE • 15

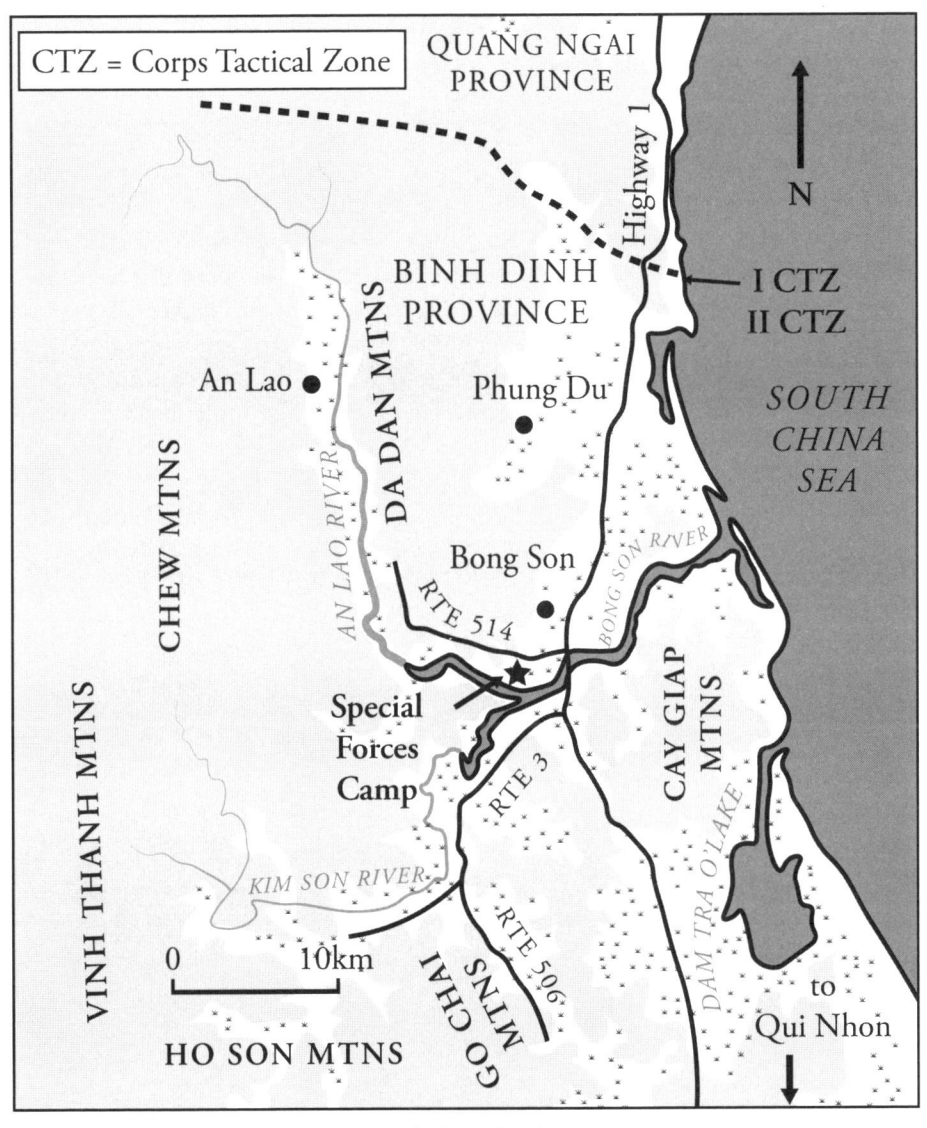

Map 4. Bong Son Area

CHAPTER TWO

Tragedy Strikes

On the morning of January 24, the 3rd Brigade kicked off its plan to move from the division's base camp at An Khe to LZ Hammond on the coastal plains, 45 kilometers south of Bong Son. Lieutenant Colonel Rutland D. Beard Jr., and the troops of the 1st Battalion (Airborne), 12th Cavalry, loaded onto helicopters for the 20-minute flight to LZ Hammond, where the battalion assumed security of the area from the ROK Capital Infantry Division. The Koreans had secured the area as part of Operation *Flying Tiger*. Lieutenant Colonel Raymond L. Kampe and the troops of the 1st Battalion, 7th Cavalry loaded onto deuce-and-a-half trucks and traveled by convoy to LZ Hammond, a distance of 60 kilometers by road from the division's base camp. There it rendezvoused with the 1/12th Cav. A second convoy for the 11th Aviation Group followed the 1/7th Cav convoy. The 1st Squadron, 9th Cavalry, and 2/20th ARA (aerial rocket artillery) provided aerial coverage for the convoys with their helicopter gunships armed with 30-caliber mini-guns, grenade launchers, and 2.75-inch rockets by reconnoitering the road ahead of the convoys searching for potential ambushes. A jeep-mounted ground cavalry rifle platoon with recoilless rifles and 50-caliber machine guns from Delta Troop, 1/9th Cav, provided ground cover. The moves were made without incident, and by midday the units had arrived at LZ Hammond and were moving northward 2 kilometers to clear the hamlets and villages they encountered.

The 3rd Brigade initiated its deception operations on the morning of January 25. The 1/7th Cav, together with an artillery battery from the 1st Battalion, 21st Artillery (105mm howitzers), moved by convoy to an assembly area northeast of LZ Hammond along the southern portion of the Cay Giep Mountains, located between Highway 1 and the South China Sea. The area was designated Position George. A firing position was established at George by the 1/21st Artillery and the 1/7th Cav initiated reconnaissance-in-force operations, attacking eastward toward a position on the coast, designated Pickup Zone Tango.

In parallel with the 1/7th Cav's operation northeast of LZ Hammond, Charlie Troop, 1/9th Cav, initiated deception operations in the Soui Ca Valley northwest of Hammond, where the 1st Cav had battled elements of the 18th NVA Regiment in mid-December. It used its observation helicopters and gunships, and Aero Rifle Platoon (the Charlie Blues), to conduct ground reconnaissance by infantry elements in the valley and surrounding foothills.

The Charlie Blues complemented the troop's aerial reconnaissance capabilities. They could be inserted onto the ground quickly to pursue enemy elements, check sightings of aerial observers, and provide bomb damage assessments following helicopter gunship and tactical airstrikes.

In its movement toward Pickup Zone Tango, the 1/7th Cav encountered moderate resistance from small groups of North Vietnamese soldiers. It was unknown if the enemy soldiers were a delaying element for a larger North Vietnamese force that was moving through the area or if they were a guard element intended to provide an early warning to the main body of the 18th NVA Regiment, which was known to be bivouacked in the vicinity of Dam Tra O-Lake south of the 1/7th Cav's route of attack. The 12th NVA Regiment, which was known to have recently separated from the Sao Vang Division, was believed to be moving from the Bong Son area to the Saigon area, where it would join its new headquarters unit, the 7th Viet Cong Division. It was possible that the enemy soldiers were a rear guard delaying element for the regiment as it moved southward through the area. However, North Vietnamese units typically moved by dispersing into small groups, intermingling with the population, and moving at night and in bad weather to avoid detection.

The Soui Ca Valley, where the 1/9th Cav conducted its deception operations, was known to be a major infiltration route into eastern Binh Dinh Province and Phu Yen Province to the south of Binh Dinh Province. The North Vietnamese would travel down the Ho Chi Minh Trail from North Vietnam and enter South Vietnam by crossing the border into Pleiku Province, working their way eastward through the Central Highlands along Highway 19. When they reached Route 3A in western Binh Dinh Province, they would follow it to the northeast through the Vinh Thanh Valley and Vinh Thanh Mountains into the Kim Son Valley. From there they would travel through the Kim Son and Soui Ca valleys on their way to join the regiments of the Sao Vang Division in eastern Binh Dinh Province or those of the Binh Tri Thien Division (325th Division) in Phu Yen Province.

Back at An Khe, the 2/7th Cav prepared for its move to the U.S. Special Forces Camp at Bong Son, 65 kilometers northeast of An Khe as the crow flies, in the coastal region in northeast Binh Dinh Province. The troops of the 2/7th Cav would move by truck convoy from their area in the base camp to the airstrip at the U.S. Special Forces Camp at An Tuc/An Khe and load onto USAF C-123 and CV-2 Caribou aircraft for the flight to Bong Son.

PFC Jim "Doc" Hackett from Goshen, Indiana, a medic with the 2nd Platoon, Alpha Company, recalled the move:

> At 0300 hours on the January 25, we were awakened so we could shave and eat breakfast before the move to Bong Son. While at the mess hall, everyone was trying to hide from their buddies the fact that they were scared. Each one of us was looking around at the familiar faces

wondering if we would see them again when we returned to base camp. After chow, everyone received their C-rations and made last minute re-checks of their equipment.

Around 0530 hours, the word to "saddle-up" and get into platoon formation was given. Our platoon leader, Lieutenant Grove, walked up and down the formation making a visual check of our equipment while his radio operator checked his commo with the other radio operators in the company. By now, everyone was really getting nervous and wanting to get this operation started. We marched down to the waiting trucks that were going to take us to the An Khe airstrip located next to the U.S. Special Forces Camp at An Tuc/An Khe outside the perimeter, adjacent to Highway 19, about four kilometers from our area inside the base camp.

When we arrived at the airstrip, the runway was jammed with USAF C-123 troop transport planes, 12 in total, and a number of CV-2 Caribou aircraft that would take us to Bong Son.[1]

The airstrip at the Special Forces camp, known as the An Khe Army Airfield, was originally built by the French during their colonial rule in Vietnam. It had been extended to support larger aircraft, such as the USAF C-123 and C-130, and modernized with perforated (or pierced) steel planking (PSP) by U.S. Army engineers in the fall of 1965 when the 1st Cav arrived in Vietnam. It was now an airstrip capable of handling aircraft in the monsoon weather as well as in the dry season, and more than one aircraft could be accommodated at the same time.

Ironically, the airstrip was the departure point for French Groupement Mobile 100, a regimental-sized task force of the French Far East Expeditionary Corps, in the pre-dawn darkness of June 24, 1954. By 1800 hours that evening, the unit ceased to exist as an effective fighting force. It was ambushed by the Việt Minh 803rd Regiment on Highway 19 west of the airstrip, just short of the Mang Yang Pass, on the way to Pleiku City and suffered one of the bloodiest defeats of the French Union in Vietnam (together with the battle of Dien Bien Phu in 1954).[2] The remnants of the unit had to brave 30 kilometers more of enemy road and were ambushed on June 28 and 29 at Dak Ya-Ayun by the Việt Minh 108th Regiment. The survivors finally reached Pleiku the following day. The battle is well documented in Bernard Fall's *Street Without Joy*.

Captain Joel E. Sugdinis, commander of Alpha Company, 2/7th Cav, recalled the move to Bong Son:

> The men of Alpha Company moved through the confusion, which habitually precedes a major air move, like professionals. They had already executed several of these moves and considered this one as routine. However, several field grade officers from division headquarters had arrived at

---

[1] In an email to the author, Jim "Doc" Hackett described Alpha Company, 2nd Battalion, 7th Cavalry's move by deuce-and-a-half trucks from its area in the base camp to the airstrip at the U.S. Special Forces Camp at An Khe, on January 25, 1966. He also described Alpha Company's flight to the U.S. Special Forces Camp at Bong Son. Email from Jim "Doc" Hackett with attachment entitled "LZ 4," dated June 2, 2011.

[2] Wikipedia, "Ambush at the Mang Yang Pass," https://en.wikipedia.org/wiki/Battle_of_Mang_Yang_Pass.

the airstrip and were attempting to get involved in the loading of the troops aboard the aircraft. These supervisory personnel were constantly running up and down the airstrip shouting to each other to make sure that the troops were prepared to board. They became quite humorous as they argued over who controlled what. The men of Alpha Company chuckled and did what they knew they had to do, regardless of the conflicting instructions. One good thing about this spectacle of frustration was that it relaxed the men.[3]

At one point in the loading of the troops, the men of Alpha Company's 1st Platoon, along with Captain Sugdinis and 1st Lieutenant Jim "Lurch" Kelly, platoon leader of the 1st Platoon, were forced to offload from the third C-123 aircraft because one of the plane's engines was experiencing mechanical problems and would not stay running, and were loaded onto another C-123 for the flight to Bong Son. The pilots of the third aircraft eventually resolved the engine problem and the men of Alpha Company's 3rd Platoon, along with a squad from Alpha Company's Mortar Platoon, loaded onto that aircraft. Crates of ammunition, grenades, and mortar rounds were also loaded onto the aircraft.

No sooner had the first three C-123s taken off from the airstrip than tragedy struck. Captain Sugdinis, who was in the second aircraft, says: "We were approximately five minutes from landing at the Special Forces Camp at Bong Son when a member of the flight crew in the rear of the aircraft suddenly rushed forward to the pilot's compartment. He, with a second member of the crew, put his ear to a head set and appeared to be listening to something of an exciting and unusual nature. This lasted for about a minute." Sugdinis soon after found out that the third C-123, with the men from Alpha Company's 3rd Platoon and a squad from the Mortar Platoon onboard, had crashed shortly after takeoff.[4]

As Captain Sugdinis's aircraft approached the dirt airstrip at the Special Forces camp at Bong Son, it was raked with enemy machine-gun fire from below, forcing the pilot to abort the landing attempt and do a fly-around. A large-caliber bullet ripped through the plane's fuselage, leaving a gaping hole the size of a man's fist and filling the aircraft with dust. The bullet came up between the legs of Bob Poos, a news reporter with the Associated Press (AP), spraying him with sawdust and splinters from the plane's sub-flooring. It rattled around in the fuselage for a while before losing its velocity and getting tangled up in the plane's web lining.

Enemy ground fire directed at airborne aircraft in the Bong Son area became a routine part of life for USAF and 1st Cav pilots. The volume of fire directed at helicopters and fixed-wing aircraft by Viet Cong local-force guerillas in the hamlets

---

[3] Captain Joel E. Sugdinas, U.S. Infantry 1966–67, U.S. Army Infantry School monograph, "Operations of Company A, 2nd Battalion, 7th Cavalry, 1st Air Cavalry Division, Near Bong Son, Republic of Vietnam, 25–29 January 1966, Masher Operation, Personal Experience of the Company Commander," 7.
[4] Aviation Safety Network, "ASN Aircraft accident Fairchild C-123K Provider 54–702, An Khe."

and villages in the Bong Son area was so heavy that it necessitated changes to the tactics used by the pilots. They would approach the airstrip from different directions, weather permitting, and on air-assaults the infantry would be offloaded on the high ground and sweep down the slopes to the low ground.

Poos and AP photographer Henri Huet were traveling with the 2/7th Cav covering the initial phase of Operation *Masher*.[5] Poos served in the U.S. Marine Corps during the Korean War. He was among the Marines who staged a fighting winter retreat in 1951 from the Chosin Reservoir, which was under attack by Chinese Communist forces who had entered the war on the side of North Korea. Poos joined the AP in 1957 and was assigned to its Saigon Bureau in 1965, quickly becoming noted for his aggressive and daring combat reporting. During the initial phase of Operation *Masher*, when the 7th Cav troops were surrounded by North Vietnamese and Viet Cong forces, Poos and Huet helped recover wounded 7th Cav troopers and stood guard over North Vietnamese and Viet Cong prisoners. Years later, when asked about his role, Poos recalled: "We figured we could be overrun and wiped out in the next 24 hours."

Huet was a French war photographer who served in the French Navy.[6] He returned to his native Vietnam in 1954 at the end of the First Indochina War and worked for the U.S. Government as a civilian photographer, and later as a photographer with AP. He died on February 10, 1971, when the helicopter he was riding in was shot down by the North Vietnamese over the Ho Chi Minh Trail in Laos and crashed, killing all onboard. His photographs were credited with helping to influence American public opinion. One of his most memorable photographs featured a wounded medic from Alpha Company, 2/7th Cav, at Phung Du with a bandage wrapped around his head while administrating first aid to a fellow wounded trooper. The photograph appeared on the cover of *Life Magazine* on February 11, 1966, and remains one of the most haunting images of the entire war.

Upon landing at the Special Forces camp, Captain Sugdinis learned that the crash of the third C-123 killed all 46 men aboard, which included most of the troops from Alpha Company's 3rd Platoon and a squad from Alpha Company's Mortar Platoon, as well as the plane's four-man crew. Less than 10 minutes into the flight, the aircraft experienced mechanical problems with one of its engines, forcing the pilots to turn the aircraft around and attempt to get back to the airstrip at An Khe. Tragically, it didn't make it, coming crashing down on the east side of the An Khe Pass along Highway 19, 10 kilometers short of the runway. It was flying in an inverted position and smashed into the side of a steep jungle-covered mountain, tumbling down the mountainside and exploding, cutting a huge swath into the burning jungle.

---

[5] USMCCCA Online, "CC Bob Poos, AP correspondent dies after a lengthy illness," https://www.usmcccaonline.com/cc-bob-poos-ap-correspondent-dies-after-a-lengthy-illness/, December 21, 2008.

[6] "Henri Huet," https://en.wikipedia.org/wiki/Henri_Huet.

The aircraft crashed near the forward command post of the 1st Battalion (Airborne), 8th Cavalry, which at the time was providing security for the An Khe Pass and Highway 19, east of the division's base camp. The troops of the 1/8th Cav and a group of radio communications specialists operating a radio relay station there saw the plane come down. They got to the crash site within minutes, but the plane started burning almost immediately and secondary explosions from the ammunition on board prevented any kind of rescue attempt.

Once the explosions died down, the 1/8th Cav troops were able to extinguish the fire and start searching through the wreckage for survivors, along with medical personnel from the division's base camp who had since arrived at the crash site. By 1500 hours, all that could be done in terms of a rescue attempt had been done, and now efforts turned to a recovery process. The 1/8th Cav troops were able to locate and remove only a handful of the bodies before darkness fell, making it impossible to do any more. At first light on January 26, the men of the 1/8th Cav resumed their efforts, and with the help of a Flying Crane helicopter, which arrived at the crash site at 1400 hours, were able to lift the wreckage, and locate and remove the remaining bodies. The recovery process was finished by late afternoon, and the bodies, which were badly torn, were placed into rubber bags and carried several hundred meters up the mountainside toward Highway 19, to a spot where they could be loaded onto helicopters and transported to Graves Registration at the division's base camp. Investigators later found evidence of a fire in the No. 2 engine, which was thought to be the cause of the crash.

PFC Jack Wagner, a rifleman with Alpha Company's 1st Platoon, remembered: "For us it was a blessing to have been removed from the aircraft that could not keep one of its engines running. But for the members of the 3rd Platoon and for a squad from the Mortar Platoon who were later loaded on that aircraft, it would be their last operation."[7]

Colonel Kenneth D. Mertel, then a lieutenant colonel, battalion commander of the 1/8th Cav at the time, recalled:

> I was about a mile east of the An Khe Pass when I heard the noise of a low-flying aircraft as it passed overhead. A few moments later, I heard a tremendous explosion as the aircraft augered into the side of a mountain.

Colonel Mertel continued:

> Our battalion was responsible for the security of the An Khe Pass at the time, so we had the job of providing immediate assistance to the crash scene since we were the closest troops. Within a few minutes the men from the battalion were at the scene, but the intense flames and the exploding ammunition prevented them from getting too close for a few minutes. It was obvious from the explosion and fire that there probably were few if any troopers left alive in the aircraft.

---

[7] Email from Jack Wagner, dated January 25, 2017.

I reached the scene within 15 minutes of the crash. It was a grim and discouraging sight. By that time the ammunition stopped popping sufficiently so that the troops could get in and extinguish the remaining flames. The first report, since it was difficult to find any bodies, indicated that the only ones onboard were the crew members. However, it turned out that the aircraft was fully loaded with troopers from the 2nd of the 7th Cav.[8]

The fourth C-123, which had not yet departed from the airstrip at An Khe, was delayed from taking off. The remaining members of Alpha Company's Mortar Platoon were instructed to leave behind their mortar tubes and related gear and were issued with M-16 rifles with full loads of ammunition. They would be organized as rifle squads and attached to the 1st and 2nd Platoons of Alpha Company once they got to Bong Son. Alpha Company would then consist of two rifle platoons of approximately 40 men each. 1st Lieutenant Larry Gwin, Executive Officer of Alpha Company, who was managing the move to Bong Son for Alpha Company at the An Khe end, was instructed by Captain Sugdinis to stay behind and attend to the plane crash by helping to identify the bodies and packing up the personal effects of the men involved.[9]

Shortly after the battalion arrived at the Special Forces camp at Bong Son, the 2/7th Cav—minus Captain Henry Thorpe's Delta Company—moved northward from the camp for 2 kilometers, clearing the villages it encountered. There was no enemy contact, just frightened and bewildered stares from the villagers, according to Captain Sugdinis. Delta Company remained at the camp providing security for the battalion command post.

The Bong Son Plain extended northward from the Bong Son River along the coast to the northernmost point of Binh Dinh Province, a distance of roughly 23 kilometers, and extended eastward from the base of the Da Dan Mountains to the water's edge of the South China Sea, a distance of about 25 kilometers at its widest point. It was vast with rice paddy fields extending as far as the eye could see. Sandy dry-crop islands with tall palm trees dotted the horizon. Numerous small rivers and streams cut across the plain, carrying rain runoff from the Da Dan Mountains to the irrigation ditches located alongside the rice paddies, filling them with fresh water before continuing eastward on their way to join the Tam Quan River and Tam Quan Bay, and ultimately the South China Sea.[10] At the northern end of the plain, the rice paddies were built on gently rolling hills and hillsides, where tiered paddies cut into mountainous spurs that jetted out into the plain. The rice paddies

---

[8] Colonel Kenneth D. Mertel, (Ret.), *Year of the Horse: Vietnam, 1st Air Cavalry in the Highlands, 1965–1967* (Atglen, PA: Schiffer Publishing Ltd, 1997).

[9] The website "Vietnam Air Losses" provided the names of the USAF personnel who died in the crash of the Fairchild C-123K Provider aircraft 54–702 in the An Khe Pass on January 25, 1966. https://www.vietnamairlosses.com.

[10] A description of the coastal plain north of Bong Son was based on maps of Binh Dinh Province, Hoai Nhon District, and Hoai An District. Interim Report of Operations, First Cavalry Division, July 1965 to December 1966.

gradually gave way to the foothills of the southern Quang Ngai Mountains at the Binh Dinh–Quang Ngai provincial boundary.

Captain Sugdinis recalled seeing Bong Son for the first time:

> The area is extremely beautiful. A person's eye can wander from the golden yellow of the rice paddies to the rich green of the coconut groves. The pure white sand is blinding as the brilliance of the sun's rays reflects back at you. It is a picture of peace and quiet. A closer look, however, at this scene immediately reveals the ugly Viet Cong trademark, entrenchments. Every sandy island, many covered with hootches and coconut trees, is virtually a spider web of trench lines, bunkers, and small round holes. It almost appears that every square foot of dry ground had been prepared for defensive combat. Oddly enough, though, the fortifications were not oriented in any one direction. Instead, all fighting positions, trenches, etc., were emplaced for the conduct of an all-around defense of each and every single island.

The Special Forces camp with its dirt airstrip was located just north of the Bong Son River (Song Lai Giang) and about 500 meters south of Route 514, the main road into the An Lao Valley. The district headquarters of Hoai Nhon District was located next to the camp, along with the troops of the ARVN 22nd Infantry Division who were garrisoned there. When the 1st Cav arrived, it extended the camp northward across Route 514, centered around a small hill mass, designated Hill 36, to accommodate the arrival of the new troops. The area was named LZ Two Bits, because the southern portion of the camp was separated from the northern portion into two parts by the road.

At 1440 hours that afternoon, the ARVN soldiers at the Special Forces camp notified the 3rd Brigade commanders there that a 1st Cav quarter-ton truck had been taken under fire by the Viet Cong at the barrier across Highway 1 at the southern end of Bong Son. The barrier had been constructed by the Viet Cong to close traffic between Bong Son and Qui Nhon. The vehicle was on its way to the Special Forces camp, 3.5 kilometers to the southwest of the town on Route 514. The driver apparently missed the turn-off for Route 514 and continued northward on Highway 1 until he approached the barrier, where the Viet Cong opened fire on his vehicle. Helicopter gunships from the 1/9th Cav and 2/20th ARA were dispatched to the location and drove away two Viet Cong platoons. No estimate of Viet Cong casualties was provided.

As it turned out, there were two quarter-ton trucks involved in the attack. They were from the 11th Aviation Group and were carrying electronic surveillance equipment to the Special Forces camp to be used to support helicopter operations in the area. When the two vehicles approached the barrier, the Viet Cong opened fire on the lead vehicle. It had three of its tires shot out and also took a single round through the engine. The driver of the vehicle was able to escape with only minor wounds. The second vehicle stopped abruptly when the firing started and backed down Highway 1 until safely out of range of the Viet Cong. The driver of that vehicle was unharmed. Shortly afterwards, the Recon Platoon, Delta Company,

2/7th Cav, was dispatched to the site and the two vehicles were secured. The lead vehicle had to be airlifted by helicopter to the Special Forces camp, but the second one was able to be driven there.

Meanwhile, Alpha, Bravo, and Charlie companies, 2/7th Cav, continued clearing the villages they encountered north of the Special Forces camp until they reached an area of high ground and dry crop plots, where they stopped and established a night defensive perimeter. The night was spent there without incident.

On the morning of January 26, an area designated Position Dog was to be secured by the 2/7th Cav for use as the 3rd Brigade's command post and forward operating base. It was located on high ground on the western side of Highway 1, 5 kilometers north of Bong Son and 2 kilometers north of where the 2/7th Cav had spent the night. It would serve as the jumping-off point for the 3rd Brigade's attack into Phung Du on the morning of January 28, D-Day.

In the first of two requests to the USAF, Lieutenant Colonel McDade requested a close-in tactical airstrike to support the 2/7th Cav's air assault into Dog. At 0630 hours, a USAF forward air controller (FAC) in a propeller-driven Cessna O-1 Bird Dog aircraft, and a pair of single-engine, propeller-driven A-1E Skyraiders, arrived over Dog. Shortly afterwards, the FAC spotted a defensive position consisting of trenches and bunkers roughly 4 kilometers west of Dog at the base on the Da Dan Mountains, and directed the Skyraiders to attack the position with high-explosive and white phosphorus bombs, napalm, and 20mm cannon fire. The attack resulted in four North Vietnamese KBA and six bunkers destroyed. The Skyraiders also struck a number of trenches northwest of Dog in a tree line occupied by North Vietnamese soldiers. The FAC reported 90 percent coverage, but damage assessment was not possible due to the thick foliage in the area.

At 0800 hours, after a 15-minute artillery preparation, the troops of Bravo and Charlie companies, 2/7th Cav, loaded onto helicopters for the air assault into Dog. The assault was met with only light resistance, which was quickly eliminated, and the remainder of the battalion landed unopposed. Once the entire battalion was on the ground, Lieutenant Colonel McDade requested a second close-in tactical airstrike on a position to the northeast of Dog. An estimated company of North Vietnamese soldiers had been spotted from the air on the approach to Dog. McDade directed Captain Myron Diduryk, commander of Bravo Company, and Captain John (Skip) Fesmire, commander of Charlie Company, to push out with their companies at the completion of the airstrike and make contact with the North Vietnamese forces. The enemy soldiers were located in a well-fortified network of trenches on the eastern side of Highway 1, less than 1 kilometer from where the 2/7th troops had set down. They were dressed in khaki uniforms with pith helmets, and were equipped with web gear and automatic weapons. A pair of Skyraiders arrived shortly afterwards and attacked the position with general purpose and white phosphorus bombs, napalm, and 20mm cannon fire.

The North Vietnamese soldiers fled northward along Highway 1 toward the hamlets of Phung Du and An Thai, chased by helicopter gunships armed with 30-caliber mini-guns from Delta Company, 229th Assault Helicopter Battalion (AHB), and aerial rocket gunships from Charlie Battery, 2/20th ARA. Although no enemy soldiers were found in the trenches, there was ample evidence of movement out of the area, and the 2/7th Cav captured 14 North Vietnamese soldiers. The enemy troops were loaded onto a CH-47 Chinook helicopter and transported to the division's base camp at An Khe for interrogation by the 1st Cav's military intelligence unit. This provided the 1st Cav with the first indication by ground contact of the presence of North Vietnamese forces in the area of operation.

Tactical air support was provided to the 1st Cav by the USAF's 2nd Air Division as the command & control authority for USAF units in South Vietnam, under the authority of the MACV.[11] It was responsible for controlling local USAF operations. The actual aircraft and pilots who provided the tactical air support, however, were part of various tactical fighter squadrons based at different airbases in South Vietnam, such as the 21st Tactical Air Support Squadron at Pleiku Air Base or the 602nd Fighter Squadron at Nha Trang Air Base. Tactical air support was used extensively by the 1st Cav to support ground operations, in addition to preparing landing zones for air assaults prior to artillery preparation. The types of ordnance used by the USAF in tactical airstrikes were 500lb general purpose bombs, 250lb fragmentation bombs, napalm and WP (white phosphorus) bombs, rockets, and 20mm cannon fire. The reaction time of the aircraft varied from a few minutes for an aircraft that was already in the area to 30–40 minutes if it had to be called from a strip alert.

Skyraiders were the most frequently used aircraft for close-in ground support for the infantry because of their four wing-mounted 20mm cannons, the loads they carried, and the length of time they could stay over the target area. Night illumination and suppressive fire support were also used extensively by the 1st Cav to support ground operations. Smokey-the-Bear, a Douglas C-47 aircraft, was used to drop magnesium-based flares to illuminate the ground at night, and a gunship variation of that, Puff-the-Magic-Dragon (or Spooky), a C-47 aircraft equipped with three 7.62mm mini-guns, provided close-in tactical support. Smokey-the-Bear was used so frequently by the 1st Cav that it was on strip alert or in the air each night for use by the infantry battalions.

Meanwhile, south of Bong Son, the 1/7th Cav and 1/9th Cav intensified their deception operations. The troops of the 1/7th Cav swept northward along the coast in the direction of Bong Son toward clearings designated Objectives Golf and Echo, where they met with sporadic enemy resistance and land mines. At Objective Echo, a booby trap was triggered, detonating a land mine that sent metal fragments through

---

[11] Military Wiki, "U.S. Air Force in Vietnam," https://military-history.fandom.com/wiki/United_States_Air_Force_in_South_Vietnam.

the air. A squad leader with Bravo Company was hit by them in the head, legs, and pelvic area and died from hemorrhagic shock before he could be evacuated to the 15th Medical Battalion aid station at Dog for treatment. He was the division's first KIA resulting from enemy contact in the operation. In the process of moving around the clearing in the tree line, the 1/7th Cav troops captured 10 North Vietnamese soldiers, who were most likely part of a guard element for the 18th NVA Regiment, which was known to be in the vicinity of Dam Trac O-Lake. The prisoners were loaded onto a Chinook helicopter and flown to the division's base camp at An Khe for interrogation by its military intelligence unit. The 1/9th Cav continued to recon the Soui Ca Valley with its observation helicopters and gunships, as well as an aero rifle platoon, reporting no further enemy activity that day.

Charlie Company, 15th Medical Battalion, set up a field site at the 3rd Brigade's Command Post at Position Dog to support the brigade's operations in the Bong Son area. The site consisted of an aid station, or medical clearing station, with medical personnel to treat wounded, injured, and sick troopers. It was designated "Charlie Med." A section of the 15th Med's Medevac Platoon was also positioned there, with multiple Huey helicopters and aviation crews to transport the troopers from the battlefield to the aid station for treatment. If the evacuation of a trooper required a hoist capability due to the terrain, a Chinook helicopter from the division's helicopter support battalion would perform the evacuation. The early models of the medevac helicopters lacked the lift capability when fully loaded with crew and armament to hoist a trooper from the ground up into the helicopter.

If surgery was required to treat a trooper, he would most likely be back-hauled by helicopter or CV-2 aircraft from the aid station to either the 2nd Surgical Hospital (Mobile Army) at An Khe or the 85th Evacuation Hospital at Qui Nhon, where they had the doctors and nurses, and medical equipment, to perform the surgery. If a trooper contracted malaria or some other infectious disease, such as scrub typhus, he might also be back-hauled to one of the surgical hospitals for treatment and recovery or might remain at the Charlie Med aid station. The aid station was equipped to handle a limited number of in-bed patients.

A medevac crew included a pilot, co-pilot, crew chief, door gunner, and medic, and the helicopters had red crosses painted on them in a subdued shade of red, so there was little to distinguish them from the other troop-carrying helicopters in the division. The 1st Cav commanders learned early on in the war that just because a helicopter had red crosses painted on it didn't mean that the enemy were not going to shoot at it. After suffering several fatalities among the medevac crews, the helicopters were armed with two M-60 machine guns, one on each side of the aircraft, for use in insecure areas. Each machine gun was initially connected via a bungee cord for free-firing; later, they were hard-mounted to the aircraft.

On January 27, D Day-1, the 2/7th Cav, upon being relieved by advanced security elements from the 3rd Brigade, moved from Dog to a position 3 kilometers to the north, designated LZ 2. From there, it continued clearing the area northwest, west, and southwest of the LZ, while the battalion's six-man long-range reconnaissance unit, the Ground Reconnaissance Intelligence Team (GRIT), proceeded to the northwest for 5 kilometers to reconnoiter the Cu Nghi area at the base of the Da Dan Mountains, where an artillery position would be established on the following morning. The position would provide artillery support for the attacking 7th Cav troops at Phung Du. The 2/7th Cav received sporadic fire from snipers, and several visual sightings were made of small groups of North Vietnamese soldiers. The enemy soldiers, however, appeared to be more interested in getting out of the area than in engaging the 2/7th Cav troops.

The 1/7th Cav, in its final deception operation, air-assaulted into a position designated LZ Alpha in the Suoi Dinh Binh Valley, east of Bong Son, between Highway 1 and the South China Sea, and conducted search-and-destroy operations north to the Bong Son River, meeting light but increasing enemy resistance. In a series of booby-trapped minefield explosions, two troopers from Alpha Company suffered multiple metal fragment wounds to the body and died from loss of blood before they could be evacuated to the 15th Med aid station at Dog.

At 1350 hours, an OH-13 observation helicopter from Charlie Troop, 1/9th Cav, was shot out of the air by enemy ground fire and came crashing down into 10-foot-high elephant grass west of Dog. It was providing aerial coverage for Charlie Company, 2/7th Cav, and was reconnoitering a suspected ambush site ahead of the advancing Charlie Company troops. It was shot down by North Vietnamese soldiers lying in wait to ambush the men of Charlie Company. The helicopter rolled end-over-end several times and came to rest upside down. The pilot was left dangling from his seat by his shoulder harness and the aerial scout was pinned under the wreckage. The pilot, with a 38-caliber handgun, and the scout, with a 60-caliber machine gun, kept enemy soldiers at bay by firing at voices in the elephant grass long enough for the Charlie Company troops to make a running assault across 200 meters and a stream to the crash site. At 1410 hours, the Charlie Company troops reached the site and extracted the pilot and scout. Both of them were seriously wounded and had to be transported to the 15th Med aid station at Dog and subsequently back-hauled to the 2nd Surgical Hospital at the 1st Cav's base camp for surgery. The scout died from his wounds the next evening at the hospital. The helicopter was a total loss and had to be scrapped.

At 1700 hours, the GRIT team from the 2/7th Cav attempted to return from its reconnaissance mission in the Cu Nghi area at the base of the Da Dan Mountains to rejoin the battalion, which was now at LZ 2. It came under heavy machine-gun fire from enemy soldiers and was unable to maneuver. Aerial rocket gunships from the 2/20th ARA were called in to neutralize the enemy position and to pick up the recon team members and transport them to LZ 2 to rejoin the main body of the battalion.

South of Bong Son in the Soui Ca Valley, observation helicopters from the 1/9th Cav received heavy automatic weapons fire while reconnoitering the northern portion of the valley and called for an airstrike on a suspected enemy position. Two Skyraiders responded and were on target within 20 minutes. They pounded the area with an assortment of high-explosive and napalm bombs, and upon completion of the airstrike the Charlie Blues were inserted into the area to do a bomb damage assessment. The Blues found the bodies of two North Vietnamese soldiers KBA and a heavy smell of burned flesh. Additional KBA were suspected, but the Blues were unable to find any additional bodies or any weapons.

By late afternoon, the 2nd Battalion, 12th Cavalry, arrived by USAF C-123 and CV-2 aircraft at the Special Forces camp, where it remained on standby ready to reinforce the troops of the 7th Cav.

Meanwhile, Major Beckwith and the members of his Project Delta teams were busy preparing for their insertion into the An Lao Valley at dusk. Huey helicopters from the 145th Airlift Platoon would transport three six-man teams into the valley and insert them at predefined locations, while helicopter gunship escorts provided cover. The teams would consist solely of U.S. Special Forces soldiers because the South Vietnamese troops who were part of Project Delta were in training and were unavailable for assignment.

The 145th Airlift Platoon, which had arrived in Vietnam in 1962, operated out of Tan Son Nhut Airbase to support MACV. At the start of 1965, it was put under the operational control of the 5th Special Forces Group at Nha Trang in direct support of Project Delta operations in I Corps and II Corps. It had a total of 10 helicopters, with six Huey troop-carrying helicopters and four helicopter gunships.[12]

Meanwhile, back at Dog, Colonel Moore and his 3rd Brigade commanders were busy finalizing their plans for the attack on the following morning.

North of Bong Son in Quang Ngai Province, the commanders of the U.S. III Marine Amphibious Force, together with those of the ARVN 4th Regiment, were also finalizing their plans for the following morning. At midnight on January 27, a company from the 2nd Battalion, 4th Marines, together with company from the ARVN 3rd Battalion, 4th Regiment, would begin a night march northward to a spot south of Red Beach, designated Hill 163, to secure the area for an amphibious landing of Marine battalions.

---

[12] Wikipedia, "Project Delta," https://en.wikipedia.org/wiki/Project_DELTA.

30 • THE BATTLE OF BONG SON

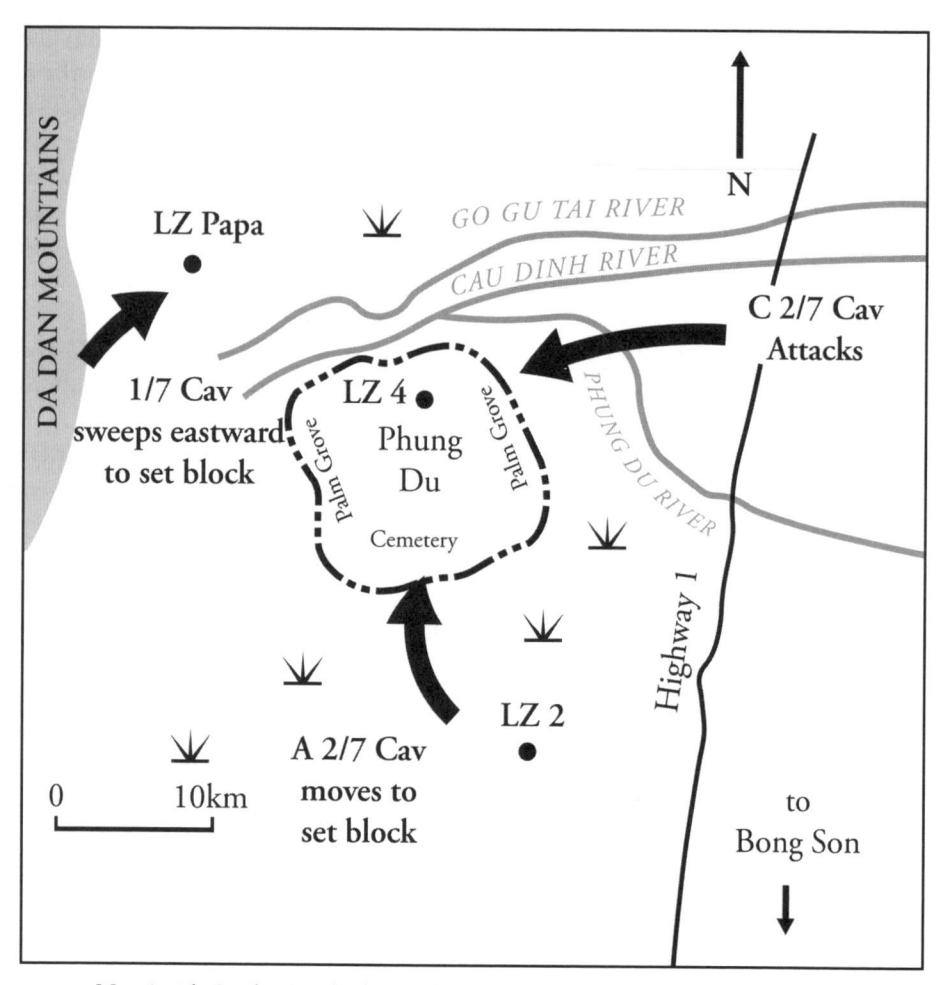

Map 5. 7th Cavalry Attacks the North Vietnamese at Phung Du, January 28, 1966

CHAPTER THREE

Attack

Colonel Hal Moore's plan for the attack on January 28, D-Day, was quite simple. Bravo Company, 2nd Battalion, 7th Cavalry, would seize and secure a position on the high ground west of Bong Son in the vicinity of Cu Nghi for artillery that would cover the target area. The position was designated LZ Steel. Charlie Company, 2/7th Cav, would attack the North Vietnamese by air assault into an area at the northern end of Phung Du, where it was believed to be concentrated, and attack southward. The area was designated LZ 4. From the south, Alpha Company, 2/7th Cav, would move from LZ 2 to the southern end of Phung Du and establish a blocking position there against which the attacking troops from Charlie Company would push the North Vietnamese forces in a classic hammer-and-anvil tactic. From the west, the 1st Battalion, 7th Cavalry, would sweep eastward from LZ Steel toward Phung Du, cutting off escape routes to the Da Dan Mountains and An Lao Valley to the west. Finally, the ARVN Airborne Brigade would conduct search-and-destroy operations east of Highway 1, blocking escape routes to the South China Sea. The 2nd Battalion, 12th Cavalry, would remain at the Special Forces camp as the reserve force prepared to join the battle when called. The plan would sandwich the enemy soldiers between the attacking 7th Cav troops and force them to fight or be destroyed if they attempted to flee.

On the morning of the attack, eastern Binh Dinh Province was firmly in the grip of the winter monsoon. Northeasterly winds from the South China Sea were blowing across the province, delivering rain and fog, severely limiting visibility. It was classic monsoon weather for January, and would likely only get worse as the day progressed, with lower cloud ceilings, frequent downpours, and dropping temperatures. In spite of this, the 1st Cav's helicopters were able to lift off by 0800 hours and begin transporting the troops to their target positions. The helicopters, however, were forced to fly at extremely low altitudes—below 300 feet—and at reduced air speeds to compensate for the weather, thereby increasing their vulnerability to enemy ground fire. Following an airstrike and artillery preparation, Captain Diduryk and Bravo Company, 2/7th Cav, air assaulted into LZ Steel to the west of Bong Son and secured it for follow-on artillery. Immediately afterwards, the lead elements of Captain Fesmire's Charlie Company, 2/7th Cav, air assaulted into LZ 4, a large open area that could accommodate multiple helicopters setting down at the same time to offload troops. Palm groves were located on the east and west sides of the LZ with clusters of hootches scattered among the palm groves. On the east side, a burial area, or graveyard, was located in the palm grove next to a large cluster of hootches, where villagers who once lived in the hamlet were interned.

Because the hamlet was heavily populated, it was not prepped with artillery fire before the troops air assaulted into it. Regardless, the initial lift was unopposed and the Charlie Company troops got on the ground and were able to secure the area for follow-on landings. When the second lift of helicopters approached the LZ with troops from Charlie Company onboard, North Vietnamese soldiers hiding in trenches, one-man spider holes, bamboo thickets, and palm groves on the east and west sides of the LZ opened up on them with mortar and machine-gun fire, hitting the helicopters and troops onboard and spraying the troops already on the ground. A pathfinder from the 11th Pathfinder Company (Airborne/Provisional), also known as "Black Hats," who had arrived in the lead helicopter of the initial lift, was on the ground guiding the helicopters into the LZ and was hit in the head with multiple metal fragments from enemy mortars, falling to the ground dead. This, plus the enemy ground fire directed at the helicopters and infantry passengers onboard, caused the flight formation to veer off to the north and south of the LZ to offload the troops. When the third lift of helicopters came in, the troops were set down about 200 meters to the east of the troops already on the ground. And when the fourth and final lift of helicopters came in, carrying members of the Mortar Platoon, they were offloaded about 100 meters behind the troops on the previous lift, next to a cluster of hootches with a graveyard nearby. The troops were able to take cover behind the burial mounds that dotted the surface. The Charlie Company troops were scattered over a distance of 300 meters or more.

By 0845 hours, Charlie Company was on the ground but it was badly fragmented, and the enemy fire directed at it was so intense that the troops were unable to maneuver or communicate with one another. When the company attempted to regroup, the sniper and mortar fire directed at it only increased in intensity. The rain and fog made the use of air support virtually impossible, and the scattered formation of the troops on the ground prevented the use of artillery. The Charlie Company troops were badly outnumbered and were forced to coil up into multiple separate and non-mutually supporting perimeters while the North Vietnamese soldiers moved through the trenches and tunnels in the hamlet to surround them.

Gerry Skelly from Mitchell, South Dakota, an RTO (radio telephone operator) with Charlie Company, remembered:

> We came in on four flights of Hueys—four helicopters per flight arranged in a diamond formation bringing in six men per helicopter, 24 per flight. Each flight offloaded the troops onboard and then returned to the pick-up zone to get the next group for transport to the LZ. Each lift was spaced three minutes apart, 12 minutes for total insertion of the company. We

rode the skids in and jumped to the ground from approximately 12 feet while the Hueys moved at about five mph in hover mode.

I came in on the first lift, the number four ship, with Captain Fesmire—I was his RTO. We took light fire on approach. We spread out to make room for the second lift, which in turn sets the troops back 100 meters behind our position. Things are beginning to spread out. This lift took heavy fire on approach and on liftoff, and the troops on the ground sustain heavy casualties. We do not have a functioning radio that is tuned to the lift frequency. The pilots are obviously communicating. At nine minutes, the third lift arrives. It sets the troops back 100 meters beyond the second lift, so now the company is spread out over more than 200 meters. At 12 minutes, the fourth and final lift arrives with the Mortar Platoon. It sets the troops down 100 meters beyond the last lift.

Captain Fesmire has no communication with the 3rd or 4th Platoons. The RTO for the Mortar Platoon is dead. The radio for the 3rd Platoon is out of communication—radio destroyed by enemy fire, and the RTO is badly wounded.

Captain Fesmire decides that he needs to know what's going on back 200 meters in the graveyard where many of the troops were set-down. He makes a wild run across 200 meters of open ground to where the men of the Mortar Platoon are located. I follow him, no stopping, no weaving. We drop 15 meters out from the jungle among the 4th Platoon dead and wounded. They are scattered 100 meters across the clearing. Doc has gone to the center of the graveyard dragging in some of the wounded. It is raining and miserable. There is sand everywhere. We yell back and forth occasionally to check on status, laughing that they'll dig a trench to the village.

Captain Fesmire gets hit by a sniper round—a minor wound in his right pinkie finger. His hand was on his head as we lay behind an 8in high circular grave—2in lower or higher and it would have hit his head or mine.

The decision is made to rejoin the reminder of the company which has regrouped with living/wounded and dead in the village. Doc yells that they will wait until we can get to them. He can't move the wounded. We run. Captain Fesmire and his rifle reach the village safely. I'm still behind in the graveyard. I run toward the village. They said that I covered the 200 meters in the wet sand in under ten seconds carrying 110 pounds of ammunition and equipment. I'm motivated by fear. Felt like it took an hour. The men at the village were cheering and yelling "You can make it." Never heard a thing. An enemy sniper tracks me but fails to hit me. I arrive alive. He did hit the radio but it is still functioning.[1]

South of Phung Du, Captain Sugdinis and Alpha Company had departed LZ 2 on foot at 0815 hours and were moving northward through the rice paddies toward Phung Du, a distance of 3 kilometers. Its movement was unopposed and there was no reason to think at the time that it would be unable to reach the southern end of the hamlet and establish a blocking position against which the Charlie Company troops would drive the North Vietnamese. Alpha Company consisted of two rifle platoons only and a command group since it lost its 3rd Platoon and a squad from its Mortar Platoon in the crash of the C-123 aircraft at the An Khe Pass three days earlier.

Captain Sugdinis recalled the company's move northward:

> The company moved forward in a column formation with the 2nd Platoon in the lead deployed over an approximate frontage of fifty meters. The company Command Group

---

[1] Email from Gerry Skelly to author, dated May 31, 2011, with attachment entitled "Regarding LZ 4 (Graveyard) January 28, 1966."

followed. It consisted of the company commander, two radio operators, one artillery forward observer with a radio operator and a reconnaissance sergeant, the company 1st sergeant with one radio operator, three ROK Army officers, three photographers—two American and one French, two American and one Australian reporters, and one official Army photographer. Needless to say, the Command Group was huge when you consider all the media personnel. Following this rather large group was the 1st Platoon, also deployed over approximately fifty meters of ground.[2]

Meanwhile, back at Position Dog, Colonel Moore and his 3rd Brigade commanders decided to scrap their plan to establish an artillery position at LZ Steel and instead focus on the enemy troops in Phung Du. Within the first hour of the operation, three Chinook helicopters enroute to LZ Steel with 105mm howitzers in sling load were hit by enemy ground fire and forced to set down. A fourth one en route to the LZ with a 105mm howitzer in sling load was so badly damaged by enemy ground fire that it started shaking violently and the pilot was forced to set the helicopter down 2 kilometers northwest of LZ 4 in close proximity to North Vietnamese soldiers on the ground. The pilot was able to release the sling and put the howitzer down on the ground, then set the helicopter down next to it while the three door gunners onboard prepared to defend the position with their M-60 machine guns. Enemy soldiers from the nearby village of Luong Tho wasted no time converging on the site, and Bravo Company, 1/7th Cav, was forced to air assault into the site to rescue the crew and secure the Chinook and howitzer. The Bravo Company troops received heavy mortar and small-arms fire upon landing and had to utilize the 105mm howitzer in a direct-fire role to repel the enemy soldiers. When Bravo Company continued to receive heavy fire from the village and areas to the north, Lieutenant Colonel Kampe decided to set aside his original mission—sweeping eastward from LZ Steel toward Phung Du, cutting off escape routes to the west—and moved the rest of his battalion to the site by helicopter throughout the day. The site was designated LZ Papa. It was later determined from interrogating captured enemy soldiers that the 1/7th Cav was battling elements of the 9th Battalion, 22nd NVA Regiment, at LZ Papa.

As Alpha Company, 2/7th Cav, continued to move northward in an attempt to reach Phung Du and establish a blocking position for Charlie Company, it started to encounter palm grove islands ringed with trenches at the perimeter, and spider holes and tunnels scattered throughout.

Captain Sugdinis recalled: "The abandoned enemy fortifications were extremely well built and prepared, and we expected to meet resistance at any time but we heard

---

[2] Captain Joel E. Sugdinis, U.S. Army Infantry School monograph, "Operations of Company A, 2nd Battalion, 7th Cavalry, 1st Air Cavalry Division, Near Bong Son, An Thi, Republic of Vietnam, 25–29 January 1966, Operation Masher, Personal Experience of a Company Commander, dated 1966–1967."

no shots. Apparently, the North Vietnamese soldiers had abandoned their positions to the south and consolidated in the vicinity of LZ 4."

By 1000 hours, Alpha Company had progressed to a low ridge area overlooking Phung Du, where the fighting was taking place. Tracer rounds could be seen going in all directions, with the smoke from grenades thrown by Charlie Company troops rising from the hamlet into the rain and fog. The Charlie Company troops were attempting to mark their positions for Lieutenant Colonel McDade, who was circling high above in his command & control helicopter. They had been unable to maneuver and remained in an unchanged situation since their landing, and were still receiving small-arms fire and sporadic mortar and 40mm rocket fire.

At this point, Captain Sugdinis changed the company formation, putting his two rifle platoons abreast of each other in a wide front in an attempt to reduce the risk of ambush. The 2nd Platoon was on the left and the 1st Platoon on the right. The Command Group was in the rear. Since the enemy forces were only 500 meters away, Captain Sugdinis suspected an ambush situation at any time. As the company moved forward, it entered a palm tree area where the ground sloped down quite rapidly and the company discovered that a relatively narrow rice paddy stood between it and Phung Du. The rice paddy bordered a cemetery on its east and southeast. The company cautiously approached the flooded rice paddy with both platoons abreast. As Alpha Company started to move forward from the palm tree area into the rice paddy, an automatic weapon opened up on the extreme left flank of the 2nd Platoon without warning, hitting the platoon leader's radio operator and killing him. Within seconds, several other weapons opened up on the 2nd Platoon troops from the far bank, forcing them to fall back to the palm tree area.

Doc Hackett remembered:

> The enemy had not seen us coming and was thrown off balance. We were about 100 meters away when they finally saw us and opened fire. Our platoon leader's RTO was shot in the chest by a sniper and fell into the knee-deep water. I went out into the rice paddy to check him but he was KIA. As I started to fall back to the tree line, Lieutenant Grove yelled to me to get the radio, which I did, but it had been rendered useless. Then a rifleman from our platoon was hit in the lungs and stomach area and later that night went into shock and died. Some of us tried to cross the open rice paddy straight toward the enemy but we were being hit by heavy fire and a 50-caliber machine gun from the far bank causing more casualties.[3]

At one point, an enemy round hit the lip of Captain Sugdinis's steel helmet, spinning it around and off his head to the ground. The round went on to nick his radio operator in the right arm, knocking him off balance. The velocity of the round indicated just how close the enemy force was to the troops of Alpha Company and how well concealed it was.

---

[3] Email from Jim "Doc" Hackett to author, with attachment entitled "LZ 4," dated June 2, 2011.

Captain Sugdinis directed Lieutenant Kelly to assault his platoon across the rice paddy to the far bank on signal and capture the enemy trenches on the island, while the 2nd Platoon put down a heavy base of fire.

Captain Sugdinis recalled:

> I gave the signal by radio. The 2nd Platoon put out devastating fire into the observed trenches, into the trees, and into the bank itself to seek out the cleverly concealed enemy. Suddenly a loud police whistle sounded, and in a beautiful movement the entire 1st Platoon moved on a dead run across the rice paddy. To everyone's surprise, not a single man was hit as the 1st Platoon stormed right up into the trenches. The enemy could be seen leaping up and fleeing the trench line to the north. The 1st Platoon quickly moved north through the trenches and into the palm grove against the enemy soldiers, firing from the shoulder as it advanced.

Seeing that the enemy soldiers were fleeing, Captain Sugdinis and the members of the Command Group moved into the rice paddy and attempted to cross. The enemy soldiers on the left front, however, opened up on them from a distance of about 100 meters, causing the majority of the group to seek cover in the knee-deep water behind the rice paddy dikes, and only Captain Sugdinis and three others successfully made it across on the first try. Captain Sugdinis then directed Lieutenant Kelly and the 1st Platoon to return to the crossing point and sweep north along the initial trench line, eliminate the enemy fire that covered the length of the rice paddy, and allow the Command Group and the 2nd Platoon to cross.

As Lieutenant Kelly and the 1st Platoon cleared the enemy soldiers from the trench line on the left front, the pinned-down members of the Command Group and 2nd Platoon worked their way across the rice paddy and onto the far bank.

Captain Sugdinis recalled:

> Under the outstanding leadership, drive, and determination of the leader of the 2nd Platoon, the squad leaders, and the individual platoon members, the entire 2nd Platoon and Command Group ran, crawled, and inched its way across the rice paddy and up into the abandoned Viet Cong trenches. The entire company, including the dead and wounded, were now on the island fortress and intact as a fighting unit.

PFC Jack Wagner remembered:

> The rice paddy seemed to be as wide as a football field and I could not see end-to-end. I was directed to stay behind as my platoon crossed and cover the rear in case we received enemy fire from behind so I was the last one in my platoon to come across. Running alongside the rice paddy dike for cover, it took me three attempts to get across. The enemy rounds would hit in front of me and behind me knocking out pieces of dirt from the dike. I would fall, place my M-16 rifle on the dike out of the water and act as though I was hit and take off running again. After three attempts to cross, I finally made it to the far bank and joined up with my platoon. To me, crossing that rice paddy was in itself hell.[4]

---

[4] In an email to author dated January 25, 2017, Jack Wagner describes the move across the rice paddy directly south of Phung Du by Alpha Company, 2nd Battalion. 7th Cav on January 28, 1966.

With Alpha Company now running dangerously low on ammunition, Captain Sugdinis knew that it needed to secure a LZ for the helicopters to bring in ammo and medical supplies. The cemetery at the southern end of Phung Du, with its white sand, large, rounded burial mounds, and occasional headstones, was chosen to be the landing zone. It was located 200 meters east of Alpha Company's present position on the far side of a palm grove, with tall palm trees and overgrown elephant grass, and hootches scattered among the palm trees.

Captain Sugdinis directed Lieutenant Kelly and the 1st Platoon to push eastward through the palm grove to the northern end of the cemetery, and Lieutenant Grove and the 2nd Platoon to move eastward toward the southern end of the cemetery. The 1st Platoon received only sporadic enemy fire as it advanced, but the 2nd Platoon was forced to move by individual fire teams and squads in short advances against increasing automatic weapons fire. Artillery from Position Dog was brought to bear on the North Vietnamese soldiers opposing the 2nd Platoon's advance, but the enemy was well concealed and occupied well dug-in positions, and the artillery appeared to be only marginally effective.

PFC Jack Wagner from the 1st Platoon commented:

> We lined up in a prone position to assault into the palm grove. When we started to move out, we received sniper fire. Lieutenant Kelly took an M-79 grenade launcher from one of the squad members and fired it into a tree. A Viet Cong sniper dropped out. As we pushed forward into the palm grove, we approached several hootches with rice baskets sitting outside and large woven basket lids strewn about. My platoon sergeant directed me and a member of my squad to clear a hole that was covered by one of the basket lids. I was directed to remove the lid and clear it while my squad member covered me. I kicked the lid aside and yelled into it "*di di mau.*" Out came two women, one a young mother with a baby. They were very frightened. I continued to yell into the hole but no one else came out. I threw a grenade into it after it was cleared. The two women followed us as we ran to catch up with the rest of the platoon but my platoon sergeant seemed peeved that we allowed them to follow and told us to take them back to their hootches. We took them back a short distance, pointed to their hootches, and told them to go back, which they did. We continued to sweep eastward toward the northern end of the cemetery with my squad. Somewhere on the sweep my squad leader was hit with enemy mortar and automatic weapons fire and killed. He was a replacement who had served with the 82nd Airborne Division in the Dominican Republic and had been diverted to the 1st Cav when he arrived in Vietnam to make up for the losses that the 1st Cav suffered in the Ia Drang Valley two months earlier. He was very conscientious and kept a close check on all of us in his squad. We heard that he was hit in the head but we later learned that he was hit in the leg and bled to death. As we approached the last set of hootches that sat between the palm grove and the cemetery, North Vietnamese soldiers opened up on us. A member of my squad was hit immediately. Then I got hit. Our squad cleared the hootches and the two of us were able to make our way to a horseshoe-shaped trench located in the middle of the cemetery that was fast becoming a collection point for the wounded and dead.

The horseshoe-shaped trench was long enough and deep enough to hold a large enemy force, such as a platoon or reinforced platoon of soldiers, and was likely part of the enemy's line of defense together with the trenches ringing the perimeter of the palm groves. For the next day or so, however, it would serve as a relatively safe spot for the wounded troops of the 7th Cavalry.

By 1530 hours, Alpha Company had reached the cemetery and encircled it, but intense enemy fire was being received from multiple directions and the troops could do little more than take cover behind the burial mounds and headstones, and dig into the sand. It was apparent that Alpha Company, like Charlie Company scattered to the north, was badly outnumbered and surrounded by the enemy. Shortly afterwards, Lieutenant Colonel McDade landed in the cemetery in his command & control helicopter to join Alpha Company and to coordinate the resupply of ammunition and reinforcements. His helicopter drew intensive small-arms and automatic weapons fire from the east and south as it approached the cemetery and lifted off to return to Dog. It was hit numerous times but was not shot down. The direction of the enemy fire indicated that the North Vietnamese had moved back into the trench line immediately north of the rice paddy that Alpha Company had just cleared, confirming that Alpha Company was now also completely surrounded by enemy soldiers.

At 1700 hours, a decision was made by McDade to reinforce Alpha Company with the troops of Bravo Company, 2/7th Cav. A heavy smokescreen of artillery was placed on the eastern side of the cemetery to provide cover for the incoming helicopters that would be approaching from the west. Six helicopters from Charlie Company, 229th Assault Helicopter Battalion, brought in a platoon from Bravo Company with Captain Diduryk and his Command Group, but again the helicopters drew intense enemy ground fire from the east and south as they approached the cemetery. A door gunner on one of the helicopters was shot and killed, and a pilot wounded. A member of Bravo Company's Command Group was also wounded.

Captain Sugdinis recalled:

> The troops of Alpha Company literally fired a "mad minute" with one magazine from each weapon as the six helicopters came in to land. The Viet Cong had been waiting and released a volume of fire which was unbelievable, hitting all six ships and wounding two members of the crew. It was apparent that we were badly outnumbered, and it was immediately decided not to bring in any more reinforcements that night. Miraculously, 28 troopers from Bravo Company jumped out of the helicopters and into the friendly trenches with fresh supplies of ammunition without the loss of a single man.

Even with the additional ammunition, it was apparent that more would be needed to defend the perimeter should the North Vietnamese soldiers launch an all-out attack against Alpha Company that night. With that, a decision was made by McDade to use a north–south approach route on the western side of the cemetery for the resupply helicopters. There had been very little fire on that side, and a sunken rice paddy there offered some cover. The area was pounded with artillery and sprayed with mini-gun fire, aerial grenades, and 2.75-inch rockets by aerial rocket gunships from Charlie Battery, 2/20th ARA. At 1830 hours, three helicopters approached the western side of Phung Du from the north, flying just a few feet above the rice paddies. The crews threw out crates of ammunition, medical supplies, water, and food as they passed a point on the dry ground with a poncho with an "X" laid out. Heavy enemy ground fire was received from seemingly everywhere, and all three helicopters were hit and damaged. One was so badly damaged that it crashed into a rice paddy. The four-man crew was unhurt and managed to climb out and maneuver through the palm grove and take refuge with the Alpha Company troops in the cemetery. They carried with them the helicopter's two M-60 machine guns and multiple boxes of M-60 ammunition. All of the supplies were recovered from the rice paddy.

Northwest of LZ 4, the 1/7th Cav had established a defensive position at LZ Papa to prevent any additional enemy soldiers from fleeing the LZ 4 area northward or from moving southward into Phung Du to reinforce the North Vietnamese at LZ 4 or at the cemetery. At approximately 1700 hours that afternoon, a Chinook helicopter from Bravo Company, 228th Assault Support Helicopter, arrived at LZ Papa to airlift out an OH-13 observation helicopter from the 1/9th Cav. It had been hit by enemy ground fire earlier that afternoon and forced to land. Luckily, the pilot was able to set it down at a spot close to friendly troops. The helicopter, whose two-man crew was unhurt, had been providing aerial reconnaissance for the 1/7th Cav. The OH-13 was strapped to the bottom of the Chinook in sling load, but as it was being lifted out, the pilot of the Chinook was shot in the head by enemy ground fire at an estimated altitude of 800 feet and killed. The co-pilot of the Chinook was able to take control of the aircraft and complete the airlift operation without crashing.[5]

As the evening progressed, the temperature continued to drop and the light misty rain turned into a hard and steady downpour, making the use of air support virtually impossible. The situation with the Charlie Company troops had not changed. They were still coiled up in three separate perimeters north of the cemetery, but as long as they didn't move and create targets for the enemy soldiers, the North Vietnamese did not fire at them. As the night progressed, however, the situation improved for the Charlie Company troops. The darkness and heavy rain gave them the cover they needed to regroup, allowing Lieutenant Colonel McDade to pinpoint their locations and call in artillery to support their move southward toward the cemetery and the rest of the battalion there, a distance of roughly 1 kilometer.

Captain Sugdinis recalled:

> Around midnight, the Charlie Company commander reported that he had regrouped his company and was prepared to move southward en masse toward the Alpha Company perimeter.

---

[5] In a document from the Center of Military History, Lieutenant General John J. Tolson described the incident of the Chinook helicopter piloted by Major Taylor D. Johnson being hit by enemy ground fire, killing Major Johnson, while airlifting out the OH-13 observation helicopter. Center of Military History, United States Army, Washington, D.C. (1999), "Vietnam Studies, Airmobility 1961–1971," CMH Pub. 90–94; 1973, 93.

The problem at this point was identifying the Charlie Company troops as they approached from the north. Since no one possessed any confidence in the assigned challenge and password, the Alpha Company commander issued instructions that any sightings on the north side of the perimeter would be greeted with a "Garry Owen" yell for recognition, the battalion motto.

Captain Fesmire's plan for the movement of Charlie Company through the hamlet to Alpha Company's perimeter called for the troops to move in a single file formation with no talking or joking, no smoking, and complete radio silence. One radio would be used by Captain Fesmire to communicate with Lieutenant Colonel McDade. They were to move slowly and cautiously, and to avoid contact with the enemy if at all possible as firing their weapons would only reveal their positions. Grenades could be used to accomplish the same purpose while allowing the troops to stay hidden in the darkness and rain. The troops would have to carry the weapons and ammunition of the wounded and dead while keeping an eye open for any troopers who might have become separated from the main body of the company in the initial air assault into LZ 4 and may still be alive in the hamlet. The troops would also have to carry the wounded as needed and the bodies of the dead, requiring four troopers to carry each body, adding to the confusion of the move and further weakening the troops. Everybody knew that the move could end up in disaster, but they also realized that there really was no alternative. At 0255 hours, the Charlie Company troops began moving south through the hamlet in the darkness and rain under the cover of artillery fire.

While Captain Fesmire and the troops of Charlie Company started to move through the hamlet, the ARVN Airborne Brigade positioned along Highway 1, 2 kilometers to the east of LZ 4, was reporting that it was under attack from a large enemy force. The size of the force was estimated to be a company-sized unit or larger, based on information obtained from captured enemy soldiers. The North Vietnamese were apparently using the darkness and heavy rain to flee the LZ 4 area eastward along the banks of the rivers that flowed west-to-east through the area to Tam Quan Bay.

Meanwhile, back at the cemetery, the North Vietnamese were aggressively probing the south side of the cemetery in an attempt to find a way to penetrate Alpha Company's perimeter. At about 0200 hours, enemy soldiers moved along the south side of the cemetery and lobbed potato masher-style grenades at the perimeter in attempt to determine if there were Alpha Company troops guarding it or if it was unmanned. Most of the grenades, however, were duds and either didn't cause much of an explosion or failed to explode at all. The heavy rain had soaked the fuses of the grenades to the point that they were rendered near useless. Once the Alpha Company troops realized this, they were able to concentrate not on the grenades being thrown at them but on the enemy soldiers who were throwing them, and they had their targets. At daybreak, there were nine new bodies littering the area south of the cemetery.

While the Alpha Company troops on the south side of the cemetery were fighting off probes from the North Vietnamese, those to the east of the cemetery were busy exchanging fire with enemy snipers and a machine gunner hidden in a tree line. At one point in the darkness and rain, a member of the 2nd Platoon crawled out of the Alpha Company perimeter on his stomach and maneuvered through the sand toward the tree line to the east—a distance of more than 50 meters—in an attempt to locate and knock out a 50-caliber machine gun that had been delivering devastating fire on the Alpha Company perimeter. As he stood up and assaulted the tree line where the 50-caliber was located, an enemy sniper opened up, wounding him in the chest, and he was unable to continue the assault or return to the Alpha Company perimeter. Seeing this, Doc Hackett grabbed his poncho and crawled out of the perimeter to where the trooper was lying. On signal, the Alpha Company troops opened up with covering fire on the tree line, allowing Hackett to slide his poncho underneath the trooper and drag him back to the perimeter, where he could receive first aid. Although Hackett got him back to the perimeter, the trooper died later that night from his wounds.

Charlie Company continued to move very slowly southward through the hamlet toward Alpha Company's position in the cemetery. Captain Fesmire reported to Lieutenant Colonel McDade that there were many enemy soldiers in the area talking very loudly and acting confused, as if they didn't know which way to go. The instructions to the Charlie Company men were to continue moving with extreme caution and avoid contact if at all possible.

At 0430 hours, the Alpha Company troops positioned at the northeast corner of the perimeter detected movement coming toward them from the north. However, this was not from any Charlie Company troops but instead from two North Vietnamese soldiers who were attempting to penetrate the Alpha Company perimeter. The two were quickly captured by Alpha Company, disarmed, and brought to the trench located in the middle of the cemetery, where their arms were tied behind their backs and their hands and feet bound. They were put under armed guard next to two other North Vietnamese prisoners who had been captured on the previous afternoon with a machine gun on wheels. Bob Poos and Henri Huet, the AP reporter and photographer, stood guard over the enemy prisoners.[6] A number of local villagers, who had taken refuge with Alpha Company when the fighting started, were situated further down the trench from the prisoners. They included the two women and the baby whom the Alpha Company troops had encountered the previous afternoon in the palm grove. They had subsequently left their hootches and sought shelter in the trench in the cemetery. The woman with

---

[6] United States Marine Corps Combat Correspondents Association, "Bob Poos, AP correspondent dies after a lengthy illness," https://www.usmccaonline.com/cc-bob-poos-ap-correspondent-dies-after-a-lengthy-illness/.

the baby had since received a serious wound to one of her hands, almost severing it from her arm—possibly from an unexploded potato masher-style grenade that detonated when she picked it up—and required medical treatment. Unfortunately, she would have to wait until daylight before she could be medically evacuated to the Bong Son Dispensary for treatment. Tragically, her baby died that night in the trench, most likely from hypothermia.

The Bong Son District Dispensary had been in operation since the summer of 1965, when a team of American and New Zealand doctors, nurses, and corpsmen opened it to provide out-patient and limited in-patient care to Vietnamese civilians living in northeastern Binh Dinh Province.[7] It operated under the control of the U.S. Agency for International Development, Program of Public Health, as assistance to the Vietnamese Ministry of Health, Social Welfare, and Refugees. It was essentially an extension of the Binh Dinh Provincial Hospital in Qui Nhon, and was staffed by all volunteers. It treated civilian war victims and accident casualties from the surrounding areas and was equipped to perform out-patient and limited surgical services.[8] It was rumored to have also treated North Vietnamese and Viet Cong soldiers who were wounded in the fighting on the coastal plains and were unable to make it to the North Vietnamese field hospitals in the An Lao Valley. Safety concerns and staffing problems eventually forced the dispensary to close in 1975 and consolidate its efforts around the provincial hospital in Qui Nhon when the threat of violence became a reality—an explosive device killed a member of the dispensary's medical team.

At 0450 hours, the lead elements of Charlie Company reached the cemetery and entered Alpha Company's perimeter, completing the linkup of Charlie Company with the rest of the battalion. They carried with them 20 wounded troopers and the bodies of eight dead. Seven Charlie Company troopers were missing. Alpha Company had suffered seven KIA in the day's fighting, bringing the total number of KIA to 15 for the battalion.

For January 28, the 3rd Brigade reported that 39 helicopters and one fixed-wing aircraft had been hit by enemy ground fire. The breakdown of the damaged aircraft was as follows: 30 UH-1D helicopters were hit, 14 were flyable, and 16 were non-flyable; three UH-1B helicopter gunships were hit, with two still flyable and one non-flyable; four Chinook helicopters were hit, one was flyable, and three non-flyable; two LOH observation helicopters were hit, one flyable and the other non-flyable, airlifted out of the area under heavy enemy fire; and one L19 (O-1) Bird Dog fixed-wing aircraft was hit by enemy fire but was able to be flown back to its base in Pleiku.

---

[7] New Zealand's Vietnam War, "Memories of New Zealand and the Vietnam War, Surgical and Medical support," https://vietnamwar.govt.nz/nz-vietnam-war/surgical-and-medical-support.

[8] Robert J. Wilensky, MD, PhD., "The Medical Civic Action Program in Vietnam: Success or Failure?" Military Medicine.

CHAPTER FOUR

Breakout from the Cemetery

On the morning of January 29, the weather started to improve on the Bong Son Plain. The rain had stopped and the low cloud ceiling began to lift, allowing air support to be brought in on the enemy positions. At 0715 hours, aerial reconnaissance helicopters from the 1st Squadron, 9th Cavalry, with helicopter gunship escorts, arrived over Phung Du and initiated reconnaissance activities. They immediately spotted a large group of approximately 100 North Vietnamese soldiers at the northern end of the hamlet, in the vicinity of LZ 4, moving southward in the direction of the 2nd Battalion, 7th Cavalry, in the cemetery. Shortly afterwards, the troops of the 2/7th Cav began receiving intense sniper fire from the north and east, but reported no additional casualties. By 0830 hours, the weather had improved to the point where tactical air support was available and Lieutenant Colonel McDade requested an airstrike on the enemy positions. The USAF responded with a FAC and two Skyraiders. The Skyraiders made multiple runs over the areas to the north and east of the cemetery, dropping napalm, white phosphorus, and high-explosive bombs. The bombs detonated enemy ammunition caches, causing secondary explosions in the deep trenches and fires. The explosions raised smoke to heights of 2,000 feet or more and sent dirt, rocks, and debris flying through the air in every direction. The troops of the 2/7th Cav had been receiving moderate to heavy machine-gun and small-arms fire through the night and early morning hours from these areas, and had been able to do little more than exchange small-arms fire with the enemy.

At 1045 hours, the troops of Alpha and Bravo companies of Lieutenant Colonel Earl Ingram's 2nd Battalion, 12th Cavalry, accompanied by the brigade CO, Colonel Hal Moore, and his sergeant major, arrived by helicopter in a dry rice paddy area 2 kilometers south of Phung Du, with no enemy contact reported. The two companies moved northward through the rice paddies toward Phung Du in a column formation, with the lead company deployed over a frontage of 50 meters, sweeping the hamlets they encountered as they went. By 1140 hours, the remaining two companies of the 2/12th Cav were on the ground south of Phung Du and were moving northward through the rice paddies to link up with Alpha and Bravo companies. The 2/12th Cav had been on standby at Position Dog and the Special Forces camp, prepared to join the battle when called. It had arrived in the Bong Son area on the afternoon of January 27 and remained there on standby, with two companies at Dog and two at the Special Forces camp. On the morning of January 28, when the 2/7th Cav became heavily engaged at LZ 4, weather conditions prevented the movement of the 2/12th Cav to Phung Du to reinforce the 2/7th Cav. Drizzle and fog with low cloud ceilings completely covered the coastal plain and nearby mountains, the ground fog so intense that air support was limited to extreme combat emergencies, so the 2/12th Cav was forced to remain where it was, waiting for weather conditions to improve.

When the two lead companies of the 2/12th Cav reached the rice paddy bordering the cemetery at Phung Du to the southwest, they changed their formation to a wide front and moved into the rice paddy. They immediately started to receive machine-gun and small-arms fire from North Vietnamese soldiers in the trenches on the far bank. The 2/12th Cav troops responded with a volume of fire that quickly overwhelmed the enemy soldiers, forcing them to abandon the trenches and flee to the north. The 2/12th Cav troops crossed the rice paddy and, firing from the shoulder, moved up into the abandoned trenches and advanced into the palm grove leading to the cemetery where the troops of the 2/7th Cav were located. The 2/12th Cav reported two enemy KIA in the exchange and no friendly casualties.

No sooner had Colonel Moore and the two companies of the 2/12th Cav reached the palm grove than all hell broke loose in the An Lao Valley. The 3rd Brigade's operations officer at Position Dog urgently radioed Colonel Moore to report that Major Beckwith and his Project Delta teams had found the enemy, in force, in the An Lao Valley.[1] One of Beckwith's three teams, Team 2—code name "Capital"—had been ambushed by enemy soldiers and suffered four KIA. The two survivors, both of whom were wounded, were pinned down in the jungle underbrush, unable to maneuver, and needed extraction. Beckwith, along with three other Project Delta soldiers, was flying to the scene in the unit's command & control helicopter to locate the survivors' position.

When the team's call came in to the Project Delta operations officer at the Special Forces camp, the helicopter gunships and troop-carrying slicks supporting Project Delta, the 145th Airlift Platoon, were either being refueled and rearmed at the camp or were on their way back to the camp, and were unable to immediately follow

---

[1] Remembrances left for SFC Marlin C. Cook, SSGT Donald L. Dotson, SFC Jesse L. Hancock, and SSGT George A. Hoaglund III, described Project Delta Team 2 on a mission on January 29, 1966. Posted by wkillian@smjuhsd.org, 2016. Vietnam Veterans Memorial Fund, The Wall of Faces, https://www.vvmf.org.

Beckwith into the valley.[2] They would have to catch up to him to extract the team when the refueling and rearming operations were completed.

Because of the weather in the valley—light drizzle and fog with a cloud ceiling below 1,000 feet—Beckwith's command & control helicopter was forced to fly at an extremely low altitude—below 300 feet—and at reduced air speeds, increasing its vulnerability to enemy ground fire. Before it reached the point beyond An Lao village where the valley narrowed, it started to receive small-arms and automatic weapons fire on the left side of the aircraft. The crew chief began firing his M-60 machine gun at anything below that moved, and Beckwith, who was sitting in the passenger seat next to the crew chief, also began firing, as did the 1st sergeant who was sitting on the floor in the passenger compartment in front of Beckwith. Moments later, Beckwith was hit in the abdomen with a round that first struck the crew chief in the hand. The round was believed to be a 51-caliber round from a Soviet DShK heavy machine gun. By now, the aircraft had been hit with numerous rounds and was shaking violently. The pilot turned the helicopter away from the enemy fire and headed back to the Special Forces camp, where Beckwith and the crew chief could get medical treatment.

Team 2 had been inserted onto the high ground northeast of the An Lao Valley at the southern end of a small river valley on the evening of January 27. The valley ran northeast–southwest, with a river running down the middle of it. The river eventually joined the An Lao River in the vicinity of Route 514, several kilometers west of the valley. The valley was home to a number of small villages, including Hoc Dien, all of which were suspected of being Viet Cong strongholds.

The second of Beckwith's three teams, Team 3—code name "Roadrunner" —had likewise encountered the enemy, but on the morning of January 28. The team made initial contact with an enemy force along a streambed at 0930 hours and was forced to execute an escape-and-evade maneuver up a nearby hillside to break contact. At 1230 hours, the team came under a hail of small-arms fire. One of the team members was hit in the left arm with multiple bullets that almost severed his arm at the shoulder. The other team members applied a tourniquet to the wound and administered morphine while they were still under fire. The team was again forced to execute an escape-and-evade maneuver to break contact, and moved about 600 meters before stopping to provide medical help to the wounded team member. Once more, the team came under fire, forcing it to split into two groups of three

---

[2] Description of the attempt by the 145th Airlift Platoon to rescue Project Delta Team 2, "Capital," which had been ambushed by the Viet Cong in the mountains north of the An Lao Valley on January 29, 1966. Duane D. Vincent, "An Lao Valley Incident," https://www.281st.com/281Remembrance/stories/an_lao_valley_incident_duane_vincent.htm, November 2006.

to evade the attacking enemy. The group with the wounded team member used the cover of a steep slope, and after dark used a streambed to hide their trail. Despite constant medical attention during the night, the condition of the wounded man steadily worsened due to the loss of blood, and he died in the early hours of January 29. The two remaining team members were forced to leave his body, hiding it in the boulders and shrubs, with the hope of returning to the site with a ready-reaction force to recover it. They continued to maneuver during the early morning and were eventually spotted by aerial observation helicopter pilots and extracted.[3]

The second group of the team successfully evaded the enemy during the daytime of January 28 and settled into a hiding place that evening. At first light on January 29, the three team members began moving again, hoping to get to an open area where they could be spotted by aerial observation helicopter pilots searching for them and extracted. At 1630 hours, the trio encountered a squad of seven Viet Cong soldiers who had stumbled upon their position in a field of tall elephant grass. The team members opened fire on the enemy, killing three of them. A brief firefight resulted; one of the team members was hit in the side with several rounds and died shortly afterwards. The remaining two men attempted an escape-and-evade maneuver when one of them was hit and killed by enemy fire. The surviving team member managed to evade the pursuing enemy and was eventually spotted by the pilot of an aerial observation helicopter and extracted. The bodies of the three KIA were not recovered.

The third of Beckwith's three teams, Team 1—code name "Eskimo"—never made it through the first night of the mission. It had to be extracted from the valley, with one member wounded, shortly after being inserted into it due to intense enemy activity.

Contrary to the plan that Colonel Moore and his 3rd Brigade commanders had developed with Beckwith, Moore had no ready-reaction force with which to support the Project Delta teams. The 3rd Brigade was fully extended at Phung Du, and the 2/12th Cav, which had been on standby waiting to be called on to reinforce the 7th Cav battalions, had since been committed to the battle. The situation with the 2/7th Cav at the cemetery and with the 1st Battalion, 7th Cavalry, north of LZ 4, was still developing, and the battalions needed reinforcements to ensure continued progress. The best that Moore could do for Beckwith at this time was to organize a rescue mission for the team that was currently in trouble. Engaging the enemy with a reaction force would have to wait.

---

[3] Remembrances left for SSGT Neil Badolati, SFC Cecil J. Hodgeson, and SSGT Ronald T. Terry, Project Delta Team 3, January 29, 1966. Posted by Clay Marston, cmarston@interlog.com, 2007. Vietnam Veterans Memorial Fund, The Wall of Faces, https://www.vvmf.org

At 1230 hours, Charlie Troop, 1st Squadron, 9th Cavalry, was alerted to mount a rescue mission in the An Lao Valley for the Project Delta team.[4] Alpha Company, 1/7th Cav, was alerted to move by helicopter to a location on the high ground east of the valley for artillery that would cover the area where the team was believed to be located. The position was designated LZ Brass. The 1st Battalion, 12th Cav, was alerted to move one company to Position Dog in preparation for deploying into the An Lao Valley to assist with the extraction if needed. The 1/12th Cav was the designated brigade reserve force for the 3rd Brigade and had been securing LZ Hammond as an aircraft laager area. Finally, tactical air support was alerted to be ready to support the extraction should it be needed.

By 1315 hours, two hunter-killer aerial teams from Charlie Troop, 1/9th Cav, consisting of observation helicopters and helicopter gunship escorts, along with aerial rocket gunships from Charlie Battery, 2/20th ARA, had located the two survivors of the team on the high ground north of the An Lao Valley. The Charlie Blues were inserted onto the ground to link up with the survivors of the team. The Blues immediately came under fire from enemy soldiers, but with aerial support from the helicopter gunships, were able to advance through the jungle toward the team's position, driving the enemy deeper into the jungle.

In parallel with the 1/9th Cav's efforts, a small ready-reaction force consisting of members of Project Delta, including Sergeant Major Walt Shumate—who later became a Special Forces legend in his role as the sergeant major for Beckwith— had arrived at the site only moments before the 1/9th Cav got there, and was first on the ground. The two ready-reaction forces moved frantically through the jungle from different directions and linked up with the two survivors by 1330 hours. They recovered the bodies of the four KIA, and with the two survivors moved to a clearing where they could be extracted. By 1516 hours, everyone had been successfully extracted from the valley and returned to the Special Forces camp.

Staff Sergeant Chuck Hiner, one of the two survivors of Team 2, later said: "You know when I knew I had made it? When I looked up and saw Sgt. Major Walt Shumate's bare ass coming over the top of that log where SFC [Sergeant First Class] Frank Webber and I had taken cover. Walt told me later that he was busting bush so hard and fast coming toward us that he busted out of his pants."

Meanwhile, back at Phung Du, Colonel Moore and the 2/12th Cav encountered stiff enemy resistance in the areas south and east of the cemetery as they attempted to move through the palm grove. Tactical air support was requested and the USAF responded with a FAC and two Skyraiders. The Skyraiders pounded the area with 500lb high-explosive bombs and napalm in an attempt to neutralize the

---

[4]   Story of Project Delta Team 3 in the mountains north of An Lao Valley, January 29, 1966. Roger L. Albertson, "The Last Survivor, A Memorial Day Tribute." http://www.projectdelta.net

enemy fire. At one point, Colonel Moore radioed the operations officer at Dog to report: "[T]he airstrikes are causing secondary explosions in the deep trenches and there are many hardcore VC located in them." At 1430 hours, Moore and the 2/12th Cav finally broke through the palm grove and reached the cemetery, linking up with the 2/7th Cav. The 2/7th Cav had been receiving machine-gun and small-arms fire from the area east of the cemetery throughout the morning and early afternoon.[5]

Al Zeller, a rifleman with the 2nd Platoon, Bravo Company, 2/12th Cav, remembered:

> When we got to the cemetery where the 2/7th Cav was located, there was a lot of expended and unexpended ordinance scattered around the area, including unexploded North Vietnamese hand grenades—the potato masher type. I picked up a 20mm projectile that had exploded into a flower shape—I still have it as a souvenir of Bong Son. There was a trench in the middle of the cemetery where the wounded 7th Cav troopers were, and where the North Vietnamese prisoners were being held under armed guard. Somebody said that one of them was a large Chinese soldier who was an advisor to the North Vietnamese and was carrying a large roll of money. There were also bloody bandages scattered everywhere in the trench from the medics treating the wounded troopers. There were also some women and children from the village at the far end of the trench who took refuge with the 2/7th Cav. Beyond the trench lay the bodies of the dead 7th Cav troopers.[6]

Once the explosions and fires from the airstrike died out, the 2/12th Cav moved out of the cemetery and proceeded northward along the eastern side of Phung Du toward LZ 4 at the northern end of the hamlet, putting out a wall of fire and flying steel and clearing the bunkers, trenches, and extensive tunneling as it went. The trenches had permitted the North Vietnamese soldiers to move freely within an area about 300 meters by 500 meters without being exposed. As the 2/12th Cav advanced, the enemy resistance stiffened; and at one point, Bravo Company encountered an enemy machine gunner who held it up for more than an hour. It was only after an airstrike—the third one of the day in the LZ 4 area—was called in that the enemy machine gunner was wounded and captured, and Bravo Company was able to resume its sweep northward. At another point, Charlie Company, which was moving north between Bravo Company on its east flank and the open area running up and down the middle of the hamlet on its west flank, found itself pinned down by at least two enemy machine guns firing at it from cross directions and could not maneuver. A fourth airstrike followed by artillery from Position Dog was needed to clear the area to allow Charlie Company to continue its sweep toward LZ 4. On the sweep northward, Alpha Company suffered one KIA and Bravo Company two KIA.

---

[5] Email from Jim "Doc" Hackett to author, with attachment entitled "LZ 4," dated June 2, 2011.
[6] Email from Al Zeller to author, dated November 11, 2019.

The area on the east side of Phung Du was originally manned by a battalion of North Vietnamese soldiers, but many of them had fled north and east during the night, leaving behind multiple platoon-sized rear guard elements intended to delay the 1st Cav's advance. It was later determined from interrogating enemy prisoners that the area had been occupied by the 7th Battalion, 22nd NVA Regiment, reinforced by a heavy weapons company.

On the sweep northward, the 2/12th Cav found four troopers from Charlie Company, 2/7th Cav, who had spent the night holed up in a foxhole in the vicinity of LZ 4. All four of them had come in on the initial air assault into LZ 4 and had set down several hundred meters east of the open area where the other Charlie Company troops were scattered about. All four had been wounded fighting off enemy soldiers and were unable to link up with the rest of the company when Captain Fesmire regrouped his troops in preparation for the move en masse southward to the Alpha Company perimeter in the cemetery. The four troopers managed to find each other in the darkness and rain, and enlarged one of their foxholes to protect the four of them as they continued to fight off the North Vietnamese soldiers. One of the four soldiers, the senior medic of Charlie Company, had received several wounds to his body during the day and had his M-16 rifle shattered by a direct hit from an AK-47 rifle as he was firing at an enemy soldier. He was able to move around and administer first aid to the other three wounded men, who could not move, and he voluntarily stayed behind to help them. At daybreak, the four of them realized that they were the only Americans still on LZ 4.

Once it was safe for a medevac helicopter to be brought in, Lieutenant Colonel McDade contacted brigade headquarters at Dog and requested evacuation of the wounded 2/7th Cav troopers in the cemetery. He also asked for the medical evacuation of the wounded villagers in the cemetery who had taken refuge with the 2/7th Cav troopers and needed to be transported to the Bong Son Dispensary for treatment. He also alerted the remainder of his battalion to move by helicopter to the cemetery. Both Delta Company and the three remaining platoons of Bravo Company had been at Dog, waiting to be called to join the rest of the battalion at LZ 4. They were brought in throughout the afternoon without further contact to help secure the perimeter at the cemetery.

Doc Hackett remembered:

> At around 1500 hours, we started to evacuate the wounded. Dr. William Shucart, our battalion doctor, was one of the first in to the cemetery to assist with it. He immediately started taking care of the seriously wounded and helped to prioritize the evacuation based on medical need. We all felt relieved that our wounded men were being flown to the 15th Med aid station at Dog where they would get the medical attention they needed. We helped the woman with the seriously injured hand onto the helicopter for evacuation to the Bong Son Dispensary. She was carrying the body of her baby.

By 1645 hours, the 2/12th Cav had reached the southern edge of LZ 4. When it attempted to maneuver out of the palm grove into the open area of the landing zone, it came under heavy machine-gun and mortar fire from multiple enemy positions to its north and northeast. A fifth airstrike was requested and the USAF responded with two Skyraiders that pounded the enemy positions with high-explosive bombs and napalm. By 2000 hours, the enemy positions had been silenced and the 2/12th Cav resumed its movement to locations at the western and eastern ends of LZ 4, where it established night defensive positions.

Al Zeller recalled:

> We came out of the palm grove on the east side of Phung Du and entered a small corn field. Sgt. Robert "Heavy Duty" Smith immediately got hit in the neck with a sniper round. SP4 [Specialist 4] Dan Gensemer, who was less than five feet from me, and Tom Day, started to crawl out into the corn field to get him but both of them were hit with enemy fire. Gensemer was hit in his left arm with a bullet that went through his arm and hit Day. We threw smoke to our front to create a smoke screen and our platoon medic, SP4 Richardson, crawled out into the corn field to recover the bodies of Sgt. Smith and Gensemer while we provided covering fire.
>
> Later that night, we pulled back from where we had been pinned down at the edge of the palm grove and carried our dead and wounded with us to a point where we could put them on choppers for evacuation. The helicopters landed about two hundred meters to our rear and we loaded the wounded and dead on them for transport to Position Dog. Rudy Jaramillo, also a rifleman with my platoon, and I carried Gensemer's body to the helicopter. Several of the other members of our squad carried the body of SSgt. Bernard Wait to the waiting choppers. SSgt. Wait was in the 1st Platoon. He got killed earlier that afternoon by enemy fire but I didn't witness it.
>
> The night of January 29 was grim, possibly one of the worst nights I spent in Vietnam. My squad had 2 KIA and 2 WIA. We lost a lot of guys that day, including my best friend, so I was pretty hollow inside. Later that evening, my fire team was sent out for the night on a listening post detail at the end of a levy [sic] where the water was pretty deep and we all got "hook worm" (i.e., rice paddy itch). It was a sleepless night for us because of the rice paddy itch and because the North Vietnamese were sniping at us all night with a 57mm recoilless rifle.

Raul (Rudy) Jaramillo remembered:

> Shortly after the helicopters picked up our wounded and dead for evacuation to Position Dog, Sgt. Belvedere told us that we would be going out on a night patrol to check out some hootches north of where Sgt. Smith and Gensemer got hit. There would be five of us and I would walk point. We moved out from the 2nd Platoon's line into an open field, crossed it, and moved down an embankment to a creek. I signaled the patrol to halt while I crossed the creek to recon the other side. Then I signaled the patrol to cross to the other side where there were several hootches. I signaled the patrol to again halt while I investigated the hootch closest to me. I opened the door and saw a family sitting there getting ready to eat. I closed the door and went back to tell Sgt. Belvedere what I had found. Sgt. Belvedere radioed Lieutenant Dean Knox, commander of Bravo Company, to report what I had found. Lieutenant Knox told us to continue with the patrol. By then it was dark and we were forced to move very slowly. We hadn't gone very far when we suddenly heard the sound of small arms fire to our rear. We learned the next morning that battalion had sent out a patrol to our south and it got ambushed. The point man was hit and died shortly afterwards. The patrol was from the 1st Platoon.
>
> No sooner did we hear the small arms fire to our rear than we heard incoming artillery rounds—155mm rounds. The rounds were landing very close to our position, almost on top

of us, and we were forced to take cover where we could—in a pigsty. Sgt. Belvedere radioed Lieutenant Knox to call off the artillery. We were getting a dirt-and-rock shower, and one of the rounds landed so close to me in the pigsty that the concussion from it knocked me unconscious. I came-to later. By then the artillery had stopped. I was bleeding from my nose, mouth, and ears, but other than that, I had survived the artillery barrage. We all had survived the artillery barrage. I felt groggy but conscious. We could hear the Viet Cong digging to our rear … I was afraid that they would attack us during the night. I didn't sleep much. I kept one eye open all night long.[7]

At 2100 hours, the 2/12th Cav reported to brigade 56 enemy KIA and 22 WIA, with three friendly KIA and 21 WIA, for the day's fighting.

The operations officer at Dog radioed Lieutenant Colonel Ingram at 2300 hours to notify him that a mechanized infantry company from the ARVN 3rd Troop, 3rd Armored Cavalry Squadron, would be arriving at LZ 4 at 0800 hours the next morning with their American M-113 armored personnel carriers (APCs) and mounted infantry to assist in clearing LZ 4. It would be a coordinated infantry/APC formation to conduct combined clearing operations at LZ 4.

The ARVN 3rd Armored Cav was an independent regiment in the South Vietnamese Army that typically supported the ARVN 22nd Infantry Division in its operations in the Pleiku and Kontum areas in the western Central Highlands and provided security for Pleiku City. It apparently would now also support the ARVN 22nd Infantry Division in its operations in northeast Binh Dinh Province.

Hook worm, or rice paddy itch as it was called by the troops, would prove to be a recurring problem for the troops of the 1st Cav.[8] It was believed to be contracted through hookworm larvae found in dirt and water contaminated by human and animal feces, such as rice paddy dikes and the banks of streams close to native villages where villagers and animals would drink. It started with itchiness and a small rash in the area of the body where the larvae touched, and was generally followed by diarrhea and abdominal pain as the hookworm parasite got into a person's system and grew in the intestines. There it could live for a period of several weeks or even months or longer before it was passed through a person's feces.

The U.S. Army eventually identified measures that could be used by the troops to minimize the occurrence of hookworm, such as wearing boots at all times when out in the field, avoiding contact with moist ground insofar as possible, avoiding the use of native villages or captured enemy campsites as bivouac areas, and properly disposing of excreta even under combat conditions.

While the 2/12th Cav was moving northward on January 29, sweeping the east side of Phung Du, the companies of the 1/7th Cav were establishing blocking

---

[7] Email from Rudy Jaramillo to the author, dated July 9, 2021.
[8] Daniel Jun Yi Wong, University of Melbourne, Australia, "Hook worm infections," https://dermnetnz.org.

positions north of LZ 4 on an east–west axis, extending from LZ Papa, 2 kilometers northwest of LZ 4, to a spot 2 kilometers directly north of LZ 4, designated LZ Romeo. The 1/7th Cav troops were being shuttled by helicopter back and forth between the two LZs along a west–east axis in an attempt to cut off enemy troops fleeing the LZ 4 area northward to avoid the attacking 2/12th Cav.

The 1/7th Cav encountered several small groups of enemy soldiers in the vicinity of LZ Papa moving northward, but the encounters were brief and the enemy soldiers scattered in multiple directions before the 1/7th Cav troops could fix them in position. However, at 1415 hours, Bravo Company came under heavy mortar and machine-gun fire from My Binh, a small rice-growing hamlet located 1.5 kilometers north of LZ Papa, adjacent to a major east–west trail that ran from the base of the Da Dan Mountains to Highway 1. Tactical air support was called in—the sixth airstrike of the day in the LZ 4 area—and the USAF responded within 20 minutes with a FAC and four Skyraiders from the 602th Fighter Squadron. The FAC spotted defensive positions consisting of trenches and bunkers, along with automatic weapons emplacements, and directed the Skyraiders to strike them with high-explosive and WP bombs, napalm, and 20mm cannon fire. At the completion of the strike, Bravo Company launched a frontal attack against the enemy positions while Charlie Company attacked them from the east. Aerial rocket gunships from the 2/20th ARA provided suppressive aerial cover as the troops advanced. The battle continued until 1650 hours, when the enemy broke contact and withdrew to the north under the approaching darkness and rain. The encounter cost the North Vietnamese a total of 44 KIA by body count, an additional estimated 60 KIA, and two prisoners. Bravo Company suffered three KIA, all from enemy gunshot wounds. Bravo and Charlie companies also suffered a total of 18 WIA in the battle, which included the commander of Bravo Company. The Battalion Commander, Lieutenant Colonel Kampe, was also wounded.

After the wounded were evacuated and the dead transported to Graves Registration, Bravo and Charlie companies moved southeast to LZ Romeo to dig in and set up a night defensive position. There was light enemy contact reported during the early evening.

At 0115 hours on January 30, all hell broke loose at LZ Romeo. Bravo and Charlie companies, 1/7th Cav came under intense fire from an enemy force of unknown size, being hit with machine-gun and small-arms fire from all directions. The 1/7th Cav troops were able to do little more than exchange fire with the enemy soldiers when they revealed their positions in the darkness and rain. Ground illumination was requested and the USAF responded with Smokey-the-Bear, which circled over the battlefield dropping magnesium-based flares to illuminate the ground. Tube artillery from Position Dog was also called in to form a ring around the perimeter to prevent the enemy from breaking through it and getting onto the LZ. The intense fire continued for over an hour until the artillery started to have an effect on the enemy, and by 0300 hours, the enemy fire had ceased and the enemy soldiers had withdrawn.

The attack on the LZ may have been a diversionary one intended to occupy the 1/7th Cav troops while an enemy force moved past their position, possibly to the northwest toward the nearby mountains, or it might have been a large enemy force that was moving, explaining the intensity and duration of the attack, since there were no reports from Bravo or Charlie Company troops of any enemy soldiers attempting to break through the perimeter.

At daybreak, Alpha and Charlie companies, 2/7th Cav, with the battalion Recon Platoon attached, swept the area in and around the cemetery at the southern end of Phung Du for weapons and equipment. The sweep was uneventful. The 2/7th Cav, along with Delta Company and the Command Group of the 2/12th Cav, had been receiving moderate to heavy sniper fire in the cemetery throughout the night from the area northwest of the cemetery. Artillery fire from Position Dog had been brought to bear on the enemy soldiers, but it appeared to be only marginally effective. Alpha and Charlie companies proceeded to move northward along the western side of Phung Du toward LZ 4. They hadn't gone very far before they came across the bodies of 17 North Vietnamese soldiers half-buried in trenches and foxholes, and another seven in the area surrounding the trenches, a total of 24 enemy KIA. The enemy soldiers were wearing khaki uniforms, and many of them still had ammunition belts strapped to their bodies. They were apparently killed by the artillery fire only hours earlier. Many of the bodies were badly burned and torn open. Sections of the trenches were partially collapsed, due to what appeared to be direct hits by artillery rounds, with body parts sticking out from under the sand, indicating that there were even more enemy troops buried there, killed by the artillery fire.

Alpha and Charlie companies continued moving northward, and by 1015 hours had run into stiff resistance from North Vietnamese soldiers left behind to delay their advance. Artillery was called in on the positions, but it still took almost an hour to dislodge the enemy soldiers from their trenches. They fled westward through the flooded rice paddies toward the Da Dan Mountains and An Lao Valley. Air support from the 1/9th Cav and USAF was unavailable at the time due to a weather-hold, and the enemy forces were able to reach the foothills of the mountains and disappear into the jungle. The 2/7th Cav suffered one KIA, who died as the result of a gunshot wound to the chest and was to be the last man in Alpha Company to die at Phung Du, and 12 WIA in the move northward to LZ 4.

By 1100 hours, the weather had improved and air support was available, but there were no clearings close by large enough to allow a helicopter to land and take out the wounded and dead, so the Alpha and Charlie company troops continued to move northward, carrying them along with their weapons and ammunition. As the two companies approached the southern edge of LZ 4, they encountered a six-man enemy rifle squad that was moving to their front. The 2/7th Cav troopers quickly engaged the squad, and by 1125 hours they were reporting six enemy KIA, while suffering six more WIA themselves.

The two companies finally reached the southern edge of LZ 4 at 1230 hours. Medevac helicopters were called in and the wounded were evacuated, with the dead picked up and transported to Graves Registration at Dog. Three enemy soldiers, who had been taken prisoner on the sweep northward, were put on a Chinook helicopter and transported to the division's base camp at An Khe for interrogation by the division's military intelligence unit. Alpha and Charlie companies reported 23 enemy KIA and three prisoners on the sweep, while suffering one KIA and a total of 18 WIA.

Alpha and Charlie companies, 2/7th Cav, spent the remainder of the afternoon progressing through the trenches and tunnels at the southern end of LZ 4, clearing them as they went. The 2/12th Cav, together with the mechanized infantry company from the ARVN 3/3rd Armored Cav, cleared the northern portion of LZ 4 and the battalions linked up at 1545 hours. Later that afternoon, Alpha and Charlie companies, 2/7th Cav, returned south to their original positions in the cemetery. The two companies were so battered by their two days at Phung Du that Alpha Company was down to 65 men available for duty and Charlie Company to just 33.

The 2/12th Cav remained at LZ 4 during the night of January 30, together with the ARVN 3/3rd Armored Cav, as a blocking force to prevent any North Vietnamese soldiers still in the area from fleeing northward during the night. At 1800 hours, the 2/12th Cav reported a total of 54 enemy KIA that day, two WIA, and one North Vietnamese soldier captured, while suffering five friendly KIA and one WIA. The ARVN 3/3rd Armored Cav reported its daily totals directly to the ARVN II Corps/Military Region 2, the combat tactical zone for South Vietnamese military units operating in the Central Highlands Region, and as such were not included in the 1st Cav's daily staff journals.

While the 2/7th Cav and 2/12th Cav were clearing the LZ 4 area, Bravo and Charlie companies, 1/7th Cav, were conducting search-and-destroy patrols north of LZ Romeo on the chance that they might encounter the enemy unit that had attacked them earlier that morning in their defensive position at LZ Romeo. After spending the better part of the day maneuvering through the rice paddies and hamlets north of Romeo, with little to show for it other than a sighting of 20 Viet Cong soldiers moving along the banks of a stream some 300 meters due east of their location, Lieutenant Colonel Kampe directed the companies to move south toward Romeo. As a precautionary measure, the companies were arranged two abreast in a wide front in an attempt to reduce the risk of ambush. Bravo Company was on the west side, with Charlie Company to the east. Alpha Company, which had been providing security for an artillery battery at LZ Brass located on the high ground east of the An Lao Valley, had rejoined the battalion only minutes earlier. It followed behind Bravo and Charlie companies in the center of the formation and was the designated reserve.

At 1635 hours, the three companies reached the northern bank of the Go Gu Tai River and started to cross it when they encountered a North Vietnamese unit moving to their front. The enemy soldiers were wearing khaki uniforms and pith helmets, and were carrying backpacks. The unit was estimated to be company-sized with a heavy weapons platoon attached. The 1/7th Cav immediately attacked the enemy force with machine-gun and small-arms fire, fixing it in position. Tactical air support was requested and the USAF responded with four Skyraiders that pounded the enemy position and nearby hamlet with napalm, high-explosive bombs, and 20mm cannon fire. The airstrike drew heavy fire from the target area and the hamlet to the east, from which sniper fire was being received. The airstrike resulted in two secondary explosions that sent smoke billowing high into the afternoon sky. Numerous structures in the hamlet were destroyed. The airstrike was followed by tube artillery from Position Dog, and by 1845 hours the enemy force had broken contact and scattered in multiple directions, leaving behind 29 KIA on the battlefield. Bravo Company reported one friendly KIA, who died from a gunshot wound to the head. After the three companies were resupplied by helicopter and the body of the KIA picked up and transported to Graves Registration, the companies crossed the river and dug in on the south side of it for the night. Sniper and mortar fire was received through the night and a flare ship was requested. The USAF responded with Smokey-the-Bear and Puff-the-Magic-Dragon, an C-17 fixed-wing gunship that provided close-in air support with its 7.62mm mini-guns. The intensity of the enemy fire noticeably increased upon each occurrence of a dud flare.

East of LZ 4 in the vicinity of Highway 1, the ARVN Airborne Brigade had been battling a steady flow of North Vietnamese soldiers fleeing the area eastward toward the heavily populated villages of Dai Dong and An Thi located between Highway 1 and the South China Sea. Many of the enemy soldiers were using as escape routes the west–east rivers that cut across the coastal plain in the vicinity of LZs Papa and Romeo and joined the Tam Quan River east of Highway 1.[9] Elephant grass along the banks of the rivers provided areas for concealment from aerial observation. The flow of enemy soldiers had started during the night of January 29 and continued through

---

[9] North Vietnamese soldiers used the west–east rivers that cut across the coastal plain in the vicinity of LZs Papa and Romeo as escape routes from LZ 4 to the east of Highway 1. Topographic Map of Vietnam. QL1/South of Tam Quan, LZ North English, LZ Tom, Truong Lam—Map Sheet 6838–3 Tam Quan. Ray's Map Room, http://www.rjsmith.com/topo_map.html

the early morning of January 30. By 0630 hours on January 30, the ARVN Airborne Brigade had been battling the flow of enemy troops for more than nine hours and had suffered eight KIA and nine WIA. The flow continued through much of the day on January 30, and by 2000 hours the ARVN Airborne Brigade was reporting 57 enemy KIA and 61 prisoners, while suffering a total of 26 friendly KIA, which included one U.S. advisor who was assigned to the brigade, and 96 WIA, which included four American advisors who were assigned to it. The ARVN Airborne Brigade had captured one heavy machine gun, four submachine guns, and nine AK-47 rifles and SKS carbines.

The three battalions of the 40th (Mechanized) Infantry Regiment of the ARVN 22nd Infantry Division had likewise been battling a steady flow of enemy soldiers fleeing the LZ 4 area. Similar to what the ARVN Airborne Brigade was seeing just north of Bong Son, the ARVN battalions were encountering squad- and platoon-sized enemy elements using the Phung Du River as an escape route out of the LZ 4 area east of Bong Son. The Phung Du River ran northwest–southeast in parallel to the hamlet of Phung Du and Highway 1, north of Bong Son, and joined the Tam Quan River east of Highway 1. Once the enemy soldiers made it to the eastern side of the highway, they were able to work their way to feeder streams south of the river to the Suoi Dinh Binh Valley, east of Bong Son. At 2000 hours on January 30, the three ARVN battalions were reporting 17 enemy KIA and eight prisoners, while suffering a total of two friendly KIA and five WIA. The four battalions of the 41st Infantry Regiment of the ARVN 22nd Infantry Division continued to secure the area along Highway 1 south of Bong Son and reported only light enemy contact, with no friendly casualties.

While the three ARVN battalions were battling the enemy soldiers along Highway 1, thousands of local civilians—mostly women, children, and old men—were caught in close proximity to the fighting with no way to escape it. Prior to the start of the 1st Cav's operations in the Bong Son area on January 26, the total number of refugees in Bong Son was 7,800, according to local government officials. But as Operation *Masher* progressed, 13,000 refugees from the coastal plain had moved to Bong Son seeking shelter and safety. Local officials, however, permitted only 3,400 of them to enter the town and forced the rest to remain out on Highway 1, north of the town. The refugees were forced to huddle together on the roadway to stay warm and wait out the fighting as best they could in close proximity to the ARVN soldiers battling the fleeing North Vietnamese. Other refugees from the coastal plain chose instead to congregate around 1st Cav battalion bivouac areas, such as the 2/7th Cav's command post in the cemetery, looking for safety and scavenging for food.

In conjunction with government officials from Hoai Nhon District, medical personnel from the 1st Cav set up medical aid stations at 19 different locations along Highway 1 and in areas adjacent to tactical operations to treat injured civilians and evacuate the seriously wounded ones to the Bong Son Dispensary. Over the course of three days, more than 2,300 civilians were treated at these aid stations, 62 of them diagnosed with serious wounds that required further treatment resulting in evacuation to the dispensary. The 1st Cav also set up food distribution stations along Highway 1 and in areas adjacent to where tactical operations were being conducted. More than 42 tons of rice, 14 tons of salt, and hundreds of chickens and pigs were distributed to civilians. Another 22 tons of rice and salt, together with chickens and pigs, were also distributed to civilians at the Special Forces camp.

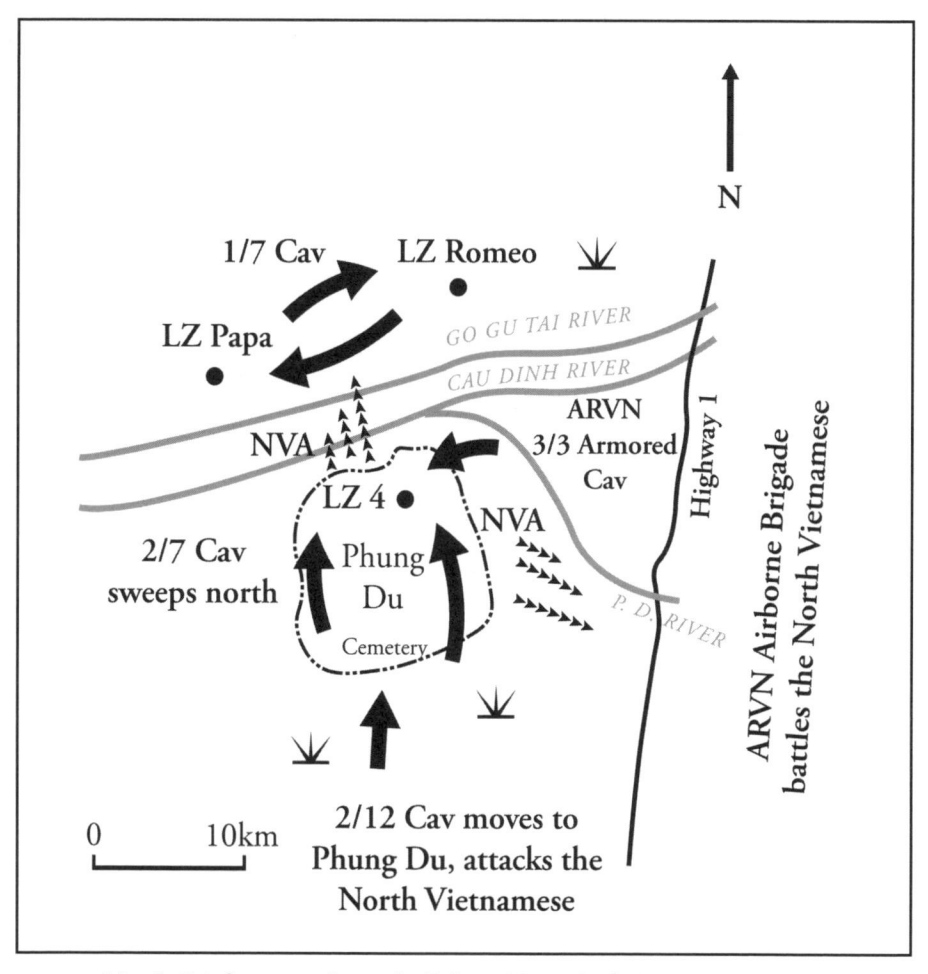

Map 6. Reinforcements Arrive, the Fighting Moves North, January 29–30, 1966

CHAPTER FIVE

A Pincer Action

The movement of enemy soldiers out of the LZ 4 area continued through the night of January 30. At 0440 hours on January 31, the troops of the 1st Battalion, 7th Cavalry, reported that an unknown number of enemy soldiers dressed in khaki uniforms, wearing pith helmets and carrying backpacks, were moving through the darkness in the direction of their perimeter south of the Go Gu Tai River, in the vicinity of LZ Romeo. At 0555 hours, Bravo and Charlie companies began receiving automatic weapons and mortar fire on the south side of the perimeter, with no casualties reported. By 0700 hours, the entire perimeter was under attack. Lieutenant Colonel Kampe requested tactical air support and the USAF responded with four B-57 twin-engine tactical bombers. The B-57s pounded the area around the perimeter with 500lb high-explosive bombs and canisters of napalm, lighting up the morning sky. After clearing the area around the perimeter, the B-57s hit a concentration of enemy soldiers in a tree line to the east of the perimeter, with resultant 90 percent target coverage. Following the airstrike, tube artillery from Position Dog and aerial rocket gunships from the 2nd Battalion, 20th ARA, were employed. The attacking enemy was estimated to be a company-sized force.

A member of Charlie Company remembered: "The high-explosive bombs landed so close to our perimeter that the concussions from the explosions actually bounced us into the air, and when the canisters of napalm exploded, they burst into fiery walls of flames that moved alongside our perimeter sucking the oxygen out of the air almost suffocating us to death."

During the attack, the enemy soldiers made multiple attempts to break through the perimeter and overrun the 1/7th Cav troops. At one point, a concentrated effort was made by the enemy to overrun a machine-gun position in Charlie Company's sector of the perimeter manned by a three-man crew. Intense automatic weapons and small-arms fire, grenades, and mortar rounds were directed at the position. The enemy made repeated attempts to break through before finally giving up and withdrawing. All three members of the machine-gun crew were wounded by the enemy fire. The machine gunner received multiple gunshot wounds to his chest and legs and died shortly afterward; the other two members of the crew were wounded but survived.[1] By 0930 hours, the enemy had broken contact and started to withdraw to the southwest. Lieutenant Colonel Kampe directed Alpha and Bravo companies to move out, two abreast in a wide front, and pursue and reestablish contact with the fleeing enemy. Charlie Company was to remain at the river to evacuate the wounded to the 15th Med aid station for treatment and transport the dead to Graves Registration, and be prepared to air assault behind the enemy's position once Alpha and Bravo companies again made contact with the enemy.

The two companies had not gone very far before Alpha Company encountered a small enemy covering force estimated to be a squad-sized unit of 10 soldiers. The Alpha Company troopers quickly overran the position, resulting in two enemy KIA. The remaining enemy soldiers managed to evade the attacking 7th Cav troops and escaped into the elephant grass along the banks of the Cau Dinh River, less than 500 meters south of the Go Gu Tai River. The second airstrike of the morning was called in and the USAF responded with a FAC and a pair of Skyraiders. The FAC quickly spotted the enemy soldiers hiding in the elephant grass and directed the Skyraiders to attack them. The airstrike resulted in eight enemy KBA.

At 1150 hours, a helicopter gunship from the 1st Squadron, 9th Cavalry, which was providing aerial coverage for the advancing 1/7th Cav companies, came under intense enemy ground fire and was hit, and came crashing down to the ground at a spot next to the Go Gu Tai River. It started to burn almost immediately, but not before the crew members onboard were able to climb out, carrying their weapons and ammunition with them. They moved away from the aircraft before it caught fire and were picked up by another 1/9th Cav helicopter. The helicopters were part of the aerial observation team that was supporting the 1/7th Cav's advance.

When the Alpha Company troops arrived at the scene of the crash to secure the helicopter, they started receiving small-arms fire from multiple directions. With a helicopter gunship from the aerial observation team providing cover, the Alpha Company men attacked the enemy soldiers and drove them from the area, capturing a 60mm mortar and 12.7mm heavy machine gun. No friendly casualties were reported in the firefight but the downed helicopter was a total loss and had to be scrapped.

The frequency and intensity of the attack on the 1/7th Cav at the Go Gu Tai River may have resulted from the fact that the North Vietnamese were virtually surrounded by the 1st Cav in the area north of LZ 4 and were trying to break out and flee westward toward the Da Dan Mountains. They may have been unaware of

---

[1] Remembrance left on the Vietnam Veterans Memorial Fund, The Wall of Faces, for PFC Charles "Chuck" Frederick from Bellevue, Ohio, described the enemy's concentrated effort to overrun the machine-gun position manned by PFC Frederick and two fellow crew members, and break through the 1st Battalion, 7th Cavalry, perimeter, on the morning of January 31, 1966, on the Bong Son Plain. Posted by Robert Garman, November 22, 2009. Vietnam Veterans Memorial Fund, The Wall of Faces, https://www.vvmf.org.

the blocking position that the 1/7th Cav had established at the Go Gu Tai River, which might have added to their desperation.

The area around LZ Romeo consisted of open rice paddies built on gently rolling hills, with several small rivers cutting through the area from west to east. The Go Gu Tai River was the northernmost river and was just north of Romeo. It was a small river that was no deeper than waist height, so it could easily be crossed by wading through it. The Cau Dinh River was located less than a kilometer south of the Go Gu Tai River. It was a larger river, but like the Go Gu Tai, it was no deeper than waist height and could be waded across. There was plenty of elephant grass with clusters of bamboo thickets and tangled vegetation along the banks of the two rivers, providing good concealment from aerial and ground observation, and there were numerous hamlets located next to the rivers where the farmers and peasants who worked the rice paddy fields lived. The fleeing North Vietnamese most likely chose to stay close to the rivers to take advantage of the concealment they offered and near to the hamlets for the protection they afforded.[2]

In an attempt to slow down the North Vietnamese withdrawal, Colonel Moore directed Charlie Troop, 1/9th Cav, to stage a diversionary landing about 2 kilometers west of Alpha and Bravo companies' current position in the hope of deceiving the enemy into thinking that a 1/7th Cav infantry element had just landed to its west and that it should establish a position to defend itself against the advancing 1/7th Cav troopers. The maneuver involved several helicopters. There was no contact in the maneuver, but the 1/9th Cav did capture a North Vietnamese soldier who was moving through the area. The lone enemy soldier was apprehended by one of the helicopter crews, disarmed, and put on the helicopter for transport to Position Dog for interrogation. After the diversionary maneuver, Alpha and Bravo companies were directed to continue their advance westward and reestablish contact with the enemy force. At that point, Charlie Company was alerted to move by helicopter from its position along the Go Gu Tai River to a spot 1 kilometer southwest of LZ Papa. The spot was designated LZ Quebec. The thinking was that Charlie Company could establish a blocking position at Quebec against which the attacking Alpha and Bravo company troops could push the North Vietnamese in a classic hammer-and-anvil tactic, shattering the enemy force.[3]

---

[2] A description of the terrain north of Phung Du on the Bong Son Plain, between LZs Papa and Romeo, was based on Topographic Digital Map Images, QL1/South of Tam Quan, LZ North English, LZ Tom, Truong Lam—Map Sheet 6838–3 Tam Quan. Ray's Map Room, http://www.rjsmith.com/topo_map.html.

[3] A description of the incident at LZ Quebec on January 31, 1966, at the base of the Da Dan Mountains, 1 kilometer west of the hamlet of Luong Tho and 7 kilometers northwest of Position Dog, was provided on the Vietnam Helicopter Pilots Association website. The incident involved the death of Captain Howard E. Phillips, pilot, who was shot in the chest and died in an air assault into LZ Quebec, on January 31, 1966. Vietnam Helicopter Pilots Association, "KIA Info by Name," https://www.vhpa.org.

LZ Quebec was a narrow strip of dry, sandy land located along the base of the Da Dan Mountains, about 1 kilometer west of the hamlet of Luong Tho and 7 kilometers northwest of Dog. Like much of the area along the base of the mountains, it was covered with clumps of scrawny-looking bushes, patches of wild grass, and rocks. It was only large enough to accommodate four helicopters at one time in single-file formation.

Prior to the air assault into Quebec by Charlie Company, the LZ was prepped with an airstrike—the third of the day in the area north of LZ 4—that lasted for about 20 minutes. It was hit with high-explosive bombs, napalm, and white phosphorus. One of the helicopter pilots at Dog awaiting the signal to lift off and proceed to the Go Gu Tai River to pick up the Charlie Company troops and transport them to Quebec, Robert Mason, a warrant officer with Alpha Company, 229th AHB, recalled: "We hung around on the ground watching the Air Force Phantoms as they hit Quebec with tons of bombs and napalm. I sat on the roof of my Huey and watched the show. At the bottom of their passes, the Phantoms would mush accelerate and they'd kick-in their afterburners to power out." Multiple runs were made over the LZ by the Phantoms.[4]

The airstrike was followed with tube artillery fire from Dog, and the helicopters carrying the Charlie Company troops timed their approach into the LZ to coincide with the completion of the artillery bombardment. The pilots were directed by their flight leader to use a north–south approach to the LZ, keeping the mountains to their right. The lead helicopter in the formation touched down at the southern end of the LZ and the Charlie Company troopers onboard jumped out and ran across the open space to the tree line at the base of the mountain. When the second helicopter started to flare to reduce its vertical and horizontal speed and land, it was hit with automatic weapons and small-arms fire from enemy soldiers located on a ridge to the west of the LZ. The helicopter lost power and fell about 15 feet to the ground, landing hard. The Charlie Company troops aboard were shaken up but were able to climb out of the helicopter and run across the open area to the tree line. Seeing what had just happened, the pilots of the two helicopter gunships from Delta Company, 229th AHB, escorting the formation, immediately veered off and attacked the enemy on the ridge with their 30-caliber mini-guns and 40mm grenade launchers in the powered nose turrets of the helicopters. The attack resulted in 10 KBA, two destroyed machine guns, and several destroyed automatic rifles.

The Charlie Company troops reported no casualties in the air assault, but the pilots were not so lucky. The aircraft commander of the second helicopter in

---

[4] A description of the airstrike on LZ Quebec on January 31, 1966, before the troops of Charlie Company, 1/7th Cav, air assaulted into the LZ, and details of the actual air assault, provided by Robert Mason in his book *Chickenhawk Chickenhawk* (New York: Viking Press, 1983).

the formation from Alpha Company, 229th AHB, received a gunshot wound to the chest and died instantly. The co-pilot attempted to take control of the aircraft and fly it out of the LZ, but was unable to do so. The hydraulics of the aircraft were apparently damaged by the enemy fire and the aircraft was not flyable. The co-pilot, crew chief, and door gunner were forced to grab their weapons and ammunition, jump out of the helicopter, and dash across the open space to the tree line to take cover with the Charlie Company troops. The helicopter would have to remain in the middle of the LZ in spite of the remaining ships in the formation needing to set down there to offload their Charlie Company troops. Once the LZ was fully secured, the body of the pilot could be recovered and the damaged helicopter could be lifted out by a Chinook and transported to Dog for repair. Once alerted, the 15th Med aid station at Dog would dispatch a rescue/recovery team to the site together with members of Graves Registration. The teams were able to complete the recovery process fairly quickly and the 228th ASHB recovered the helicopter and transported it to Dog for repairs.

At 1640 hours, Alpha Company, in its advance westward, encountered an estimated reinforced enemy company 500 meters directly north of LZ Papa and 1.5 kilometers northeast of Quebec. An intense firefight resulted and Charlie Company, which had just started to move out of Quebec northward on foot, was directed to assist Alpha Company by attacking the enemy's southern flank. By this time, the aircraft commander's body had been recovered from the helicopter in Quebec and transported to Graves Registration, and the damaged helicopter had been lifted out of the LZ and taken to Dog for repair. The fourth airstrike of the day in the area north of LZ 4 was requested by Lieutenant Colonel Kampe to cut off any attempts by the North Vietnamese to break contact and withdraw to the foothills to the west.

By 1725 hours, Charlie Company began receiving heavy automatic weapons fire from the vicinity of Luong Tho to its northeast. The fire became so intense that Charlie Company was unable to continue moving northeast to flank the enemy force. A fifth airstrike was requested by Lieutenant Colonel Kampe, the USAF responding with a FAC and two Skyraiders. The FAC pinpointed the locations from which the automatic weapons fire was coming and where large concentrations of enemy soldiers were located. The two Skyraiders pounded the positions with general purpose bombs and napalm, making 10 passes in all. Prior to the airstrike, the firefight had been at such close quarters that it was difficult to bring in supporting fire. Bravo Company, which had been sweeping the area north of the Go Gu Tai River east of LZ Papa, was committed to help extract Alpha Company from its position. Together with aerial rocket gunships from the 2nd Battalion, 20th ARA, Bravo Company put down a base of fire that allowed Alpha Company to break contact with the enemy and pull back to a safe position with its wounded and dead. Charlie Company, meanwhile, was also able to break contact and pull back with its wounded and dead, and maneuver to the east and north to link up with Alpha and Bravo companies. By 1800 hours, the enemy had started to break contact and withdraw in small groups to the north, northwest, and west.

Darkness was setting in and Alpha Company had a dozen badly wounded troopers who likely would not make it through the night unless they were evacuated to the 15th Med aid station at Dog where they could receive medical treatment. Unfortunately, the darkness and enemy fire made it impossible for any medevac helicopters to land and pick up any wounded troopers till daybreak. However, the company commander of Alpha Company, 229th AHB, Major Bruce Crandall, was returning from an air assault mission with the 1/12th Cav north of the 1/7th Cav's position and heard the company commander of Alpha Company, Captain Tony Nadal, his friend and fellow veteran of LZ X-Ray, on the radio requesting medical evacuation of his wounded troopers. Major Crandall immediately changed course for Alpha Company, 1/7th Cav's position, using the light from exploding grenades and tracer rounds to guide him. He radioed Captain Nadal that he was coming in, but that he would have to come in without his searchlight or landing lights on so as not to attract enemy ground fire or backlight the troopers defending the perimeter. Nadal and his troops would have to use their flashlights to guide Crandall's helicopter into the area in a vertical descent while avoiding the surrounding palm trees and branches. Crandall had to abort his first approach when the flashlights were turned off due to enemy fire. He then decided to land to a single flashlight that he asked Captain Nadal to put in the center of the touchdown area, approaching the flashlight straight down in order to minimize his chances of striking any unseen trees. His second attempt to set down under intense enemy fire was successful and he was able to pick up six wounded troopers and transport them to the 15th Med aid station at Dog. He then returned to Alpha Company's position and completed a second successful lift of the remaining six wounded under the same conditions.[5]

After the evacuation of Alpha Company's wounded troopers, the three companies of the 1/7th Cav regrouped and moved southward as a battalion in the dark through the rice paddies and palm groves toward LZ Papa, a distance of 1 kilometer. Prior to closing on Papa, Captain Sugdinis and Alpha Company, 2nd Battalion, 7th Cavalry,

---

[5] A description of Major Bruce Crandall landing his helicopter under enemy fire and picking up wounded troopers of Alpha Company, 1/7th Cav, on the night of January 31, 1966, and transporting them to the 15th Med aid station at Position Dog for medical treatment, is described in the United States Air Force biography. Major Crandall responded to the request of Captain Tony Nadal, Company Commander, Alpha Company, 1/7th Cav, to evacuate his wounded troops who would likely not make it through the night without medical treatment. "United States Air Force, A Gathering of Eagles, Biography of Bruce P. Crandall," https://en.wikipedia.org/wiki/Bruce_P._Crandall.

arrived by helicopter to link up with the 1/7th Cav in order to reinforce it for the night. Alpha Company, 2/7th Cav, had been securing Position Dog and keeping it clear of enemy snipers shooting at the artillerymen firing in support of the infantry battalions. At 2000 hours, the 1/7th Cav, with Alpha Company, 2/7th Cav, attached, closed into Papa.

Shortly after establishing their night defensive position, Lieutenant Colonel Kampe requested harassment & interdiction (H&I) fire into the area northwest and west of the hamlet of Luong Tho to cut off the enemy's withdrawal into the foothills of the Da Dan Mountains. The H&I fire would last throughout the night and into the early hours and would consist of no more than a few rounds fired at random intervals, seeking to deny the enemy freedom of movement.

The day's encounter with the 1/7th Cav cost the North Vietnamese 67 KIA, numerous machine guns and Type 56 Chicom assault rifles, seven SKS carbine rifles, and a large number of 60mm mortar rounds. Losses for the 1/7th Cav were six KIA—four from Alpha Company and two from Charlie Company—and 33 WIA.

While Alpha and Bravo companies, 1/7th Cav, were chasing the North Vietnamese westward along the Go Gu Tai River, Lieutenant Colonel Ingram and the 2nd Battalion, 12th Cavalry, were moving north from their night defense position at LZ 4 in an attempt to intercept the fleeing North Vietnamese and envelop them in a pincer action with Alpha and Bravo companies, 1/7th Cav. The 2/12th Cav had moved out of LZ 4 on foot at 0745 hours while the 1/7th Cav was still under attack by the North Vietnamese. The 2/12th Cav had not moved very far north before the battalion's Recon Platoon, which was walking point for the battalion, reached a hamlet and found numerous women and children huddled together for protection in a corner of a hootch, along with two enemy soldiers who were waving white flags and had Chieu Hoi Passes—safe conduct passes to encourage NVA and Viet Cong soldiers to defect—wanting to surrender to the 2/12th Cav. Ingram had no choice but to keep his battalion moving northward, so the best he could do for the women and children was to direct them to Highway 1 to the east and to the refuge center in Bong Son. The two enemy soldiers were disarmed and told to fall in with the battalion Command Group. When the battalion reached a location where a helicopter could be brought in, they would be put on it and transported to the division's base camp at An Khe for processing.

At 1150 hours, the 2/12th Cav reached the Cau Dinh River just in time to see black smoke raising into the air from the 1/9th Cav helicopter that had been shot down by enemy ground fire and came crashing down to the ground next to the Go Gu Tai River. The crash site was roughly 1 kilometer west of the 2/12th Cav's current position. Lieutenant Colonel Ingram contacted the operations officer at Dog and offered to send a squad from Bravo Company to secure the site and rescue the crew, but the 1/7th Cav was closer to the crash site and had already been dispatched to it.

Bravo Company, 2/12th Cav, was the first company in the battalion to reach the Cau Dinh River and cross it. Once across, they cleared the far bank of hiding places and caves, with no enemy contact reported, while the rest of the battalion crossed the river. At approximately 1340 hours, the Bravo Company troops spotted an estimated platoon-sized force of North Vietnamese fleeing the area from the direction where the 1/9th Cav helicopter had been shot out of the air. It was fleeing to the northeast along the north side of the Go Gu Tai River. Lieutenant Knox called in tube artillery on the fleeing enemy soldiers and requested support from aerial rocket gunships. Shortly afterwards, a pair of gunships from Charlie Battery, 2/20th ARA, arrived and started to pursue the North Vietnamese. No estimate of enemy casualties was reported. At that point, Colonel Moore directed Lieutenant Colonel Ingram and the 2/12th Cav to scrap the original plan to link up with the 1/7th Cav in a pincer action, and instead continue moving north and establish contact with the enemy force that was fleeing the area.

As the 2/12th Cav continued to move northward in pursuit of the retreating North Vietnamese, it received occasional sniper fire from small hamlets along the way. At one point, a platoon had to be sent into one of the hamlets to silence the sniper in order for the battalion to move beyond that point. The sniper managed to escape before the platoon could locate him. As the battalion continued to move northward in the direction of An Qui, 3 kilometers north of the Go Gu Tai River, the tempo of the sniper fire accelerated dramatically and Lieutenant Colonel Ingram radioed the operations officer at Dog to request aerial coverage to support the battalion's continued advance.

At 1515 hours, the 2/12th Cav reported that it was still moving northward and had reached beyond a small hamlet and onto a dry crop island, 300 meters west of the hamlet of An Qui and 600 meters south of the village of Lieu An. The island was ringed with palm groves with tall palm trees, and was surrounded by flooded rice paddies on the north and west sides. It was roughly 1 kilometer long, north to south, and 200–300 meters wide. There were clusters of hootches scattered among the palm groves on both sides of the island, with small corn fields and potato patches, and fenced-in areas for chickens and pigs located nearby. The lead element of the 2/12th Cav almost immediately came under fire, receiving automatic weapons, small-arms, and mortar fire from the palm groves to the north and east. The troops returned fire into the trees to their east with their M-16s and M-79 shoulder-fired grenade launchers, thinking that the small-arms fire was coming from snipers in the trees. Then someone noticed that the enemy fire was coming from the base of the trees and not from the tree tops. The enemy soldiers had carved out small notches in the tree trunks just above the ground, where the barrel of an AK-47 rifle or SKS carbine could be positioned and pointed at the Americans, allowing the North Vietnamese to fire at them as they passed while remaining unnoticed behind the trees. The 2/12th Cav silenced the snipers and reported one North Vietnamese KIA.[6]

The automatic weapons and mortar fire were being received from a trench 300 meters to the north. The trench was set down behind a small hill and stretched the width of the island, east-to-west. A platoon or reinforced squad of North Vietnamese soldiers was in the trench firing at the 2/12th Cav troops. The enemy soldiers were wearing khaki uniforms and pith helmets, and carrying AK-47 assault rifles. Lieutenant Colonel Ingram requested tube artillery from Dog to support the battalion's advance, and for tactical air support to be available if needed. Ingram also directed Alpha and Bravo companies to change their formations to a wide front, with Bravo Company on the west and Alpha Company on the east, and attack and capture the trench on signal when the artillery fire ended. Charlie Company was to flank the position.

Smoke grenades and flares were used to screen the advance by the troops of Alpha and Bravo companies, but the smoke screen did not work very well and the men were forced to maneuver in short advances through the palm grove in individual fire teams and squads against automatic weapons and small-arms fire from the trench. The volume of fire being put out by the 2/12th Cav eventually forced the enemy soldiers to abandon the trench and flee into the open rice paddies to the north and east toward An Qui, dragging their dead and wounded with them.[7] Snipers were left behind in the palm grove to delay the 2/12th Cav's advance.

The companies of the 2/12th Cav pursued the North Vietnamese beyond the trench and into the open rice paddies. As they started to move to the east, a large

---

[6] In phone conversations, June–July 2021, Rudy Jaramillo described the following: enemy soldiers shot at 2/12th troopers from behind trees with notch at base of tree for rifle to stick out; 2nd Battalion, 12th Cav, troops attacked enemy soldiers in trench forcing enemy soldiers to abandon trench and flee into open rice paddies; the ARVN 3rd Troop, 3rd Armored Cavalry Squadron, arrived at the 2nd Battalion, 12th Cavalry's position with its APCs and mounted infantry, under heavy enemy fire, with a resupply of ammunition, water, and medical supplies. The 2/12th Cav had married up with the ARVN 3/3rd Armored Cav and was moving north. The move stalled because of heavy enemy fire. Bravo Company, 2/12th Cav, was directed to pull back to a safe position to evacuate its wounded. Rudy Jaramillo, "Vietnam 1965–1966 Conversations in Their Own Words, B 2/12 Cav, The Rice Paddy."

[7] Description of the infantry/APC attack on Lieu An by the 2/12th Cav and ARVN 3rd Troop, 3rd Armored Cav. The attack stalled and the 2/12th Cav troops were forced to pull back to a palm grove carrying their wounded and dead with them. The 2/12th Cav and ARVN 3/3rd Armored Cav received heavy automatic weapons and small-arms fire during the night. Rudy Jaramillo, "Vietnam 1965–1966 Conversations in Their Own Words, B 2/12th Cav, The Rice Paddy." Dated June–July 2021.

enemy force suddenly emerged from a palm grove on the southern side of Lieu An, approximately 600 meters to the north, and began to advance toward them while firing. It seemed that the 2/12th Cav had triggered an ambush when it moved out of the palm grove into the rice paddy. The enemy force was arranged in a wide front and was putting out a heavy volume of fire that immediately halted the 2/12th Cav's advance and forced the troops to dig in as best they could behind the rice paddy dikes.

The 2/12th Cav troops were already low on ammunition and needed an immediate resupply if they were to defend themselves against such a large enemy force. Lieutenant Colonel Ingram radioed the operations office at Dog to request immediate tactical air support and a resupply of ammunition, water, rations, and medical supplies. The operations office informed him that the ARVN 3/3rd Armored Cav was reporting that it was just now arriving at the southern end of the island where the 2/12th Cav was in contact. It carried with it a resupply of ammunition, water, and medical supplies. The 3/3rd Armored Cav had been moving north along a dirt road from the LZ 4 area in parallel to the movement of the 2/12th Cav across the Cau Dinh and Go Gu Tai rivers, and was now preparing to link up with the 2/12th Cav.

When the troopers of the 2/12th Cav heard the noise of the APCs coming toward their position from the south, they immediately thought that they were being attacked by the Viet Cong and that it was time for them to fix bayonets. Then someone recognized the APCs and guided them to where the 2/12th troops were dug in. Upon seeing the APCs, the North Vietnamese immediately pulled back into the palm grove from where they had come.

At about 1750 hours, Alpha and Bravo companies, along with the 3/3rd Armored Cav, initiated their attack northward toward Lieu An, where the North Vietnamese were located. Lieutenant Knox and Bravo Company were on the left, Alpha Company was on the right, and the 3/3rd Armored Cav was on Alpha Company's right flank, leading the way with its APCs. As the companies moved out of the palm grove into the open rice paddies, Bravo Company started to receive automatic weapons fire from the northeast. The 3/3rd Armored Cav had apparently got ahead of Bravo Company, and when it emerged from behind a cluster of hootches in the palm grove it spotted the Bravo Company troops and opened fire on them, mistaking them for North Vietnamese. There was firing going on by all of the units, including the North Vietnamese. The ARVN and Bravo Company firing stopped once they realized who they were firing at. The APCs then started to attack northward across the rice paddies, with the dismounted ARVN troops following close behind on foot. The APCs accelerated so quickly that the 2/12th Cav men were unable to get behind them. Lieutenant Knox and his radio operator ran at full speed through the flooded rice paddies to catch up with the APCs and get them to slow down long enough for the 2/12th Cav troops to catch up.

By 1854 hours, the troops had progressed to within 300 meters of the palm grove at Lieu An, when suddenly all hell broke loose. The North Vietnamese released an incredible volume of fire that knocked the machine gunners off the tops of the APCs and into the rice paddies. Backup machine gunners quickly climbed up on top of the APCs and took over the machine-gun positions, but the volume of fire directed at them and at the dismounted infantry and 2/12th Cav troops was overwhelming. The attack stalled and the troops were forced to take cover behind the APCs. Seeing this, the North Vietnamese directed their fire at the bottoms and sides of the APCs, hoping that the bullets would ricochet off the metal and hit the troops taking cover behind them.

With casualties mounting, Lieutenant Colonel Ingram directed Alpha Company to pull back a safe distance into the palm grove and form a perimeter. Charlie Company, which had been held in reserve, was ordered by Ingram to move to the rear of Alpha Company and assist with the withdrawal. At 1938 hours, Ingram ordered Lieutenant Knox and Bravo Company to also pull back into the palm grove and consolidate its position with the rest of the battalion. It would then prepare to evacuate its wounded once it was safe to bring in medevac helicopters. The Bravo Company troops carried their wounded and dead with them as they pulled back. In the confusion, the best that the ARVN soldiers could do was to form a perimeter in the rice paddies and gather up their wounded for evacuation. The wounded, however, would have to be carried back to the palm grove under the cover of darkness once it was safe to do so. The remaining ARVN soldiers would secure the APCs in the rice paddies.

Tactical air support was called in by Lieutenant Colonel Ingram and the USAF responded with a FAC and two Skyraiders. The Skyraiders pounded the palm grove on the south side of Lieu An where the enemy soldiers had withdrawn with 500lb high-explosive bombs, napalm, and white phosphorus, and raked the area with 20mm cannon fire.

Forrest Brewer, a sergeant with the 2nd Platoon of Bravo Company, remembered:

> We started to receive enemy fire when we initially entered the palm grove. I took cover behind a small tree and started shooting at the muzzle flashes from across the open area. I was also being fired on, as bullets were hitting the front of the tree and the dirt in front of it. One bullet hit the tree, about a foot above my head. I can't remember who was to my left, but he said that the VC must be behind us, but it was the only round that came from that direction.
>
> Then someone popped a violet smoke grenade and a few minutes later, a chopper was flying overhead firing on us. Someone hollered for a medic because he had been hit. I don't know how much time had passed but I know I was getting low on ammunition and I didn't want to shoot until I was certain of a target. Later, off to my right, an ARVN APC emerged from a cluster of hootches to the east and began coming toward us. The ARVN soldiers must have been confused as they were firing on us. A member of our platoon was hit by their machine-gun fire, and I called for a medic to help him.
>
> Then someone said that we [were] going to get up and assault across the rice paddy. I was right beside an APC when we began the assault. Bad move, as bullets were bouncing off the

APC. I moved over toward my right. During the assault, my M-16 jammed but I didn't want to lag behind so I finished the assault with only my bayonet. From then until dark, I don't remember much except that we pulled back to the palm grove and dug in, and one of the platoon members and I were sharing a fox hole. Next thing I know, I'm in the hospital being treated for a head wound.

I will never forget that day or the names and faces of the men we lost. I think about them all the time.[8]

Back in the palm grove where the 2/12 Cav had established its night defensive position, enemy sniper fire continued to be received, so Lieutenant Colonel Ingram directed the pathfinders assigned to the battalion to delay the arrival of the medevac helicopters until the snipers could be eliminated. With the help of the 2/12th Cav troops, the snipers were quickly located and silenced and the pathfinders were able to bring in the helicopters. Twenty troopers from the 2/12th Cav and 30 from the 3/3rd Armored Cav were transported to the 15th Med aid station at Dog for treatment. By 2240 hours, all of the WIA had been evacuated.

Meanwhile, the weather had taken a turn for the worse, with rain and fog moving into the area and limiting visibility. A Chinook helicopter, which was on the ground in the palm grove being loaded with enemy prisoners for transport to Dog, would be the last aircraft into or out of the area for the night. The bodies of the friendly KIA would be transported to Dog in the morning. Illumination from Smokey-the-Bear and suppressive fire from Puff-the-Magic-Dragon would not be available during the night due to a weather-hold. Conditions were not expected to improve much before morning, and artillery fire from Dog would be limited because of the scattered formation of the ARVN troops and their APCs in the rice paddies.

Rudy Jaramillo remembered:

> January 31, a hot day, walked and fought the entire day. Started to cross the rice paddy but came up short. Low on ammo, we dug in. I was counting the few slugs I had left. Gene was tapping his bayonet to Thumper (M-79 grenade launcher). He also was low on ammo for both his 45 Cal and M-79. I was down in the hole when Gene sat down and looked at me and said, "Rudy, tell my mother I loved her." I saw his face. I looked up and saw them coming on line across the rice paddy, this time at us. Then someone said, "We got VC to the rear." Someone engaged them but as it turned out, it was friendly troops in APCs. Gene and I hugged each other. We looked up and saw the VC and NVA start running back. We got re-supplied with ammo, rations, and water.
>
> We started to move. APCs up front with mechanized infantry, 2nd Platoon behind them, our squad in the lead. The APCs crossed the rice paddies, got half way when all hell broke loose. The ARVN soldiers manning the 50-caliber machine guns on top of the APCs, started to fall off the tracks. Gene was to my left, pounding away with Thumper. Sgt. Belvedere pushing forward, "move it, move it" then I looked back to see him get hit. Big huge round, 51 cal took off his right arm as he was waving the rest of the company forward. I saw the bullet deflect

---

[8] Description of the coordinated infantry/APC attack on Lieu An by the 2/12th Cav and ARVN 3/3rd Armored Cav. Forrest Brewer, "Vietnam 1965–1966 Conversations in Their Own Words, B 2/12 Cav, The Rice Paddy."

downward. As I watched it hit the rice paddy water, I saw it bounce up as it sizzled, saw the steam, the splash, and upward movement. I turned as fast as I could, but felt the thud, the push, the spin, the pain, and saw I was in the air. When I saw Gene, he was fighting, firing. I called for the medic. He was attending to Sgt. Belvedere. Gene pointed to me and the medic came running. Rolled me over, told me to knock it off, that I was okay. The bullet tore the shoulder strap, my T-shirt and bruised me pretty bad. He went back to Sgt. Belvedere.

The order came to pull back. I saw a lot of ARVN dead and wounded in the paddies. When we pulled back to a trench, Crosby said, "Let's go get some of the ARVN wounded." I said, "let's go." I last saw Gene in the trench told him to stay back. We went into the rice paddy, but I lost Crosby, he went back because of the intense enemy fire. It was really bad. I crawled to a ditch and saw an ARVN officer trying to put a battlefield dressing on. I helped him and carried him back. I saw a few others, so I went back several more times. When I returned to the trench where Gene was, I was told that Gene was killed in the trench by roving enemy soldiers. He had killed four VC before they got him. The firefight in the rice paddy seemed like forever, yet it was all in slow motion. Gene, I miss you, you will always be with me.

The day's totals for the 2/12th Cav included 63 enemy KIA, 13 prisoners, and 39 North Vietnamese suspects. It suffered eight friendly KIA, and 20 troopers required evacuation to the 15th Med aid station at Dog for treatment. The ARVN 3/3rd Armored Cav reported that it had engaged a reinforced company that resulted in 40–50 enemy KIA after they joined the fight, while suffering five friendly KIA and 30 WIA needing evacuation to Dog for medical treatment.

While the 2/12th Cav and ARVN 3/3rd Armored Cav were pursuing the fleeing North Vietnamese north of the Go Gu Tai Rivers on January 31, toward Lieu An, Lieutenant Colonel Beard and the 1st Battalion (Airborne), 12th Cavalry, were busy moving by helicopter from LZ Hammond to an area 5 kilometers north of LZ Romeo to cut off escape routes to the foothills of the Quang Ngai Mountains in southern Quang Ngai Province for any North Vietnamese who might attempt to flee the LZ Romeo area northward. The spot was designated LZ Tom.

The 1/12th Cav was the designated brigade reserve force for the 3rd Brigade and had been securing LZ Hammond as an aircraft laager area awaiting orders to move north to Bong Son and join the brigade's infantry battalions. By 1030 hours, the troops of the 1/12th Cav were on the ground at Tom. Almost immediately they started receiving small-arms fire from a tree line 200 meters to their east. Artillery fire from Dog was called in on the target to neutralize the enemy position. Meanwhile, the troops of Alpha Company had started moving southward and came across a school house where an estimated 20 women and children were huddled together inside in one corner. The 3rd Brigade civil affairs officer at Dog was notified of the situation and Lieutenant Colonel Beard later received word from the brigade operations officer that a helicopter would be dispatched to the site to evacuate these women and children and transport them to the refuge center in Bong Son, if they wanted to go.

At 1330 hours, a five-man long-range patrol (LRP) team from Bravo Company, 1/12th Cav, stumbled into an enemy position and an intense firefight ensued. The LRP team overran the North Vietnamese, resulting in seven enemy KIA and two captured soldiers. The LRPs reported no friendly casualties. The team had been reconnoitering the area roughly 500 meters west of the main battalion as it moved southward toward Romeo. A helicopter was dispatched to the site to extract the prisoners and transport them to Dog for interrogation.

As Bravo and Charlie companies, 1/12th Cav, moved south, they encountered moderate to heavy automatic weapons and small-arms fire from the west and were unable to maneuver. A pair of aerial rocket gunships from the 2/20th ARA was called in to neutralize the enemy fire. After the gunship strike, the troops of the 1/12th Cav searched the area but found no KBA and only one enemy WIA who had been left for dead. Multiple enemy KBA were suspected, but the 1/12th Cav troops were unable to find any bodies. Charlie Company suffered two friendly KIA and four WIA in the encounter. The WIA were evacuated to Dog for medical treatment and the bodies of the two KIA were transported by helicopter to Graves Registration at Dog. The companies of the 1/12th Cav resumed their movement southward toward Romeo, with no further enemy contact reported. At the direction of Colonel Moore, the battalion consolidated for the night at 2000 hours in a position 2 kilometers south of Tom and 3 kilometers north of Romeo. The position, coincidently, was 1.5 kilometers directly west of the village of Lieu An, where the 2/12th Cav and 3/3rd Armored Cav were battling the North Vietnamese.

On the sweep southward from LZ Tom, the troops of the 1/12th Cav found numerous documents from their encounter with the North Vietnamese, which provided intelligence information on the Quyet Tam Regiment (22nd NVA Regiment). One of the documents was a letter from a company commander to his battalion commander which stated: "The men are defecting ... we are surrounded by ARVN and US troops ... request permission to consolidate and attack tomorrow." Evidently, the battalion commander did not give the company commander permission, for the running battles with the 1st Cav troops continued into the day.

While the 1/12th Cav was moving south toward LZ Romeo, Lieutenant Colonel Frederick Ackerson and the 1st Battalion, 5th Cavalry, were moving by helicopter to LZ Hammond from the division's base camp at An Khe, where it had been clearing the area around Highway 19. Upon arrival at Hammond, the 1/5th Cav assumed the security role for the area as an aircraft laager area and forward support base, and became the 3rd Brigade's reserve force. It would remain there awaiting orders to move north to the Bong Son Plain and join the infantry battalions of the 3rd Brigade.

East of Highway 1, the ARVN Airborne Brigade continued to battle the North Vietnamese fleeing the LZ 4 area eastward toward Tam Quan and the South China Sea. The ARVN Airborne Brigade had established blocking positions along Highway 1 and the banks of the rivers in the area that led to the Tam Quan River and Tam Quan Bay from the vicinity of LZs Papa and Romeo. The rivers provided good concealment from ground and aerial observation and were likely escape routes for any enemy soldiers wanting to flee to the east.

At 2130 hours on January 31, the ARVN Airborne Brigade reported 100 enemy KIA and 25 prisoners. It also captured 21 machine guns, AK-47 rifles and SKS carbines, while suffering 49 friendly KIA, which included one American advisor, and 173 WIA, which included five American advisors.

The three battalions of the 40th (Mechanized) Regiment of the ARVN 22nd Infantry Division, which were operating south and east of Bong Son, continued to battle enemy soldiers attempting to flee the area eastward to the Suoi Dinh Binh Valley. They reported 17 enemy KIA, eight enemy prisoners, and one captured AK-47 rifle. In doing so, they suffered two friendly KIA and five WIA. The four battalions of the 41st Regiment of the ARVN 22nd Infantry Division continued to operate in the vicinity of Highway 1 south of Bong Son, reporting only limited enemy contact with no friendly casualties.

By 2400 hours on January 31, the locations of the 3rd Brigade's infantry battalions were as follows: the 1/7th Cav, together with Alpha Company, 2/7th Cav, was in a night defensive position at LZ Papa, 4 kilometers northwest of LZ 4; the 2/12th Cav was in a night defensive position in the palm grove 600 meters south of Lieu An, 5 kilometers north of LZ 4; and the 1/12th Cav was in a night defensive position 4 kilometers north of the 1/7th Cav at LZ Papa and 1.5 kilometers directly west of the 2/12th Cav's position in the palm grove south of Lien An, 6 kilometers northwest of LZ 4. The ARVN 3/3rd Armored Cav was securing its APCs in the rice paddies north of the palm grove 500 meters south of Lieu An and 5 kilometers north of LZ 4. The three battalions of the 40th (Mechanized) Regiment of the ARVN 22nd Infantry Division were positioned in the area east and south of Bong Son in the Suoi Dinh Binh Valley, and the four battalions of the ARVN 41st Regiment, 22nd Infantry Division, were spread out along Highway 1 south of Bong Son.

74 • THE BATTLE OF BONG SON

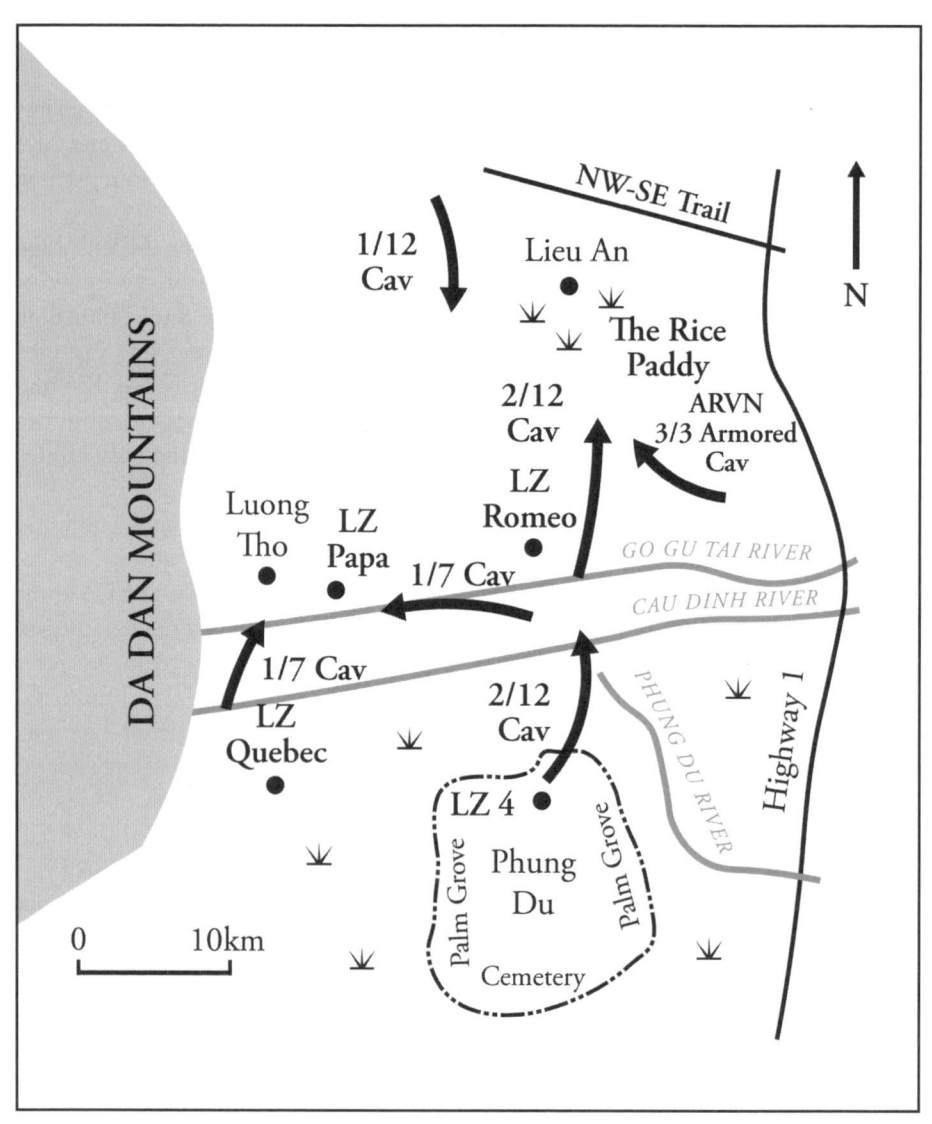

Map 7. Heavy Fighting Continues North and Northwest of Phung Du, January 31–February 1, 1966

CHAPTER SIX

Closing Out Phase I

The night of January 31 was rainy and cold, and visibility in the LZ 4 area was poor. Conditions could not have been better for any North Vietnamese soldiers who might still be in the area following the previous day's fighting at Luong Tho and now wanted to flee westward toward the Da Dan Mountains and An Lao Valley. Shortly after midnight, a squad-sized ambush team from Bravo Company, 1st Battalion, 7th Cavalry, found itself in a grenade-throwing contest with an enemy force of unknown size that was moving westward past its position. The squad had set an ambush along an east–west trail several hundred meters west of the 1/7th Cav's main battalion perimeter at LZ Papa in an attempt to catch any North Vietnamese soldiers fleeing the area under the cover of darkness and rain. The poor visibility made it nearly impossible for the squad members to detect and engage the enemy soldiers with mortar and small-arms fire as they moved along the trail, and instead forced them to engage them with grenades when they revealed their positions. The action resulted in three enemy KIA with no friendly casualties reported.

Several hours later, at 0438 hours, the troops of the 1/7th Cav, together with those of Alpha Company, 2/7th Cav, came under mortar attack in their night defensive position at LZ Papa. Enemy soldiers to the north were firing mortars at them, but the rain and ground fog prevented the troops from pinpointing the location where the mortars were being launched and they were able to do little more than take cover in their foxholes and keep their heads down. The attack lasted only a few minutes and resulted in no casualties. It was most likely a diversionary move by the North Vietnamese to allow one of its units to move past the 1/7th Cav's position without being detected.

In 1966, starlight scopes were standard issue for ground units in South Vietnam, but the devices didn't work very well in a tropical climate, such as that of South Vietnam, where it was rainy and foggy much of the year. They were based on technology that dated back to World War II and required moonlight to work. While not very heavy, they were bulky and awkward to carry. As such, many of the units chose not to take them on field operations in monsoon conditions.

At 0645 hours, the 1/7th Cav pulled in its ambush teams. As they were moving back to LZ Papa to rejoin the rest of the battalion, the Bravo Company troops guarding the perimeter spotted multiple North Vietnamese soldiers moving directly in front of their section of the perimeter and engaged them with shoulder-fired M-79 grenade launchers. The enemy soldiers did not return fire and were able to flee while avoiding the ambush teams that were reentering the battalion perimeter. At daybreak, a search of the area failed to turn up any enemy bodies or blood trails. The 1/7th Cav reported no friendly casualties in the encounter.

Three kilometers northeast of the 1/7th Cav at LZ Papa, Lieutenant Colonel Ingram and the 2nd Battalion, 12th Cavalry, spent a long and anxious night in the palm grove south of Lieu An. Heavy automatic weapons and small-arms fire was received throughout the night and the troops were forced to fight off multiple probes by the North Vietnamese. Because of the rain and fog, illumination from Smokey-the-Bear and suppressive fire from Puff-the-Magic-Dragon were unavailable, and tube artillery from Position Dog was limited to H&I fire directed at the palm grove in Lieu An north of the rice paddy.

By 0755 hours, the fog had lifted and air support was available. The operations officer at Position Dog radioed Lieutenant Colonel Ingram to notify him that aerial reconnaissance helicopters from the 1st Squadron, 9th Cavalry, with helicopter gunship escorts were on their way to his position and would be arriving shortly. The helicopters had been requested the previous night to pick up and transport his eight KIA to Graves Registration at Dog. The five KIA from the ARVN 3/3rd Armored Cav would also be picked-up at that time and transported to Dog. The operations officer informed Ingram that the North Vietnamese soldiers whom the 2/12th Cav had captured the previous evening in the fighting told their interrogators that 300–400 North Vietnamese were in Lieu An the previous afternoon and had started to withdraw to the north and west as darkness approached, leaving behind only a delaying force.

Shortly afterwards, aerial reconnaissance helicopters arrived over the palm grove to initiate their activities in the Lieu An area. The scouts reported that the hamlet was empty of enemy soldiers and that the force that the 2/12th Cav had battled on the previous day had fled. A multi-platoon-sized enemy force, however, was spotted in a trench about 1 kilometer north of Lieu An, adjacent to several nearby hamlets. It had fired on the observation helicopters with automatic weapons when they flew over the area.

Based on the information from the scouts, Lieutenant Colonel Ingram requested an airstrike on the trench and the USAF responded with a FAC and two Skyraiders. The FAC immediately spotted the enemy soldiers and directed the Skyraiders to make multiple passes over the trench, dropping high-explosive bombs and napalm, and raking it with 20mm cannon fire. No assessment of damage was provided.

At 1000 hours, Ingram sent out two patrols in the direction of Lieu An in an attempt to draw fire from any enemy soldiers who might still be in the hamlet. Lieutenant Knox and Bravo Company moved across the open rice paddies to where the ARVN APCs were positioned and swung west on an east–west axis along the APCs' defensive line. Bravo Company failed to draw any enemy fire, but it did capture a North Vietnamese soldier who was making a run for it to the west across its front. At 1052 hours, Bravo Company returned to the palm grove with its prisoner. While Bravo Company was moving to the north and west, Charlie Company was moving to the east and north in the direction of An Qui. It too failed to draw any enemy fire, but it encountered a group of Vietnamese civilians attempting to flee Lieu An to the east in the direction of the hamlet of Gia An and the Man Tan Mu River. The river ran southwest–northeast through the area and provided an avenue of escape in the direction of Highway 1 and Tam Quan. The group consisted of 10 young men of military age dressed in civilian clothes. They were detained by the Charlie Company troops and taken back to the palm grove for interrogation where the rest of the 2/12th Cav was located.

Shortly afterwards, Lieutenant Colonel Ingram notified his company commanders that together with the 3/3rd Armored Cav, the 2/12th Cav was to resume its attack northward toward Lieu An. The 3/3rd Armored Cav would lead the attack with its APCs and mounted infantry, together with the companies of the 2/12th Cav, in a coordinated infantry/APC formation. The attack would continue past the hamlet of Lieu An for a distance of 2.5 kilometers until it reached a northwest–southeast trail that cut across the area leading to Tam Quan. The trail was 1 kilometer south of the Binh Dinh–Quang Ngai provincial boundary and base of the southern Quang Ngai Mountains. Lieutenant Knox and Bravo Company, however, were to proceed north with the attacking force only until it reached Lieu An, where it would turn west and sweep through the hamlet, driving any North Vietnamese there into a blocking position established by the 1/12th Cav 1.5 kilometers west of the hamlet. Alpha, Charlie, and Delta companies, 2/12th Cav, were to continue attacking northward with the 3/3rd Armored Cav. Aerial rocket gunships from the 2/20th ARA would provide coverage for the infantry and APCs in the attack, which would commence at 1350 hours.

In parallel with the 2/12th Cav's sweep northward, Lieutenant Colonel Beard and the 1st Battalion (Airborne), 12th Cavalry, would move to the northeast parallel to the 2/12th Cav's advance in an attempt to cut off escape routes to the west for any enemy soldiers in Lieu An trying to flee the attacking 2/12th Cav. The 1/12th Cav had spent the night roughly 1.5 kilometers directly west of the 2/12th Cav's night defensive position in the palm grove south of Lieu An.

The 2/12th Cav and 3/3rd Armored Cav received only light small-arms fire as they advanced northward across the open rice paddies. The enemy fire was from what appeared to be a rear guard element left behind by the North Vietnamese. At 1440 hours, the attacking force reached the hamlet of Lieu An, where Bravo Company turned to the west and proceeded to move through the hamlet, with no enemy contact. As reported by the aerial scouts from the 1/9th Cav, the main body of the battalion-sized enemy force was no longer in the hamlet. It was deserted except for some women, children, and old men who were huddled together in hootches. Web gear, grenades, and Viet Cong flags from the previous day's action littered the area. As the rear guard element attempted to flee westward to avoid the attacking Bravo Company troops, it ran into the blocking position set by the 1/12th Cav, which had consolidated its position earlier that day directly west of Lieu An. After an initial exchange of small-arms fire, the North Vietnamese soldiers scattered and the troops of the 1/12th Cav were forced to chase them down in a series of running firefights. The 1/12th troops captured 11 of them while reporting one enemy KIA and no friendly casualties.

Alpha, Charlie, and Delta companies, 2/12th Cav, together with the 3/3rd Armored Cav, continued to sweep northward through Lieu An for 2 kilometers, meeting scattered to moderate resistance. At 1726 hours, the attacking force reached the northwest–southeast trail. They had been receiving scattered enemy fire as they advanced. There was no report of enemy KIA in the advance, but the 2/12th Cav suffered four KIA in the day's operation.

While Alpha, Charlie, and Delta companies were sweeping northward with the 3/3rd Armored Cav, Lieutenant Knox and Bravo Company were alerted by Ingram to move by helicopter to a mountaintop position 4 kilometers northwest of Lieu An and 2 kilometers northwest of the northwest–southeast trail, and establish a blocking position there in an attempt to catch any North Vietnamese soldiers fleeing the Lieu An area northward to avoid the attacking 2/12th Cav. Alpha, Charlie, and Delta companies, along with the 3/3rd Armored Cav, would spend the night at the northwest–southeast trail, while Bravo Company would remain in its blocking position on the mountaintop.

Rudy Jaramillo remembered:

> We moved by helicopter to a mountaintop north of Lieu An where we established a blocking position. The area was surrounded by heavy jungle but the mountaintop was wide open and clear. We had a great view of the Bong Son Plain below for what must have been miles. That evening they brought in hot food for us—steaks, potatoes, and drinks. It was a nice break from what we had been going through the last four days. They told us that we had to go back down there the next morning and battle the North Vietnamese again. Then I got sick to my stomach.[1]

During the Vietnam War, the ARVN pioneered the use of the American M-113 APC as an infantry fighting vehicle by fighting "mounted" rather than using it simply as a

---

[1] In phone conversations with the author in June and July 2021, Paul (Rudy) Jaramillo described the move of Bravo Co, 2/12th Cav, by helicopter to a mountaintop location north of Lieu An, where it established a blocking position.

vehicle to transport personnel and equipment into battle.² The ARVN 3rd Armored Cav Squadron used the tactic so proficiently and with such heroism in numerous battles against the North Vietnamese and Viet Cong in the Vietnam War that then U.S. President Richard M. Nixon awarded a Presidential Unit Citation to the unit for their actions in Pleiku Province in 1968.

In one of the last significant encounters with the North Vietnamese in the LZ 4 area, a 13-man recon team from Delta Troop, 1st Squadron, 9th Cavalry, came under heavy automatic weapons fire late on the morning of February 1 from an estimated multi-platoon-sized force, 4 kilometers west of Position Dog. The team had been inserted onto the ground to locate an enemy machine-gun crew that had been firing at 1st Cav helicopters as they approached Dog. The team had only moved about 500 meters when the point man realized that he had walked into an ambush, and he immediately opened fire on the enemy soldiers charging their position. He was cut down by the enemy fire, but his actions alerted the rest of the team to the ambush and it was able to take cover. The team, however, took several casualties in a matter of minutes and was fragmented by the enemy fire. A ready-reaction team from Delta Troop, which had been on standby at Dog ready to come to the assistance of the recon team should the need arise, landed shortly afterwards and quickly moved to the recon team's position. A helicopter gunship from the 1/9th Cav had been providing aerial cover for the recon team and was able to pinpoint the location of the enemy soldiers as being 200 meters from the teams' position. The helicopter made firing passes on the enemy soldiers to keep them pinned down while the two teams attacked the enemy's position.³

The point man of the ready-reaction team was in the middle of the fight when he was hit by machine-gun fire and severely wounded. He died shortly afterwards from his wounds en route by helicopter to the 15th Med aid station. The North Vietnamese soldiers withdrew in disarray up a draw into the Da Dan Mountains. Tactical air support was requested while the helicopter gunship chased after them. Within 10 minutes of the request, two USAF B-57 tactical bombers arrived on station, dropping general purpose and fragmentation bombs and napalm, and raking the area with 20mm cannon fire. Once the explosions and fires died down, the two

---

2   A Presidential Unit Citation (Army) document provided a description of how the ARVN 3/3rd Armored Cav pioneered the use of the American M-113 APC as an infantry fighting vehicle by fighting "mounted" rather than using it simply as a vehicle to transport personnel and equipment into battle. The Presidential Unit Citation (Army) Award for Extraordinary Heroism, 3rd Armored Cavalry Squadron, Army of the Republic of Vietnam. Signed by President Richard Nixon, March 25, 1971.
3   Remembrances left by Lieutenant Colonel Teddy H. Sanford, Jr. (Ret.) for SP4 Douglas McArthur Wetmore, Williamsburg, Kentucky, and PFC John Howard Griffith, Mount Vernon, New York. Vietnam Veterans Memorial Fund, The Wall of Faces, posting dated May 23, 2014, https://www.vvmf.org.

teams pursued the enemy and reestablished contact with them several times, but were unable to fix them in position. As the afternoon dragged on and darkness set in, the teams were extracted and no bomb damage assessment was possible due to the darkness. Delta Troop suffered two KIA and multiple WIA in the encounter.

The rifle platoons of Delta Troop were elite economy-of-force units. They were small and mobile and could be deployed quickly. They were used as both ground and air cavalry to provide armed escorts for convoys in areas subject to ambush by North Vietnamese and Viet Cong forces. They could also conduct bomb damage assessments and ground reconnaissance activities in force, such as the one on February 1, and provide general infantry support and ready-reaction forces to the brigades.

With the completion of the airstrip at Position Dog by the division's 8th Engineer Battalion, and with the landing of the first aircraft there on February 1, Position Dog was renamed LZ English in honor of SP5 Carver J. English, Jr., Headquarters Company, 8th Engineer Battalion. Construction of the airstrip was completed by Alpha Company, 8th Engineers, working around the clock for 70 hours. The airstrip was capable of accommodating USAF C-123 aircraft.

Late on the afternoon of February 1, Colonel Moore requested a B-52 strike for the following morning in the foothills of the Da Dan Mountains, west of Luong Tho. Repeated firing at 1st Squadron, 9th Cavalry, aircraft reconnoitering the area indicated the presence of a large enemy force there—likely that which the 1/7th Cav had battled at Luong Tho for the last several days.

At 1000 hours on February 2, a flight of three USAF B-52s from Guam arrived over the foothills of the Da Dan Mountains and dropped their bombs. The strike zone covered an area 2 kilometers long, north to south, and 1 kilometer wide, west to east. Immediately after the airstrike, a platoon from Delta Troop, 1/9th Cav, entered the area to assess damage and search for enemy soldiers who might have survived the airstrike, or weapons that might still be intact. No enemy contact was reported. At 1159 hours, the 1/7th Cav was inserted into the area to join the platoon from Delta Troop, 1/9th Cav. Again, there was no enemy contact reported. Alpha Company moved to the north, Bravo Company to the west, and Charlie Company to the south. At 1456 hours, the 1/7th Cav reported that it had encountered five North Vietnamese soldiers, and engaged them resulting in five enemy KIA. There were no friendly casualties in the encounter. The 1/7th Cav also reported that it found the wreckage of a Huey helicopter. The weapons and components of the aircraft had been removed and the aircraft had been camouflaged with leaves and jungle vegetation. There were no helicopters from the 1st Cav reported missing at that time, but when the MACV Sector Advisor at the Special Forces camp was contacted, he said that an American helicopter had gone down in that area on December 30, 1965, and that an American soldier onboard the helicopter had survived the crash. He was injured and was captured shortly afterwards by the Viet Cong, and was being held in a POW camp in the mountainous Gia Ket area.

Colonel Hal Moore, 3rd Brigade commander. (Army News Service, February 16, 2017)

General Westmoreland. (National Archives)

Troops sweep area north of Phu Cat in Deception Phase. (National Archives)

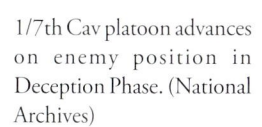

1/7th Cav platoon advances on enemy position in Deception Phase. (National Archives)

Bravo Battery, 2/21th Arty at Position George north of Phu Cat. (National Archives)

1/7th Cav troopers take cover from enemy sniper north of Phu Cat. (National Archives)

1/7th Cav troops stand guard over captured North Vietnamese soldiers in Deception Phase. (National Archives)

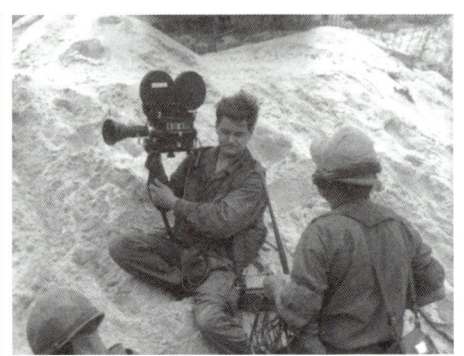

CBS News camera crew travels with 1/7th Cav. (National Archives)

Search-and-destroy north of Phu Cat. (National Archives)

Republic of Korea (ROK) troops on patrol in Phu Cat area. (National Archives)

2/7th Cav troopers preparing for move to Bong Son. (National Archives)

2/7th Cav troops load onto deuce-and-a-half truck for ride to airstrip. (National Archives)

2/7th Cav troops move by truck convoy from base camp to airfield at Special Forces Camp at An Khe. (National Archives)

Truck convoy makes its way through Phu Cat area on way to Bong Son. (National Archives)

The Golf Course at 1st Cav's base camp at An Khe. (National Archives)

2/7th Cav troops at airstrip prepare for flight to Bong Son. (National Archives)

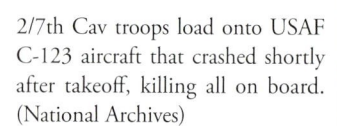

2/7th Cav troops load onto USAF C-123 aircraft that crashed shortly after takeoff, killing all on board. (National Archives)

2/7th Cav command post at Special Forces Camp at Bong Son. (National Archives)

1/7th Cav troops help wounded North Vietnamese soldier. (National Archives)

Villagers huddle together as 2/7th Cav troops sweep village in Bong Son. (National Archives)

2/12th Cav medics hold sick call for villagers at LZ Hammond. (National Archives)

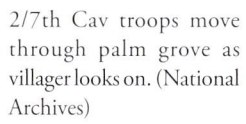

2/7th Cav troops move through palm grove as villager looks on. (National Archives)

Troops check out cave built into rice paddy dike. (National Archives)

2/7th Cav troops return fire at enemy position in palm grove. (National Archives)

Troops cautiously advance on enemy position in palm grove. (National Archives)

2nd Brigade firing mortars. (National Archives)

Charlie Battery, 1/21st Artillery at Position Dog fires in support of troops at Phung Du. (National Archives)

Protestant Chaplain Captain Lavera W. Cardia conducts service at Position Dog. (National Archives)

2/7th Cav troops take cover behind burial mounds in Phung Du. (National Archives)

Medevac helicopter lifts off from cemetery at Phung Du. (National Archives)

Position Dog with Da Dan Mountains in background. (National Archives)

Troops offload from CH-47 Chinook. (National Archives)

At 1440 hours on February 2, Colonel Moore alerted Lieutenant Colonel Ingram that the companies of the 2/12th Cav were to move by helicopter from their current positions north of Lieu An to a location in the far northwestern corner of the Bong Son Plain along the Binh Dinh–Quang Ngai provincial boundary. The location was designated LZ Sue.

The companies of the 2/12th Cav closed into LZ Sue at 1535 hours with no enemy contact reported. Bravo Company, the first company on the ground, seized and secured the position for the rest of the battalion. Alpha and Charlie companies immediately began to sweep to the southeast, while Bravo remained at Sue.

The units of the 3rd Brigade continued to fight daily skirmishes with the North Vietnamese in the LZ 4 area over the next couple of days, but the frequency and intensity of the encounters diminished. With that, Major General Kinnard ordered an end to Phase I of Operation *Masher*, effective 1200 hours February 4.

In eight days of sustained fighting, January 28–February 4, 1966, preceded by four days of deception operations, the 1st Cav virtually destroyed the 7th and 9th Battalions of the 22nd NVA Regiment, killing 603 enemy soldiers by body count, and an additional 956 estimated, based on debris left on the battlefields, totaling more than 1,500. Two hundred and forty-two enemy soldiers were taken prisoner. It also forced the 7th and 9th Battalions of the 22nd NVA, which had long threatened Bong Son and Highway 1 from Qui Nhon to Bong Son, to flee a formerly "secure" base area and seek refuge in the jungle-covered mountains to the west to avoid the attacking 1st Cav. This, however, came at a steep price—90 Americans died on the battlefield, an additional 46 died in the crash of the USAF C-123 Provider aircraft shortly after takeoff from the 1st Cav's base camp at An Khe, and more than 220 were wounded in action.

The ARVN likewise paid a heavy price for its participation in the fighting. Although it did not release a summary of casualty figures on a per-battle basis, the ARVN did report daily casualty figures on a tactical unit basis to the operations group of the 3rd Brigade. The ARVN Airborne Brigade suffered 27 KIA and 100 WIA on January 30 and another 22 KIA and 73 WIA on January 31, totaling 49 KIA, including one U.S. advisor, and 173 WIA, including five U.S. advisors. The 40th (Mechanized) and 41st Regiments of the ARVN 22nd Infantry Division suffered seven KIA and five WIA on the night of January 30 and two KIA and five WIA on January 31, totaling nine KIA and 10 WIA. The ARVN 3/3rd Armored Cav Squadron did not report casualty figures to the 1st Cav.

In Operation *Double Eagle/Lien Ket 22*, there was no heavy fighting along the boundary with Binh Dinh Province in spite of the extensive commitment of troops and equipment by the Marines and ARVN. Marine units encountered only small groups of enemy soldiers. According to the commander of Foxtrot Company, 2nd Battalion, 3rd Marines, "the Viet Cong would hit us, pull out, hit us and pull out. They wouldn't stick around." Although firefights were the exception rather than the rule, the Marines did inflict a heavy toll on local enemy forces, and in two separate engagements on February 2 in the coastal region north of Red Beach, Lieutenant Colonel Young's 3rd Battalion, 1st Marines, battled small groups of Viet Cong engaged in hit-and-run attacks, resulting in 31 enemy guerillas KIA.

As for equipment, the 1st Cav had 21 helicopters damaged by enemy ground fire during the diversionary maneuvers, with one being shot down. The one shot down was recovered, but was damaged beyond repair and was scrapped. During Phase I, 91 helicopters were damaged by enemy ground fire, with six being shot down. All six of them were recovered, but two were so badly damaged that they too had to be scrapped.

Figures released by local government officials in Bong Son showed that a large number of refugees and war victims resulted from the fighting on the coastal plain. The number already in Bong Son on January 26 when the fighting started was 7,800, but as the fighting progressed, that figure increased to more than 21,000. While many civilians fled the fighting seeking safety and shelter in Bong Son, others did not, remaining in their hootches for fear that if they abandoned them the Viet Cong would confiscate their land and redistribute it to more dedicated supporters.

CHAPTER SEVEN

Into the An Lao Valley

With the end of Phase I on February 4, the 3rd Brigade, under the command of Colonel Hal Moore, was to shift its efforts west from the coastal plain north of Bong Son to the An Lao Valley and initiate search-and-destroy operations there in what would be Phase II of Operation *Masher*. The 2nd Brigade, under the command of Colonel Lynch, was to move from the division's base camp at An Khe to Position Dog, now named LZ English—Position Dog was renamed LZ English with the completion of the airstrip there by the 8th Engineer Battalion and the landing of a USAF C-123 Provider aircraft—and join Colonel Moore and the 3rd Brigade. Phase II would target the North Vietnamese operating in the An Lao Valley and the headquarters of the Sao Vang Division, believed to be located on the high ground north of the valley.

Although enemy strength and disposition in the valley was unknown at the time, recent intelligence reports received from the MACV Sector Advisor at the Special Forces camp indicated that the 8th Battalion, 22nd NVA Regiment, was garrisoned in the valley, and that the enemy soldiers who had exfiltrated the coastal plain in Phase I had taken refuge in it. Repeated firing at 1st Squadron, 9th Cavalry, aircraft reconnoitering the valley, as well as the experience of Major Beckwith and his Project Delta teams, further indicated the presence of hostile forces there.

The An Lao Valley was 13 kilometers west of the coastal plain where Phase I was conducted. It was 30 kilometers long from north to south, and three kilometers wide at its widest point. It was a rich, fertile valley through which the An Lao River (Song An Lao) flowed. Mountain peaks and razorback ridges dominated the valley, with the Da Dan Mountains in the east rising to heights approaching 663 meters and the Cheu Mountains in the west reaching heights of 400 meters. The mountains were covered in double- and triple-canopy jungle, with tangled vegetation at the ground level, and slopes with huge rock formations and natural caves. The mountains were nearly impenetrable. The valley had numerous smaller, or side, valleys and draws that were heavily forested, providing areas with concealment from aerial observation. The An Lao River was a long, twisting river that ran down the middle of the valley, with Route 514 in parallel to it much of the way. The valley had long been known to be a major Viet Cong north–south logistics and communications route between enemy bases in Quang Ngai Province to the north and Binh Dinh Province, and was believed to contain rice caches and resupply points for North Vietnamese and Viet Cong units.

The valley had an estimated population of 7,500 inhabitants, most of whom lived in An Lao village about halfway up the valley, adjacent to the An Lao River. Others lived either in the villages of Hung Long or Thuan An, immediately north of An Lao village, or in Long Khanh, south of it. The areas around the villages were heavily cultivated, but much of the land north of Hung Long and Thuan An was jungle and uninhabited, while the area south of Long Khanh was only moderately populated.

The plan for clearing the valley of the North Vietnamese and Viet Cong called for a coordinated effort among the 2nd and 3rd Brigades of the 1st Cav, the 40th (Mechanized) and 41st Regiments of the ARVN 22nd Infantry Division, and the U.S. III Marine Amphibious Force, together with the 4th Regiment of the ARVN 2nd Infantry Division. The ARVN 40th (Mechanized) and 41st Regiments would seal the southern entrance to the valley to prevent the North Vietnamese from escaping to the south. The U.S. Marines, together with the ARVN 4th Regiment, would cross into Binh Dinh Province from neighboring Quang Ngai Province and seal the head of the valley, thereby stopping the North Vietnamese from escaping to the north. The two brigades of the 1st Cav would air assault onto the high ground and sweep down the slopes into the valley, destroying the enemy as they went.

For Phase II, the 3rd Brigade would consist of the 1st and 2nd Battalions, 7th Cavalry, the 1st Battalion (Airborne), 12th Cavalry, from the 1st Brigade, and Charlie Troop, 1st Squadron, 9th Cavalry. The 1/12th Cav would remain under the operational control of the 3rd Brigade for the duration of Phase II. The three battalions would air assault onto the mountaintops on the east and west sides of the valley in the vicinity of Long Khanh and sweep down the slopes into the valley, thus upsetting probable enemy expectations that the landings would be in the valley. They would destroy any North Vietnamese forces encountered, as well as supply bases, rice caches, and other establishments, and aid in the return of the valley to South Vietnamese government officials. Charlie Troop, 1/9th Cav, would provide aerial and ground reconnaissance with its observation helicopters, gunships, and aero rifle platoon.

The 2nd Brigade would consist of the 1st and 2nd Battalions, 5th Cavalry, the 2nd Battalion, 12th Cavalry, and Bravo Troop, 1st Squadron, 9th Cavalry. The 1/5th Cav and 2/12th Cav would return to the control of the 2nd Brigade at the start of Phase II. The 2nd Brigade would also include aerial and tube artillery batteries, aviation units, engineering companies, and other support units. The two 5th Cav battalions would air assault onto the mountaintops on the western side of the valley in the vicinity of An Lao village and Thuan An, then sweep down the slopes into the valley. The 2/12th Cav would air assault into LZ Brass located on the high ground to the northeast of the valley, and seize and secure the position for follow-on artillery. It would also link up with the U.S. Marines' Golf Company, 2nd Battalion, 4th Marines, which would cross into Binh Dinh Province from southern Quang Ngai Province. The 2/4th Marines would be accompanied by a small communication platoon detachment that would provide security and radio communication for the site. The 2nd Battalion, 9th Marines, would also cross into Binh Dinh Province from southern Quang Ngai Province at the same time, sweep down the slopes, and link up with the 2nd Brigade units. Bravo Troop, 1/9th Cav, would provide aerial and ground reconnaissance. Alpha Battery, 1st Battalion, 30th Field Artillery (155mm howitzer), and Alpha Battery from the 2nd Brigade's direct support artillery unit, the 1st Battalion, 77th Artillery (105mm howitzers), would fire in support of 1st Cav and Marine units in the valley. The big guns of the 1/30th Field Artillery would also support Marine units in southern Quang Ngai Province. And finally, ship-to-shore naval gunfire from the USS *Barry* and USS *Orleck* would be used to support the 2nd Brigade units,

In addition, the 2/12th Cav, 2/4th Marines, and 2/9th Marines would conduct extensive search-and-destroy sweeps on the high ground north of the valley in search of the headquarters of the Sao Vang Division. They would also search for the bodies of the three members of the Special Forces, Project Delta, Team 3, which had not been recovered from the January 29 incident. Team 3 had been searching for the headquarters of the Sao Vang Division in the same general area where the three battalions would be conducting operations, when it encountered the North Vietnamese. At the completion of the search-and-destroy sweeps, the three battalions would attack south from the high ground into the valley to catch the enemy between the two closing forces.

The 1st Battalion, 30th Field Artillery, was an independent regiment in the Army that supported 155mm howitzers. It had arrived in South Vietnam in November 1965 and had been actively supporting various U.S. Army units and Korean Tiger Division units in II Corps. In February 1966, Alpha Battery of the regiment was attached to the 1st Cav to support operations in the An Lao Valley. Special slings were fabricated by the 1st Cav Support Command to be used by Flying Crane helicopters to lift Alpha Battery's 14,000lb 155mm howitzers to mountaintop positions. These positions would otherwise not have been accessible to towed artillery because of the lack of roads, showing that towed howitzers could now virtually go anywhere that the smaller and lighter artillery howitzers, such as 105mm howitzers, could go. Alpha Battery would remain attached to the 1st Cav until April 1971, when the 1st Cav left South Vietnam and returned to the U.S.

Both the 2nd Brigade's operation on the western slopes and the 3rd Brigade's operation on the slopes in the southern portion of the valley would be conducted using tear gas as part of landing zone preparatory fires, and the various objectives would be swept by troops wearing gas masks. The helicopter crews would also wear gas masks.

Bravo Company, 15th Med, would establish a field site at the Special Forces camp to support the 2nd Brigade's operations in the valley. It would include an aid station and a section of the 15th Med's Medevac Platoon. It was designated "Bravo Med." The Charlie Company aid station at LZ English, along with a section of the Medevac Platoon located nearby, would continue to support the 3rd Brigade's operations.

Marginal flying weather delayed the movement of troops into the valley by helicopter on February 5 and 6. Drizzle and fog with low cloud ceilings prevailed, completely covering the mountain areas where the troops would be operating. When the move did finally take place, the operation carried a new name—Operation *White Wing*. President Johnson had reacted angrily to the name *Masher* when he first heard it as he was preparing to meet with the leaders of South Vietnam at the Honolulu Conference on the Vietnam War in Hawaii to discuss pacification efforts. He felt that the name *Masher* was too crude in view of the heated discussions on U.S. operations in Vietnam expected in the Security Council of the United Nations and in the U.S. Congress, and he directed McGeorge Bundy, his National Security Advisor, to change it. Shortly afterwards, General Westmoreland received the following cable from Gen. Earle G. "Bus" Wheeler, Chairman of the Joint Chiefs of Staff:

> I have been quietly approached by McGeorge Bundy with the request that we choose neutral designations for our combat operations in South Vietnam. He cited "Masher" as the type of designation which should be avoided. I told him that most names used were quite innocuous and gave several examples, such as "Mallard," etc. He agreed that the nomenclature generally used is in line with his request and asked if I could, without putting a lot of directives on paper, see that all operational names are of like nature. I assured him that I could.
>
> Since I am sure that guidance of this character will cause you no difficulty, I have no hesitancy in asking you to comply. In this connection, and in contravention of an earlier directive from me, I suggest that at some convenient break in Masher its designation be changed to some innocuous term upon which even the most biased person cannot seize as the theme of a public speech.[1]

The new name chosen by General Westmoreland and his commanders at I Field Force Vietnam was rumored to be *White Dove*, but at the last minute they thought better of their choice and settled instead on *White Wing*.

On February 7, the weather had improved, permitting USAF tactical air support to be utilized for LZ preparation in order to neutralize any antiaircraft weapons that might be in the area. The air assaults by the 3rd Brigade troops onto the high

---

[1] General Earle "Bus" Wheeler, Chairman of the Joint Chiefs of Staff, sent a memo to General Westmoreland, Commander of the Military Assistance Command, Vietnam (MACV), requesting that the name *Masher* be changed to something "quite innocuous," upon which even the most biased person could not seize as the theme of a public speech. Earle "Bus" Wheeler, "Wheeler Washington to Westmoreland Saigon," copy LBJ Library, dated February 1966.

ground on the western side of the valley in the southern portion of the valley were unopposed, and the battalions of the 3rd Brigade swept down the slopes, from east and west, into the valley by combined air and ground moves without major contact. The slopes were steep and heavily forested, and movement down them was slow. Aerial observation teams from Charlie Troop, 1/9th Cav, reported receiving small-arms fire, time-fused mortar and rocket launcher fire at aircraft, and an incident of automatic weapons fire at aircraft, while providing aerial sweeps with their reconnaissance helicopters. The 1/12th Cav reported receiving small-arms fire from the hamlet of Long Khanh in the valley as it moved from the eastern side of the valley toward the river. The 2/7th Cav encountered no resistance as it moved down the western slope into the valley. Although there was no significant enemy contact, the sweeps did succeed in uncovering a remarkable system of trenches and fortifications and large caches of rice and salt.

The air assaults onto the high ground on the western side of the valley in its central and northern portions by the battalions of the 2nd Brigade were likewise unopposed. The troops of the 1/5th Cav, however, encountered a punji stake field hidden in the elephant grass at their landing zone, designated LZ Copper, approximately 2 kilometers northwest of An Lao village, resulting in five friendly WIA. Several hours later, and approximately 2 kilometers southwest of LZ Copper, Charlie Company, 2/5th Cav, likewise encountered a punji stake field, resulting in two WIA. The punji stakes were new and were oriented toward the south—the direction from which the 2/5th Cav had approached the area.

Punji stakes were a crude yet extremely effective weapon of the North Vietnamese and Viet Cong that could severely limit the effectiveness of an American unit. They were sharpened pieces of bamboo, 1–2 feet in length. They were typically hardened by fire and had an extremely sharp point that would last for long periods of time. To increase their wounding potential, the points on the stakes would be smeared with poison, or animal or human excreta. The North Vietnamese and Viet Cong would place the punji stakes in areas where American troops would likely pass through, such as helicopter landing zones, and camouflage them in elephant grass and in holes in the ground. Unsuspecting U.S. soldiers would either step into the holes and onto the punji stakes, resulting in puncture wounds to the bottom of their feet, or walk into them, tearing the muscle and flesh in their lower legs. The wounds seldom proved to be fatal, but almost always required that the troopers be evacuated by helicopter to a field hospital for medical treatment, thereby delaying the advance of the units.

The search-and-destroy sweeps on the high ground by the 2/12th Cav and the two Marine battalions failed to locate the headquarters of the Sao Vang Division, but on February 8, Golf Company, 2/9th Marines, did find the body of an American soldier, believed to be one of the three missing Special Forces troopers from Project

Delta, Team 3 ("Roadrunner").[2] It was found in the general area where the three Special Forces soldiers were believed to have been in contact with the North Vietnamese. However, there was no identification on the body, nor were there any markings on the soldier's uniform, so it was not possible to say with any certainty that the body was one of the Special Forces soldiers. A helicopter was brought in to pick up the body and transport it to Graves Registration at LZ English. Golf Company continued to search the area for the next two days but failed to find anything that might have led to the whereabouts of the bodies of the other two Special Forces soldiers.

On the sweep down the eastern slope, the 2/12th Cav encountered a number of enemy soldiers who were "out for a walk in the jungle." Several of them stopped abruptly when they spotted the 2/12th Cav troopers approaching, while others ducked into the bushes trying to hide. None of the enemy soldiers was carrying a weapon or a rucksack, and upon questioning by the ARVN interpreter who was traveling with the 2/12th Cav, they said that they were from a hospital located in a nearby cave and were recovering from wounds received in recent fighting with the 1st Cav in the Bong Son area. A Psy War (Psychological Warfare) team was dispatched to the site to help lure the remaining enemy soldiers and medical personnel out of the cave.

The results of the 2nd Brigade's operations weren't much better than those of the 3rd Brigade. They showed that large North Vietnamese forces had occupied the area on the western slopes in the central and northern portions of the valley a few days prior to the 2nd Brigade's sweep, but were no longer in the area in any large numbers. The slopes were honeycombed with recently abandoned bunkers, foxholes, caves, and hidden caches of rice, salt, and ammunition, and more. Some of the caves were 30–40 feet deep.

The rice and salt were hauled to nearby clearings by the 5th Cav troops so they could be loaded onto Chinook helicopters and transported to the Bong Son District Headquarters to be used at the refugee camps in the area, while the medical supplies were taken by helicopter to the Bong Son Dispensary. Where there were no nearby clearings, combat engineers from Bravo Company, 8th Engineer Battalion, cut back areas of the jungle-covered slopes large enough to support helicopter landings and lift-offs, often climbing down ropes from hovering helicopters to the jungle floor with their chainsaws and explosives strapped on their backs. The bunkers, many of which were booby trapped with

---

[2] According to entries posted on the Coffelt Database of Vietnam casualties, Golf Company, 2/9th Marines, found the body of an American soldier in the area north of the An Lao Valley who was believed to be one of the three missing soldiers from the Special Forces, Project Delta, Team 2 (Capital). "Operations log for the 2nd Battalion, 9th Marines, for 07 and 08 Feb 1966," http://www.coffeltdatabase.org.

grenades, Claymore mines, sticks of dynamite, and the ammunition inside them, were destroyed. The questioning of Viet Cong prisoners who were captured during the sweeps provided a wealth of information on past unit activities and morale, but was received too late to be acted upon.

Patrolling in the valley didn't yield much, either. Sniper fire was received from several of the villages, but the marksmen were long gone by the time the 5th Cav units maneuvered into position to sweep the villages and all that was left were shell casings on the ground. However, on February 8, future Army Chief-of-Staff Lieutenant Colonel Edward "Shy" Meyer and his 2/5th Cav succeeded in driving the Viet Cong political organization and local-force company from the An Lao District Headquarters at An Lao village.[3] The headquarters had been occupied by the Viet Cong and North Vietnamese since December 1964, when the North Vietnamese arrived in the valley in force and together with Viet Cong guerrillas drove the South Vietnamese government officials and ARVN troops garrisoned there out of the district headquarters and valley.

After four days of maneuvering down the slopes and patrolling in the valley with little to show for it, Major General Kinnard ordered Colonel Moore and the 3rd Brigade to redirect its efforts southward from the An Lao Valley to the Kim Son Valley, effective 1200 hours, February 11, in what would be Phase III of Operation *Masher/White Wing*. The Kim Son Valley was 15 kilometers south of the An Lao Valley and 20 kilometers southwest of Bong Son. It had long been a sanctuary for the North Vietnamese and Viet Cong, and Kinnard and his brigade commanders felt that it was ripe for an operation. The 3rd Brigade would lead the operation. The 2nd Brigade would continue to concentrate its efforts on completing search-and-destroy operations in the An Lao Valley. It would target the western slopes of the Da Dan Mountains in the vicinity of An Lao Village and patrol the eastern slopes of the mountains to ensure that enemy soldiers were not fleeing the valley and returning to the coastal plain north of Bong Son. The U.S. Marines—with the 2nd Battalion, 4th Marines, and 2nd Battalion, 9th Marines—would continue to sweep down the slopes into the valley from the high-ground to the northeast, destroying any North Vietnamese forces encountered.

Late on the afternoon of February 11, an aerial observation team from Bravo Troop, 1/9th Cav, reported receiving automatic weapons and small-arms fire from a location along the An Lao River, southeast of An Lao village. The observation team was reconnoitering the area in support of Charlie Company, 1/5th Cav, which was conducting reconnaissance-in-force patrolling along the river in search of a suspected

---

[3] Wikipedia, "Battle of An Lao," https://en_wikipedia.org describes how future Army Chief-of-Staff Lieutenant Colonel Edward "Shy" Meyer and his 2nd Battalion, 5th Cavalry, succeeded in driving the local Viet Cong political organization from the An Lao District Headquarters at An Lao village on February 8, 1966.

enemy hospital. Lieutenant Colonel Ackerson alerted Bravo Company, 1/5th Cav, to move to the location and clear it. Bravo Company had been patrolling north of Charlie Company's position with little to show for it.

At 1600 hours, Bravo Company set down several hundred meters north of where the enemy fire was coming from and started to move south. Almost immediately it began to receive small-arms fire, and aerial rocket gunships from Bravo Battery, 2/20th ARA, were requested to support Bravo Company's advance. By 1620 hours, Bravo Company was receiving heavy automatic weapons and mortar fire from an enemy force estimated to be a company-sized unit reinforced by a heavy weapons unit. Lieutenant Colonel Ackerson requested a tactical airstrike and the USAF responded with a FAC and two Skyraiders. The FAC was able to quickly locate the enemy position and the Skyraiders made multiple passes over it, dropping 500lb high-explosive bombs and napalm, resulting in secondary explosions that sent smoke high into the sky and dirt and rocks flying through the air for several hundred meters in every direction. Artillery fire from LZ English followed the airstrike.

At 1800 hours, a recon patrol from Bravo Company was sent into the area to assess the bomb damage and observe enemy activity. It spotted multiple enemy KIA scattered around and a squad-sized unit of between seven and 11 soldiers. It also observed a large number of enemy soldiers who were moving out of the area to the south toward the Da Dan Mountains, using flashlights for illumination. With that, Bravo Company moved in. Shortly afterwards, it reported that it captured 32 enemy soldiers. In parallel with Bravo Company's movement, Charlie Company to the north encountered a large group of enemy soldiers moving northward in an apparent attempt to avoid the attacking Bravo Company troops. It captured 17 soldiers initially and another 10 shortly afterwards.

It wasn't known if the captured enemy soldiers were patients at the hospital suspected to be in the area or if they were part of a hospital guard element. Bravo Company reported 15 enemy KIA, while suffering five friendly KIA and a number of WIA. One of the wounded troopers lived long enough to be evacuated to the 15th Med aid station at the Special Forces Camp where he died the next day from his wounds. Charlie Company reported six enemy KIA. Smokey-the-Bear and Puff-the-Magic-Dragon were called in to support Bravo and Charlie companies and remained in the area throughout the night.

On the morning of February 12, Bravo Company initiated search-and-destroy patrolling east of An Lao village along the western side of the Da Dan Mountains, moving south. At mid-morning, Bravo Company linked up with Alpha Company, 1/5th Cav, which had been moving north along the western side of the mountains. Alpha Company was commanded by Captain George Forrest, who had distinguished himself in the fighting at LZ Albany in the Ia Drang Valley in November. Sporadic small-arms fire was received throughout the day by both companies. Several caves were discovered by the two companies; some were 30–40 feet deep and stocked with mortar rounds, weapons, and web gear. The companies also found several large caches of rice and salt, but no enemy soldiers.

Alpha and Bravo companies, 1/5th Cav, continued to sweep the area along the western side of the mountains with little to show for it. However, at 1430 hours on February 13, an aerial observation team from Bravo Troop, 1/9th Cav, spotted a platoon-sized North Vietnamese force consisting of 25 armed soldiers moving north along the eastern side of the mountains, 3 kilometers northwest of LZ 4 and less than 1 kilometer northwest of LZ Romeo. The enemy soldiers were engaged by aerial rocket gunships from the 2/20th ARA and tube artillery from LZ English and scattered toward the base of the mountains and into the tree line, but not before the ARA gunships got two KBA.

At 1530 hours, an aerial observation team from Bravo Troop, 1/9th Cav, again spotted a group of North Vietnamese soldiers, believed to be part of the larger group of 25 that scattered into the mountains earlier that day. The group was attacked by the team's helicopter gunships, resulting in two KBA, two WIA, and two automatic weapons destroyed. The 2/12th Cav, which had also been patrolling the area along the eastern side of the mountains, approximately 2 kilometers south of where the 1/9th Cav aerial team spotted and engaged the group of North Vietnamese soldiers, was alerted to move a rifle company by helicopter to a position 2 kilometers north of where the enemy soldiers were spotted. The position was designated LZ Jim, where it was to establish a blocking position. All available lift ships attached to the 2nd Brigade were utilized, and Lieutenant Knox and Bravo Company, 2/12th Cav, along with the Reconnaissance Platoon from Delta Company, 2/12th Cav, were on the ground at LZ Jim by 1905 hours after aerial rocket gunships from the 2/20th ARA prepped the area with its 2.75inch rockets. Bravo Company and the reconnaissance platoon immediately moved south to establish contact with the enemy unit. At 1910 hours, the helicopter gunships from Bravo Troop, 1/9th Cav, again spotted the enemy unit and opened fire, resulting in four additional KBA, while Bravo Company made contact with it on the ground, leading to another four enemy KIA. Bravo Company also captured 11 North Vietnamese soldiers in the encounter. The remaining enemy soldiers were observed in a state of confusion while aerial rocket gunships from the 2/20th ARA and tube artillery from LZ English were called in on the target. Interrogation of the captured soldiers indicated that a company-sized force was in the area and that it had about 40 WIA with it. Bravo Company suffered one KIA and one WIA in the encounter. One rifleman from the 2nd Platoon suffered a gunshot wound to the head and died before he could be evacuated for treatment to the 15th Med aid station at the Special Forces camp.

In an unusual night operation, Lieutenant Knox and Bravo Company, 2/12th Cav, and the battalion's Reconnaissance Platoon pulled back into a night defensive position at LZ Jim while at the same time sending out platoon-sized patrols to keep pressure on the enemy. At 2350 hours, Charlie Company, 2/12th Cav, was alerted to move by helicopter to an area 2 kilometers south of where the enemy platoon was spotted and attack northward, driving them into Bravo Company and the Reconnaissance Platoon. Smokey-the-Bear provided illumination during the night to help spot enemy soldiers trying to slip between the two closing forces. The 2/12th Cav continued to sweep the area until daybreak, at which time it was alerted to withdraw from the area. ARVN forces moved in to complete the search-and-destroy operation.

On February 15, Alpha Company, 2/12th Cav, was patrolling the area southeast of An Lao village along the western side of the Da Dan Mountains when it discovered an abandoned 60-bed hospital with an operating room, stretchers, medical supplies, and 5 tons of rice. A mess hall was located nearby. The complex was in the area southeast of where Bravo Company, 1/5th Cav, made contact with North Vietnamese forces on the afternoon of February 11. The medical supplies and equipment were loaded onto a Chinook helicopter and transported to the Bong Son Dispensary, while the rice was transported to the Special Forces camp to be used at the refugee camps in the area. The hospital complex was destroyed.

Major General Kinnard ordered an end to the 2nd Brigade's operations in the An Lao Valley and to Phase II of Operation *Masher/White Wing*, effective at 2400 hours on February 15, and directed the 2nd Brigade to move to the Kim Son Valley to join the 3rd Brigade in Phase III, Operation *Masher/White Wing* (*Eagle's Claw*).

Although Phase II didn't result in any decisive encounters with the North Vietnamese or Viet Cong, it did lead to the 1st Cav driving the 8th Battalion, 22nd NVA Regiment, out of the valley and helping local South Vietnam government officials regain control of it. On February 8, Lieutenant Colonel Meyer and his 2/5th Cav arrived at An Lao village to find that the NVA had already vacated the district headquarters rather than staying and trying to defend it.

Phase II was also a success in uncovering large caches of rice and enemy installations in the valley. Information gained about enemy trails, systems of trenches and fortifications, fields of punji stakes, enemy movement, and patterns of supply bases would be helpful in future operations. The capture of 126 105mm artillery rounds would limit the use of the two 105mm howitzers the North Vietnamese had captured from the ARVN in December 1964 when they overran the An Lao District Headquarters. The loss of many tons of rice and salt would further limit the enemy's ability to conduct large-scale operations in the area for some time to come. Three field hospitals supporting the North Vietnamese and Viet Cong were also captured and destroyed.

In spite of the large stores of rice and salt that were captured, and the networks of trenches and fortifications that were located and destroyed, Major General Kinnard and his brigade commanders had to have been disappointed with the results of Phase II. After nearly 10 days of scouring the east and west slopes of the valley and patrolling on the valley floor, there was only one major engagement with the enemy—the hospital battle on the east side of the valley involving Bravo Company, 1/5th Cav, on February 11—and no sign of the headquarters of the Sao Vang Division that was believed to have been located on the high ground north of the valley. Kinnard and his brigade commanders speculated that the enemy had fled into the nearly impenetrable mountains to the northwest of the valley when they learned of the 1st Cav's plans to sweep the valley, and were hiding in caves there. The two-day delay of February 5 and 6 due to monsoon weather provided the enemy with ample time to flee without fear of the 1st Cav's helicopters spotting them. The operation did net 47 enemy KIA by body count, and an estimated 122 additional KIA, but it was believed that most of the enemy dead, with the exception of those killed on the afternoon of February 11, were part of rear guard elements left behind to harass the American troops. Friendly losses were seven KIA and 49 WIA.

Phase II, however, did underscore that weather must be taken into account when operating in areas where it precluded air assault operations and that alternate plans including ground attacks needed to be implemented in such cases.

As for the 40th (Mechanized) and 41st Regiments of the ARVN 22nd Infantry Division, neither regiment encountered significant enemy contact in Phase II, only light resistance from Viet Cong local guerillas, and by February 11 they began to redeploy back to their normal areas of operations.

For Operation *Double Eagle/Lien Ket 22*, Task Force Delta—consisting of the U.S. III Marine Amphibious Force, together with the 4th Regiment of the ARVN 2nd Infantry—failed to produce any significant engagements with either the 18th NVA Regiment or 2nd Viet Cong Regiment of the Sao Vang Division in the areas along the Binh Dinh–Quang Ngai provincial boundary.[4] The two enemy regiments were reported to be operating in southern Quang Ngai Province, although their base camps were believed to be located further south in northeastern Binh Dinh Province. Operation *Double Eagle* concluded on February 17. Task Force Delta reported 312 enemy KIA, most of which were from actions in the Red Beach area well north of the provincial boundary. The task force suffered 24 friendly KIA. A total of 18 individual weapons and a large quantity of small-arms ammunition were captured by Task Force Delta.

As for refugees, some 4,500 of the valley's inhabitants chose to leave the valley under American escort and move to refugee camps in Bong Son rather than remain. Of these, 3,491 were transported by helicopter. Bong Son now contained 15,836 refugees, and Highway 1 north of the town had an additional 11,806 evacuees, totaling more than 27,000 refugees and evacuees.

---

[4] The document "Operation Double Eagle, Operation Masher, Operation Thang Phong II, Operation Lien Ket 22, Operation White Wing" summarized the results of Operation *Double Eagle/Lien Ket 22*. Task Force Delta encountered significant enemy forces in the Red Beach area well north of the Binh Dinh–Quang Ngai provincial boundary but failed to produce any significant engagements with either the 18th NVA Regiment or the 2nd Viet Cong Regiment of the Sao Vang Division. Operation *Double Eagle* concluded on February 17, 1966. Source: 1st Battalion, 3rd Marines, 3rd Marine Division.

94 • THE BATTLE OF BONG SON

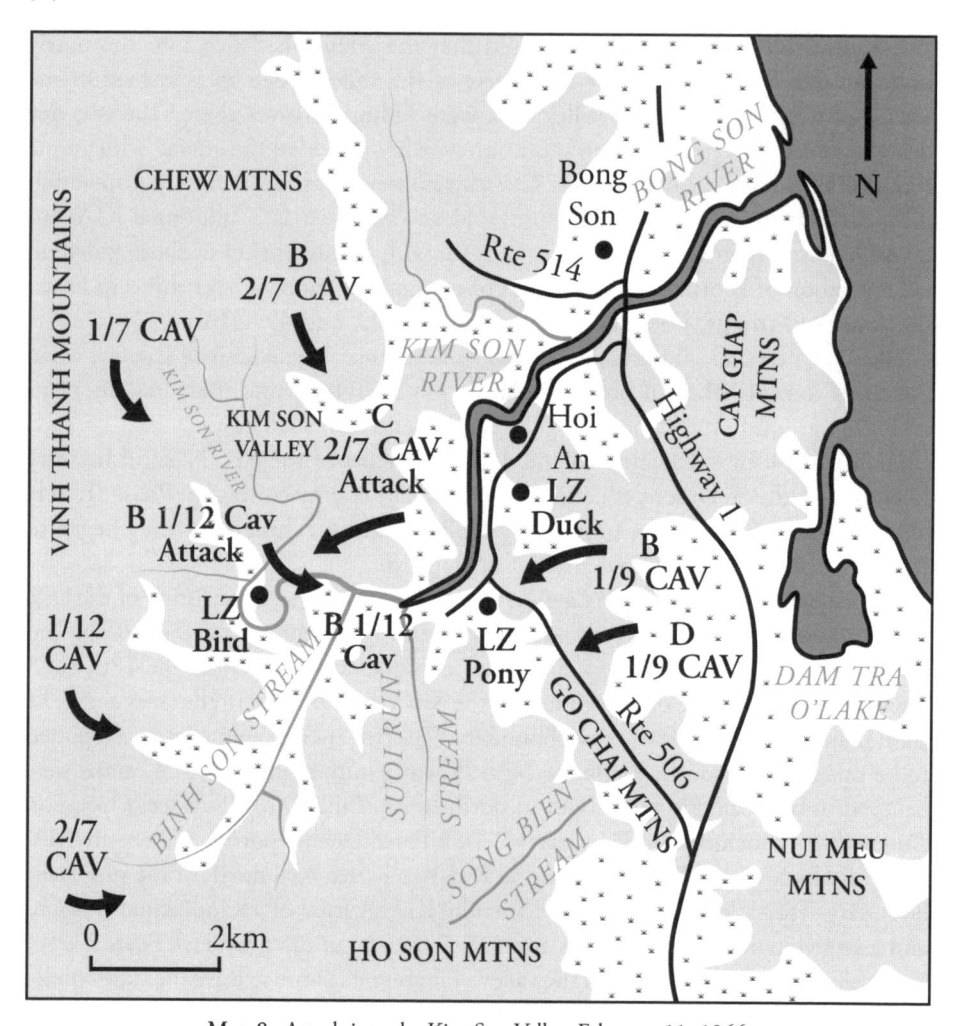

Map 8. Attack into the Kim Son Valley, February 11, 1966

CHAPTER EIGHT

The Eagle's Claw

The Kim Son Valley, like the An Lao Valley, had long been under the control of the Viet Cong and North Vietnamese. Because of its remoteness and rugged terrain, it served as an ideal safe haven for enemy units seeking refuge from government forces.[1] It was known to be used as a marshaling area for regimental-sized enemy units, where arriving personnel, equipment, material, and supplies from North Vietnam or from other regions in South Vietnam were reassembled and control returned to the unit commanders for onward movement to other destinations. It was also known to be used as part of the Viet Cong infiltration route system in Binh Dinh Province. Enemy units coming down the Ho Chi Minh Trail from North Vietnam would enter South Vietnam via Kontum or Pleiku provinces and work their way eastward through the highlands to the Kim Son Valley on their way to join either the Sao Vang Division in eastern Binh Dinh Province or the regiments of the Binh Tri Thien Division in Phu Yen Province to the south. The valley also served as a training base for newly arrived troops from North Vietnam for indoctrination to operations in the South.

The valley was actually a valley complex. It was not long and narrow with a river running down the middle of it like most of the valleys in the Central Highlands. Instead, it had a large open area, roughly 5 kilometers long by 2 kilometers wide, from which multiple twisting ridges branched outward in various directions, compressing the valley floor into seven side or feeder valleys with steep slopes. The feeder valleys ranged in length from a few kilometers to as many as 10 kilometers or more. Several of the feeder valleys themselves branched out in multiple directions, creating even more feeder valleys. Steep jungle-covered mountains, rising to heights of 400 meters, surrounded the valley complex, limiting access into and out of it. The Ho Son Mountains on the south side separated the valley complex from the Soui

---

[1] Description of Kim Son Valley and inland plains of Hoai An District based on maps of Binh Dinh Province, and Hoai An District, Interim Report of Operations, First Cavalry Division, July 1965 to December 1965, and author's recollection.

Ca Valley to the south, the Chew Mountains on the north side separated it from the inland plains southwest of Bong Son, and the Go Chai Mountains on the east side separated it from the 506 Valley to the east. Finally, the Vinh Thanh Mountains on the west side separated it from the northern Vinh Thanh Valley, where an old French fort was located at the head of the valley.

The slopes of the mountains were covered with thick interwoven jungle vegetation, crevices, and large rock formations with natural caves that were 30 feet deep or more, providing ideal hiding places for weapons, food, and the like. The mountains were nearly impenetrable, and because of the constant heat and high humidity in the valley, they were loaded with leeches, snakes, and mosquitoes, making it some of the worst terrain in all of South Vietnam. Because of the way the valley appeared on topographical maps, it was commonly called the Crow's Foot or Eagle's Claw; therefore, Phase III of the operation was named Operation *Masher/White Wing* (*Eagle's Claw*). It would start on February 11 and was expected to run until February 28.

A series of streams from the feeder valleys converged in the center of the valley complex to form the fast-flowing Kim Son River (Song Nuoc Luono). The Kim Son River flowed northeasterly to the neighboring 506 Valley and then directly north past the village of Hoai An toward Bong Son, where it merged with the Bong Son River on its way to the South China Sea.

The population of the valley was estimated to be 7,000, most of whom lived in the hamlet of Kim Son in the center of the valley or in the areas adjacent to the streams in the feeder valleys to the south. The areas around the hamlets were heavily cultivated and consisted of rice paddies flooded with knee-deep water and small, sandy dry-crop islands covered with palm groves, bamboo thickets, and thatched-roof hootches, similar to the hamlets on the coastal plain north of Bong Son. The rice paddies were divided by dikes that partitioned them into individual fields and helped to control the water in them. The dikes provided the North Vietnamese and Viet Cong with positions from which automatic weapons could be used to direct grazing fire across the rice paddies at approaching American troops.

Provincial Route 3A (TL3A) was the only way into and out of the valley by road. It entered the valley from the northeast and ran to the center of it, where it turned south into one of the feeder valleys and continued southward through the feeder valley adjacent to a small stream and then westward. From there, it continued through a pass in the Vinh Thanh Mountains and came out in the Vinh Thanh Valley. It eventually intersected with Highway 19 in the vicinity of the An Khe Pass, just east of the 1st Cav's base camp. The valley provided controlled entrances and well-positioned hiding places for the North Vietnamese and Viet Cong, with various escape routes through the mountains. It was an ideal enemy base that dated back to the 1940s, when the Communist Viet Minh used it to battle post-colonial government forces who sought to keep Route 3A open to civilian travel between the villages in the valley and Bong Son and Phu My to the east.

Intelligence reports from the district police of Hoai An District indicated that in mid-February a Viet Cong main force regiment, possibly the 210th Viet Cong, was garrisoned in the valley, and that a Viet Cong local force company, and possibly one or two Viet Cong main force battalions, were also there. The reports also indicated that a division-sized or higher control headquarters, possibly that of the Sao Vang Division, was in the valley, explaining why the 1st Cav had been unable to find it on the high ground north of the An Lao Valley—it had moved to the Kim Son Valley. One other major unit, the 18th NVA Regiment, was thought to be east of Highway 1 in the Phu Cat area, with the reported intention of returning to the Kim Son Valley. Because of the continuous movement into and out of the valley, numerous unit identifications were associated with it, and the current extent and disposition of forces there was hazy.

For Phase III, the 3rd Brigade would consist of the 1st and 2nd Battalions, 7th Cavalry; the 1st Battalion (Airborne), 12th Cavalry; the Aero Rifle Platoons of Bravo and Charlie troops, 1st Squadron, 9th Cavalry; and the Ground Cavalry Rifle Platoons of Delta Troop, 1/9th Cav. The rifle platoons would provide general infantry support to the brigade. The brigade would also include aerial and tube artillery batteries, aviation units, engineering companies, and other support units.

Colonel Moore's plan for clearing the valley of the Viet Cong and North Vietnamese called for the establishment of artillery positions east of the valley on the inland plains of Hoai An and at the head of the neighboring 506 Valley to support the initial air assault into the valley. Once the artillery batteries were in place, the 2nd Battalion, 7th Cavalry, would air assault into the center of the valley and seize and secure a position for follow-on infantry, direct-support artillery, and headquarters elements. Next, blocking forces from the 1/7th Cav, 2/7th Cav, and 1/12th Cav would land near the heads of the feeder valleys and establish blocking positions along likely escape routes through the mountains. Then, "beater" forces from the three battalions would land at the entrances to the feeder valleys and attack up the valleys toward the blocking positions. Artillery would be used extensively in front of them as they advanced to drive the enemy into the blocking positions or into the open, where they could be destroyed by tactical air power. Finally, the rifle platoons of the 1/9th Cav would establish a landing zone at the head of the Go Chai Mountains on the eastern side of the valley and conduct search-and-destroy sweeps southward through the Go Chai Mountains.

In this plan, the feeder valleys were assumed to be the escape routes. The blocking forces were to land unobtrusively by helicopter at the heads of the feeder valleys, move stealthily to blocking positions, and maintain them in secrecy. They were to adhere to strict radio silence, with no radio communication back to the battalions unless absolutely necessary. There would be no tactical air support or artillery, and no assistance of any kind from the other units. They were to avoid contact with smaller enemy formations if at all possible until they made contact with the larger units. They were to carry enough food and water and other supplies for 48 hours. Based on observed movement away from the beater forces, artillery and air interdiction would also be used on routes between the beater and blocking forces at night.

Intense ground fog on the morning of February 11 delayed the movement of troops into the valley. However, the weather on the inland plains of Hoai An was clear and dry, permitting the movement of artillery to target positions there in preparation for the air assault of troops into the valley. At 0800 hours, 155mm howitzers from Charlie Battery, 1st Battalion, 30th Artillery, were transported in sling load by a Flying Crane helicopter to a position on the high ground adjacent to Route 3A at the Hoai An District Headquarters. The position was 5 kilometers north of the entrance to the Kim Son Valley via road and 8 kilometers northeast of the center of it as the crow flies. It would support the 2/7th Cav's air assault into the valley. The position was designated LZ Duck.

In parallel to the movement of the 155mm howitzers by helicopter to LZ Duck, the 8-inch self-propelled M-110 howitzers of the 3rd Battalion, 18th Field Artillery, moved by road to LZ Duck.[2]

At 0930 hours, the Bravo Blues, 1/9th Cav, air assaulted onto the high ground adjacent to Route 3A where it intersected with Route 506, 5 kilometers south of LZ Duck and 7 kilometers east of the center of the Kim Son Valley. The air assault was preceded by artillery preparation by aerial rocket gunships from Bravo Battery, 2/20th ARA. The Bravo Blues seized and secured the position for artillery that would also support the 2/7th Cav's air assault into the valley. The position was designated LZ Pony.

The Bravo Blues immediately started receiving small-arms and automatic weapons fire from the nearby hamlet of Tan Thanh, adjacent to Route 506, less than a kilometer southeast of the landing zone. Aerial reconnaissance scouts from Bravo Troop, 1/9th Cav, attempted to pinpoint where the enemy fire was coming from, but were unable to do so, and at 0940 hours, one of the observation helicopters circling above the village at 100 feet was hit by intense enemy small-arms fire and was badly damaged and forced to return to LZ English. Tactical air support was requested and two USAF Skyraiders arrived on station, pounding the hamlet with high-explosive and WP bombs and napalm, and raking the area with 20mm cannon fire. The Charlie Blues, 1/9th Cav, were inserted onto the ground 1 kilometer south of Tan Thanh and moved north in an attempt to prevent any enemy soldiers from escaping southward. Shortly afterwards, the Bravo Blues on LZ Pony reported that they were no longer receiving fire from the hamlet. The 105mm howitzers of Charlie

---

[2] The 3rd Battalion, 18th Field Artillery Regiment (8-inch self-propelled howitzers) was an independent artillery regiment in the U.S. Army that arrived in South Vietnam in late October 1965 and was assigned to I Field Force—Vietnam. Alpha Battery, 3/18th Artillery, was subsequently attached to the 1st Cav and remained attached until 1971, when the 1st Cav returned to the U.S. Wikipedia, "3rd Field Artillery Regiment (United States)," https://en_wikipedia.org.

Battery, 2nd Battalion, 17th Field Artillery, were then transported in sling load by Chinook helicopters to Pony.[3]

The 3rd Battalion, 18th Field Artillery, with its 8-inch self-propelled howitzers, and the 2nd Battalion, 17th Field Artillery, with its 105mm howitzers, were independent artillery regiments in the Army. The units had arrived in South Vietnam in late October 1965 and were assigned to I Field Force—Vietnam. Alpha Battery, 3/18th Artillery, and Charlie Battery, 2/17th Artillery, were subsequently attached to the 1st Cav and deployed to the Pleiku area in the western Central Highlands to support the 1st Cav in its operations in the Ia Drang Valley. Along with the direct support artillery units of the 3rd Brigade, these units operated out of LZ Columbus, 4 kilometers to the east of LZ X-Ray, and Landing Zone Falcon, 8 kilometers northeast of LZ X-Ray, supporting Lieutenant Colonel Hal Moore and the 1st Battalion, 7th Cavalry, in the infamous battle at LZ X-Ray, and Lieutenant Colonel Robert McDade and the 2nd Battalion, 7th Cavalry, in the battle at LZ Albany. These batteries fired thousands of rounds in support of the 7th Cav troops in the battles of the Ia Drang Valley.

Unlike the terrain on the coastal plain north of Bong Son, where the 3rd Brigade battled the 7th and 9th battalions of the 22nd NVA Regiment in Phase I of Operation *Masher/White Wing*, the terrain in the Kim Son Valley was not flat. Instead, it was mountainous with steep jungle-covered slopes, twisting ridges, and narrow valleys. Unlike the artillery support that the 1st Cav units got on the coastal plain north of Bong Son, the artillery support they would likely get in the Kim Son Valley would be problematic. Clear trajectories to target areas without high-angle elevation, with rapid ascends and descends, would be required to ensure muzzle velocity, good range performance, and accuracy of the artillery guns. The artillery batteries at LZ Duck and LZ Pony would be able to provide good coverage for operations in the center of the Kim Son Valley, but they would do little for operations in some of the feeder valleys, especially those on the east side of the valley complex with narrow valley floors. For that, artillery guns would have to be transported in sling loads by helicopters and placed on narrow ridges that provided clear trajectories to target areas. Most of the ridges in the feeder valleys, however, were narrow and jungle-covered and had to be cleared by combat engineers from the division's 8th Engineer Battalion before any artillery pieces could be positioned on them. Also, many of the ridges were prone to intense fog in the evenings and early morning,

---

[3] The 2nd Battalion, 17th Field Artillery Regiment (105mm howitzers) was an independent artillery regiment in the U.S. Army that arrived in South Vietnam in late October 1965 and was assigned to I Field Force—Vietnam. Charlie Battery, 2/17th Artillery, was subsequently attached to the 1st Cav and remained attached until 1971, when the 1st Cav returned to the U.S. Wikipedia, "2nd Battalion, 17th Field Artillery," https://en_wikipedia.org.

and ground security was a concern. The 1st Cav, with its airmobile capability, relied heavily on ready-reaction forces that could be rapidly deployed by helicopter to sites when an SOS was sent out from it. But if a site was socked-in with fog, the helicopters would be unable to reach it and the ready-reaction force would not be able to get to the site and reinforce the unit there. This would be an ongoing concern for the 1st Cav in Operation *Masher/White Wing* (*Eagle's Claw*), as well as in future operations in other mountainous areas in the highlands.

By 1020 hours, the fog in the valley started to lift and Charlie Company, 2/7th Cav, together with the battalion's Reconnaissance Platoon, air assaulted into the center of the valley at a spot adjacent to the Kim Son River, designated LZ Bird. The assault was preceded by a tactical airstrike from USAF Skyraiders and a 15-minute artillery preparation from the 8-inch and 155mm howitzers at LZ Duck. The assault was unopposed, with the exception of sporadic small-arms fire received from a tree line 200 meters to the east of the landing zone. Once on the ground, Lieutenant Colonel McDade directed Captain Fesmire and Charlie Company to move to the tree line and eliminate the enemy fire. Charlie Company killed three North Vietnamese soldiers and captured 10, four of whom were women—one very pregnant. The remaining enemy soldiers managed to get into the jungle underbrush to the north and escape. The remainder of the 2/7th Cav was on the ground by 1055 hours.

On the assault into Bird, several aircraft were hit by enemy ground fire and one was forced to execute an emergency landing because of damage to its hydraulics. The four-man crew was unhurt and was able to climb out of the helicopter and maneuver to the 2/7th Cav's position at Bird, carrying the helicopter's two M-60 machine guns and multiple boxes of M-60 ammunition.

The 2/7th Cav troops at Bird continued to receive enemy fire, not from the tree line 200 meters east of the LZ but from a small hamlet on the south side of the Kim Son River, roughly 600 meters to the southeast. Using artillery fire from LZ Pony and mortar fire from the battalion's Mortar Platoon at Bird to cover their advance, Captain Diduryk and Bravo Company—at the direction of McDade—attacked the hamlet and quickly seized and secured it. The enemy soldiers, however, had fled and the hamlet was empty. Multiple blood trails leading in the direction of the river to the east indicated that the enemy had suffered a number of WIA and possible KIA. The Bravo Company troops captured a 50-caliber machine gun, a number of individual weapons, backpacks, web gear, and grenades, along with brass cooking utensils.

LZ Bird was located at the elbow in the Kim Son River. It was enclosed to the west and south by the river, and to the north by the Chew Mountains. It sat on a narrow jungle-covered ridge that sloped downward ever so slightly to the river's edge, roughly 300 meters to the west. The only way into it was by helicopter. Route 3A would take you to within a kilometer or so of it, but then you had to cross the river, and the only way to do that was on foot. In the dry season, that was not usually a problem because the water level in the river was low and the current weak, but in the winter monsoon season, crossing it was very dangerous. The water level was significantly higher because of the monsoon rains and the current significantly stronger because of the volume of water flowing. By mid-February, however, the winter monsoon had started to peter-out and the water level in the river had dropped significantly, allowing the troops to cross it on foot.

At 1430 hours, an aerial reconnaissance team from Charlie Troop, 1/9th Cav, spotted a company-sized North Vietnamese unit moving down the feeder valley directly north of LZ Bird in the direction of it to assist the enemy platoon that had been driven off earlier that day. McDade directed Captain Fesmire and Charlie Company to move into the feeder valley and engage the enemy unit. Charlie Company utilized artillery fire while its maneuver elements moved to contact to repulse and defeat the force, with aerial support from the helicopter gunships of Charlie Troop, 1/9th Cav, and aerial rocket gunships from Charlie Battery, 2/20th ARA. The enemy soldiers scattered and fled back up the valley in disarray, with the helicopter gunships chasing after them. The troops of Charlie Company confirmed 13 enemy KIA, with no friendly casualties reported.

The enemy unit that Charlie Company, 2/7th Cav, engaged upon its landing at LZ Bird was estimated to be a platoon-sized force. It was guarding a large quantity of communication equipment and documents, possibly indicating that a headquarters unit of some type was located there. This might have explained why the enemy had initially decided to stay and fight instead of immediately fleeing the attacking 2/7th Cav troops. The equipment and documents were collected and loaded onto a Chinook helicopter, along with the 10 captured enemy soldiers, and transported to the 1st Cav's base camp at An Khe for interrogation by the division's military intelligence unit.

By 1700 hours, the clearing operation around LZ Bird was complete and the 2/7th Cav, along with the 3rd Brigade's direct support artillery unit, the 1st Battalion, 21st Artillery—with its 105mm howitzers—and the attached 1st Battalion, 30th Field Artillery—Alpha Battery, with its 155mm howitzers—were in place at Bird. By 1800 hours, the companies of the 1/7th Cav had air assaulted into positions astride the heads of the feeder valleys directly to the north and west of Bird and had established blocking positions along likely escape routes through the mountains. Alpha and Charlie Companies, 1/12th Cav, along with Alpha Company, 2/7th Cav, had air assaulted into positions at the heads of the feeder valleys to the south and southwest of Bird and established blocking positions there. Bravo Company, 1/12th Cav, would be the beater force for the feeder valley directly south of Bird when it arrived from the An Lao Valley. The blocking forces were to maintain their positions in secrecy and only make contact with large enemy forces attempting to flee the valley.

The Ground Cavalry Rifle Platoons of Delta Troop, 1/9th Cav, had moved by helicopter to LZ Pony and initiated search-and-destroy operations in the Go Chai Mountains south of the LZ along known escape routes through the mountains to the 506 Valley to the east. The Charlie Blues continued with their search-and-destroy operations along the eastern slopes of the Go Chai Mountains south of the hamlet of Tan Thanh.

At 2150 hours, Delta Troop reported that it was receiving light enemy probes from an estimated platoon-sized force in an ambush position it had established along a heavily used trail roughly 8 kilometers southeast of Pony. The ambush position was designated LZ Saber. Artillery fire from Pony was called in, followed by helicopter gunships from the 1/9th Cav and aerial rocket gunships from the 2/20th ARA. The enemy action ceased shortly afterwards.

At daybreak on the morning of February 12, Charlie Company, 1/12th Cav, in its blocking position at the head of the feeder valley directly south of LZ Bird, ambushed a platoon-sized enemy unit that was moving along a trail that it was monitoring. The ambush resulted in one enemy KIA and 10 enemy WIA who had survived the ambush but were too badly wounded to flee and were left for dead where they fell. Multiple blood trails heading away from the ambush site indicated that the number of KIA and WIA was likely higher. Multiple Chicom Type-56 assault rifles—the Chinese-made variant of the Soviet-designed AK-47 rifle used by North Vietnamese and Viet Cong soldiers—along with ammunition were captured. Three Charlie Company troopers were wounded by enemy grenades in the ambush and had to be evacuated by helicopter to the 15th Med aid station at LZ English for medical treatment.

By 0800 hours, the beater forces that had landed around LZ Bird on the previous afternoon were attacking outward from Bird, and Bravo Company, 1/12th Cav, which was the designated beater force for the feeder valley directly south of Bird, started to move by helicopter from the An Lao Valley to the Kim Son Valley. It had spent the night in the An Lao Valley awaiting availability of helicopters. By 1400 hours, Captain Stephen Klein and Bravo Company, 1/12th Cav, arrived in the Kim Son Valley and established a company position at the entrance to the feeder valley directly south of LZ Bird. The spot was designated LZ Jim. The feeder valley was referred to as the Binh Son Valley because the hamlet of Binh Son was located in it. Bravo Company was to attack south into the valley, using artillery in front of it as it advanced. Alpha and Charlie companies, 1/12th Cav, along with the battalion's Reconnaissance Platoon, and Alpha Company, 2/7th Cav, which was attached to the 1/12th Cav, had arrived in the Kim Son Valley on the previous afternoon and established ambush sites at the head of the Binh Son Valley and along likely escape routes through the mountains.

The Binh Son Valley ran due south for approximately 5 kilometers before it split into two branches, one that turned due west toward the hamlet of Binh Son and another that continued due south toward the hamlet of Phu Ninh and ended about 5 kilometers beyond Phu Ninh at the base of the Ho Son Mountains. The due-west branch continued for about 3 kilometers and then split into several smaller feeder valleys, two of which turned south and ended at the base of the Ho Son Mountains, and one that continued due west. Route 3A ran up the middle of the due-west branch. Charlie and Alpha companies, 1/12th Cav, were located in ambush positions at the head of the due-west branch, while Alpha Company, 2/7th Cav, conducted search-and-destroy operations along the ridge southwest of the Binh Son Valley.

Captain Klein's plan for the valley was to progress halfway up it before sundown, but because of the lateness in the day in arriving in the Kim Son Valley, he realized that his company would be lucky to reach its first objective before nightfall—a Cao Dai pagoda set on a small hill mass about 1 kilometer south of the entrance to the valley.[4] There were several larger hill masses covered with heavy jungle vegetation commanding the pagoda area that would have to be cleared in order for Bravo Company to advance beyond that point. To secure the position, Klein directed 1st Lieutenant George Quigley and his 2nd Platoon, and 1st Lieutenant Roger Baker and his 3rd Platoon, to maneuver to the east and west, respectively, and clear the larger hill masses.

At 1415 hours, Captain Klein reported that the 2nd and 3rd Platoons were pinned down by automatic weapons and small-arms fire from an unknown number of enemy soldiers located on one of the larger hill masses overlooking the pagoda. At least one of the automatic weapons was a 50-caliber machine gun. Artillery fire from LZ Bird was requested, along with aerial rocket gunships from the 2/20th ARA. Under the cover of the aerial rocket gunships, the two platoons attacked the enemy position and overran it. The position looked like it had been occupied by a platoon-sized force that had fled to avoid the attacking 1/12th Cav troops. The enemy left behind four dead soldiers, a tripod for a 50-caliber machine gun, a Chicom Type-56 assault rifle, and numerous cigarette lighters with the number "403" inscribed on them. There was also a pool of blood and numerous blood trails leading into a tunnel, indicating that there were WIA or possible KIA that had been dragged into it. Bravo Company reported no friendly casualties in the encounter.

Captain Klein requested an airstrike on the position, and at 1845 hours the USAF responded with a FAC and two Skyraiders. Klein briefed the FAC on the situation on the ground and the FAC directed the two Skyraiders to pound the hill masses with high-explosive and white phosphorus bombs, and napalm, and rake the areas with 20mm cannon fire. By 2200 hours, Captain Klein and the troops of Bravo

---

[4] In an unpublished manuscript, Captain Stephen Klein provided a detailed description of Bravo Company, 1/12th Cav, moving through the Kim Son Valley as the designated beater force for the feeder valley directly south of LZ Bird. Captain Stephen Klein, U.S. Army Infantry, 1966–67, "Operations of Company B, 1st Battalion (Airborne), 12th Cavalry, 1st Cavalry Division (Airmobile), on a search-and-destroy operation on 12 and 13 February 1966 in Binh Dinh Province, Republic of Viet Nam. (Personal experience of a company commander)," 6.

Company had cleared the two hill masses and reached the pagoda. Local security was put out in all directions, the Mortar Platoon completed its registration fire, and Bravo Company settled in for an uneventful night.

Cao Dai pagodas, or temples, were very distinctive in their architecture, with towers or steeples with multiple tiers. In 1966, the South Vietnamese government estimated that there were between 4.5 and 6 million followers of Caodaism in South Vietnam.

While Captain Klein and Bravo Company, 1/12th Cav, were moving to the Binh Son Valley, Captain Sugdinis and Alpha Company, 2/7th Cav, were conducting search-and-destroy operations along a ridge 6 kilometers southwest of the Binh Son Valley. At 1230 hours, Sugdinis reported that Alpha Company encountered a squad-sized enemy force to its front and engaged it, resulting in one enemy KIA and 11 enemy soldiers being captured. No friendly casualties were reported in the firefight. As it turned out, the enemy soldiers were guarding several weapons caches that were hidden in long deep trenches covered with leaves, tree branches, and other jungle debris. The caches contained numerous weapons and ammunition, including four American M-1 rifles, nine Chicom carbines, three Chicom 12.7mm heavy machine guns, 10 Russian carbines, two 30-caliber light machine guns, two American Thompson submachine guns, one American M3 submachine gun, four Chicom mines, smoke grenades, rifle grenades, small-arms ammunition, and 80lb of explosives. Six Chinook sorties were required to transport all of the weapons, ammunition, and explosives from the site back to the 1st Cav's base camp at An Khe. The discovery lent credence to the earlier intelligence reports that sizable North Vietnamese forces were bivouacked in the Kim Son Valley.

Thirteen kilometers east of Captain Klein and Bravo Company's position in the Binh Son Valley, the rifle platoons of the 1/9th Cav were conducing search-and-destroy patrols in the Go Chai Mountains. A platoon from Delta Troop had been pursuing an enemy formation estimated to be a platoon-sized unit since earlier that morning, when the enemy force attacked the platoon in its night defensive position at LZ Saber. Artillery fire from LZ Pony and aerial rocket gunships from the 2/20th ARA were used to halt the attack, and the enemy broke contact and fled. Heavy ground fog at the time prevented the troopers from pursuing the fleeing enemy. Delta Troop reported five enemy KIA by body count, an additional 10 estimated KIA, and 10 estimated WIA in the attack. One enemy soldier was taken prisoner. Several Chicom SKS carbine rifles were captured. By 1030 hours, the ground fog had started to lift and the prisoner was put on a helicopter and transported to LZ Bird for interrogation by the division's military intelligence unit.

With the help of an aerial reconnaissance team from the 1/9th Cav, the troopers of Delta Troop pursued the fleeing enemy and attempted to reestablish contact with it, but were unable to do so. At 1845 hours, the aerial reconnaissance team reported that it had spotted a small enemy force, estimated at 15–20 soldiers, in foxholes along a ridge in the general direction that the fleeing enemy had been moving. Illumination was requested from the USAF, and Smokey-the-Bear arrived on station. Artillery fire from LZ Pony and aerial rocket gunships from the 2/20th ARA were employed. By 2200 hours, the aerial reconnaissance team reported that there were at least six enemy KBA on the ridge and that the other enemy soldiers had slipped away in the darkness down the slope to the northwest.

Coinciding with the contact on the ridge, another rifle platoon from Delta Troop at LZ Saber observed an unknown number of individuals moving on a southwest–northeast trail in the direction of LZ Saber, and sprang an ambush on them that had been set on the trail. The ambush killed 10 enemy soldiers and wounded 10 more. Multiple weapons were captured. Delta Troop reported no friendly casualties in the encounter. Because of the darkness, it was not possible to evacuate the wounded enemy soldiers so they were moved for the night to LZ Saber, where they were put under armed guard. They would have to hang on until daybreak, when a helicopter could be brought in to transport them to the aid station at the Special Forces camp.

For February 12, the 3rd Brigade reported no major engagements with enemy forces but numerous small engagements that resulted in 51 enemy KIA by body count, an additional 73 estimated KIA, and 21 captured. Thirty-nine individual weapons and nine crew-served weapons were captured, along with 2 tons of rice and 25 tons of salt.

At first light on February 13, Captain Klein and Bravo Company, 1/12th Cav, moved out of their night defensive position and resumed their attack up the valley. The platoons were disposed three abreast, the 2nd, 1st, and 3rd, from left to right in a wide front. The company Command Group and the Mortar Platoon followed behind the 1st Platoon in the center. Captain Klein directed Lieutenant Roger Baker and his 3rd Platoon to focus its attention on guarding the right flank, which was commanded by high, thickly vegetated hills. Consequently, two of the platoon's squads were put into the tree line and only its third squad remained in the open valley. Two OH-13 observation helicopters from Charlie Troop, 1/9th Cav, circled in front of the company as it advanced to screen its forward movement.

After sweeping through the village of Kim Son and finding little of interest, Bravo Company continued moving up the valley. It had proceeded no more than 100 meters when the accompanying observation helicopters started receiving sniper fire from the hamlet of Phu Ninh across the valley. Phu Ninh was located at a fork where the valley split into two branches—one that continued due west in the direction of Bing Son and the position designated Gold, with Route 3A running up the center of it, and the other that continued southward toward Phu Ninh and ended about 3 kilometers beyond the hamlet at the base of the Ho Son Mountains. The two scout ship pilots continued to report that they were being shot at, but that they could not pinpoint the source from which the fire came. However, they were both low on fuel and had to return to LZ English to refuel.

Realizing that Bravo Company could not proceed up the valley without first eliminating the sniper fire coming from Phu Ninh, Captain Klein directed Lieutenant Quigley and his 2nd Platoon to clear Phu Ninh and deal with the sniper. The other platoons were to remain in position ready to assist the 2nd Platoon if it uncovered a larger force that it could not handle. The 2nd Platoon then attacked across the open rice paddies toward Phu Ninh in short rushes of two or three men, moving from dike to dike, without drawing further fire. When the platoon reached the cover of a palm grove, the Psy War team, which had accompanied the 2nd Platoon, started broadcasting into the village. The villagers were instructed to stand outside their hootches and were warned that if the platoon was fired at, artillery fire would be directed on their village. The 2nd Platoon then quickly moved through the village and searched it, but without finding the sniper or his weapon.

The 1st and 3rd Platoons then resumed moving due west and came abreast of the 2nd Platoon. The Mortar Platoon followed by leaps and bounds, about 300 meters behind. It kept its mortar trained on Phu Ninh, with instructions to fire on it should the sniper start shooting again.

At about 1230 hours, the battalion S-3 radioed Captain Klein that an aerial rocket gunship from the 2/20th ARA had spotted an enemy heavy machine-gun position about 1,000 meters further up the valley from Bravo Company's current position in the vicinity of Binh Son, and that it had been fired upon from the same general location. Bravo Company was directed to check out the area. This answered the question for Captain Klein as to which direction Bravo Company should go when it reached the second fork, where one of the branches headed toward Bing Son and Position Gold, where Alpha and Charlie Companies, 1/12th Cav, had established blocking positions. Bravo Company would continue moving due west toward Bing Son.

At this point, Captain Klein changed the company formation, putting the 2nd Platoon from the left flank position in a reserve position behind the 1st Platoon. The company now had only two platoons abreast, but it had a reserve platoon which could be maneuvered to either side.

At about 1330 hours, the lead elements of the 1st Platoon reached the hamlet of Binh Son. It was deserted. The members of the 1st Platoon moved warily through it, kicking open doors, peering into bomb shelters, and probing the piles of straw and rice with their bayonets. As they reached the western edge of the hamlet, they passed beneath a row of coconut trees and clambered down an embankment toward a rice paddy that was about 200 meters wide. No sooner had the point man reached the edge of the rice paddy than a hail of fire was received from the far bank, which rose about 6 meters above the water level and was concealed by tall elephant grass. The 3rd Platoon, which was abreast of the 1st Platoon to the right, was in a field of high elephant grass and was approaching a finger of trees that ran down from the hills on the right. It had temporarily lost visual contact with the 1st Platoon. It too came under heavy enemy fire from the far bank. Both platoons returned fire. Lieutenants Lewis Anderson and Roger Baker reported that no causalities had been taken in the initial contact. Captain Klein later concluded: "This was a matter of sheer luck. The enemy had fired prematurely on the 1st Platoon and had allowed it to regain the sanctuary of the village. Had the enemy held its fire until the 1st Platoon was deployed into the rice paddy, initial casualties would have been high."

Captain Klein directed Quigley and his 2nd Platoon to establish flank and rear security, and hold his present position. Without waiting, the members of the Mortar Platoon were putting its mortar into position to be ready to fire as directed.

As Lieutenant Anderson and the members of the 1st Platoon continued to exchange fire with the enemy soldiers, they began to identify positions on the far bank where the enemy gunners were located. They also identified a location on the crest of the bank where a heavy machine gun was positioned.

On the right flank of the 1st Platoon, Lieutenant Baker and the members of the 3rd Platoon could not as easily define the enemy opposing them because of the elephant grass and trees on the far bank that concealed their positions. Baker did, however, radio Captain Klein that the 3rd Platoon was opposed by an estimated two squads to its front that had been identified by sound, but not location, and that the enemy had three machine guns, one of which was a heavy machine gun. He also reported that snipers were in the trees near them.

Captain Klein radioed Bravo Company's situation to Lieutenant Colonel Beard at LZ Bird, reporting that it was opposed by possibly a platoon, which was well dug in and reinforced by multiple machine guns, including one heavy machine gun. Beard directed Klein to attack the enemy and destroy them, and continue movement toward Position Gold. Klein realized that to do this, Bravo Company first needed to establish fire superiority over the enemy force and maneuver against it.

By the time that Bravo Company's forward observer, 2nd Lieutenant John Piper, was able to call in aerial rocket gunships from the 2/20th ARA against the enemy positions, Bravo Company had pretty much achieved fire superiority over the enemy. This allowed Piper to direct extremely accurate fire from the gunships because so many enemy positions had been identified. At the same time that the aerial rocket gunships were attacking the enemy positions, Piper was placing a call-for-fire request to the direct support artillery battery at Bird. Once the aerial rocket gunships emptied their rocket pods, a full battery of 105mm howitzers, reinforced by a battery of 155mm howitzers, would engage the enemy on the far bank.

Lieutenant Piper shifted the artillery fire to the right, where Baker was reporting that the sniper fire directed at the 3rd Platoon was becoming more accurate. The artillery volleys quickly silenced the enemy snipers and the artillery was then shifted back and forth, from the enemy in front of the 1st Platoon to that in front of the 3rd Platoon. The volleys were a mixture of high-explosive and white phosphorus rounds, with fuse-super-quick and fuse-delay, with the intention of destroying both surface and dug-in targets.

In spite of the volume of artillery fire directed at the far bank, the heavy machine gun in front of the 1st Platoon was still firing and the enemy leader was still directing his part of the battle. Captain Klein then ordered the 90mm recoilless rifle teams from the 1st and 2nd platoons to fire their 90mm rounds at the three machine-gun positions and enemy leaders on the far bank. Two of the three machine guns were destroyed. The enemy, however, was still active, as one of the 90mm gunners was struck twice by enemy bullets as he fired his 90mm rounds at the machine-gun position.

By 1415 hours, Bravo Company had sufficiently achieved fire superiority over the enemy force on the far bank. Captain Klein then directed Lieutenant Quigley to take his 2nd Platoon, which had been held in reserve behind the 1st Platoon, and maneuver, concealed by the palm trees, through the line of palm trees in which the 1st Platoon was deployed, to a position as close as possible to the southern flank of the far bank. Then it was to attack across the rice paddy in short dashes of two or three men, from dike to dike, covered by the other two squads. The 1st Platoon was to support by fire the 2nd Platoon's attack, maintaining a slow but steady volume of fire on the far bank, and only lift its fire when the 2nd Platoon began its final assault. 2nd Lieutenant Piper was to have the artillery continue to fire on the far bank, but to lift it when the 2nd Platoon left the concealment of the palm trees.

The attack across the rice paddy went as planned. When the 2nd Platoon reached the base of the far bank, two squads formed an assault line and swept up and over the crest of the hill, while the third squad provided flank security to the west. The 1st Platoon lifted its fire as the assault squads of the 2nd Platoon moved forward, and the fight was quickly over. Only three enemy soldiers were still alive on the far bank in front of the 1st Platoon, and they were quickly dispatched by grenades. Lieutenant Baker and the 3rd Platoon met only light resistance in their advance across the rice paddy on the right. The 3rd Platoon swept forward over what had been the enemy's position and halted, on order, abreast of the 2nd Platoon. Captain Klein then directed Anderson to move the 1st Platoon forward across the rice paddy and establish security on the far bank while the 2nd and 3rd Platoons searched the area.

The bodies of nine enemy dead were found on the far bank facing the 1st Platoon, all in deep fighting holes that were well concealed. Their uniforms showed that they were North Vietnamese soldiers. Their weapons were Chicom Type-56 assault rifles. The heavy machine gun was also found; it was a 12.7mm Chicom heavy machine gun, twisted out of shape, most likely from being hit by one of the 90mm rounds. Its tripod, transportation wheels, and antiaircraft accessories were also found.

No bodies were found on the far bank facing the 3rd Platoon; there were only discarded uniforms, numerous blood trails, and more than a dozen rucksacks scattered around the area. Although the two machine guns used against the 3rd Platoon were not found, the antiaircraft accessories for them were discovered. It was believed that the enemy soldiers had taken the guns when they withdrew into the jungle-covered hills to the north.

Shortly after Bravo Company overran the enemy on the far bank, Colonel Moore and Lieutenant Colonel Beard landed in their helicopter in the rice paddy separating Binh Son and the far bank. Colonel Moore expressed his concern about a heavy machine-gun position located further west that USAF fighter bombers had attacked earlier that day, and he directed Bravo Company to continue its movement up the valley toward Position Gold and Charlie Company. He wanted Bravo Company to retrieve the heavy machine gun before the enemy did. Bravo Company, however, needed a resupply of ammunition before it could be committed to action again, and it wasn't until after 1700 hours that a helicopter arrived with fresh ammunition and removed the captured enemy weapons. Because of the delay, Bravo Company was forced to establish a defensive position in place and set up local security. The company then spent another uneventful night.

While Captain Klein and Bravo Company were battling the North Vietnamese at the hamlet of Binh Son, Captain Drake reported that Alpha Company, 1/12th Cav, found what appeared to be a grenade factory with an estimated 2 tons of scrap metal, grenade housings, fuses, and explosives. A 20-bed hospital and a mess hall were also found in the same area. Shortly afterwards, a helicopter with a squad of combat engineers onboard from Charlie Company, 8th Engineer Battalion, arrived over Alpha Company's position and rappelled down ropes to the jungle floor, carrying chainsaws and other tree-cutting equipment strapped onto their backs. An area large enough for a Chinook helicopter to set down was cleared, and the scrap material and other grenade-making material was loaded onto multiple helicopters and hauled out to LZ English. The hospital structure and mess hall were destroyed.

In the Go Chai Mountains to the east of Captain Klein and Bravo Company in the Binh Son Valley, the rifle platoons of Delta Troop, 1/9th Cav, battled enemy units southeast of LZ Pony in six separate encounters. In one clash, documents were found on the bodies of dead Viet Cong that proved to be very valuable in locating enemy units in the area. They included a map of the Go Chai Mountains with circles drawn on it, indicating the location of a battalion from the Sao Vang Division in the Soui Run Valley.

In another of the encounters, a 13-man reconnaissance team from Delta Troop had been inserted onto the ground by helicopter earlier in the day to conduct reconnaissance-in-force patrolling.[5] Shortly after being inserted, the team came under

---

[5] Remembrances left for SP4 Roger A. Bise, Morgantown, West Virginia, PFC John W. Houston, Little Rock, Arkansas, and SP4 Charles L. Richtmyre, Wanetta, Illinois. Vietnam Veterans Memorial Fund, The Wall of Faces, posted by Lieutenant Colonel Teddy H. Sanford, Jr. (Ret), dated May 23, 2014, https://www.vvmf.org, https://www.vvmf.org.

heavy fire from an estimated platoon-sized unit and a ready-reaction force from Delta Troop was moved to the area to reinforce the team. The only available spot for a helicopter to set down to offload the troopers of the ready-reaction force was a small clearing on top of a narrow jungle-covered ridge that was only large enough for one helicopter at a time to land. When the first helicopter in the formation approached the clearing and flared to reduce its vertical and horizontal speeds to allow the troopers onboard to climb out onto the skids and jump to the ground, enemy soldiers came charging out of the jungle, firing their automatic rifles at them. Captain Ed Fritz, the Troop Commander of Delta Troop, and his RTO, and six other men onboard, found themselves in hand-to-hand fighting as they hit the ground. The pilots of the helicopter were able to maintain control of it long enough for the troopers to get on the ground. They were then able to fly it out of the clearing in order for the next helicopter in the formation to land. Almost immediately after Fritz and the troopers finished off the attacking enemy soldiers, they came under fire from an enemy force on the high ground along a very confined and steep ridge. Fritz directed 1st Lieutenant Teddy Sanford, Jr., a platoon leader in Delta Troop who was now on the ground with about 30 other troopers, to attack up the hill and destroy the enemy position to help secure the clearing for the other helicopters to land. The helicopter gunships that were escorting the formation provided aerial cover for the attacking troops. Sanford and the troopers reached the ridge, destroyed a machine gun, and neutralized the position. The ready-reaction force suffered three troopers killed in the encounter, plus multiple troopers wounded.

For February 13, enemy losses were 62 KIA by body count, an additional estimated 36 KIA, and three captured. Seven individual weapons were seized, along with three crew-served weapons, including two 50-caliber machine guns. A spare barrel and a set of wheels for a 50-caliber machine gun were also captured. Additionally, 600lb of rice and 6 tons of salt were taken. Friendly casualties were four KIA, including the three from Delta Troop, and multiple WIA.

On the morning of February 14, Captain Klein and the troops of Bravo Company, 1/12th Cav, resumed their attack up the Binh Son Valley and finally reached the head of it without further enemy contact, linking up with Captain McMillan and Charlie Company, 1/12th Cav, at Position Gold. On the way up the valley, Bravo Company was able to locate and capture the heavy machine gun that the USAF fighter bombers had attacked on the previous day, as well as numerous enemy knapsacks. Captain Klein and Bravo Company spent the next several days conducting search-and-destroy patrols in the area west of the Binh Son Valley, with only scattered enemy contact reported.

CHAPTER NINE

Yelling Like Madmen

On the afternoon of February 14, Lieutenant Colonel McDade directed Captain Diduryk and Bravo Company, 2nd Battalion, 7th Cavalry, to move by helicopter to the Suoi Run Valley, to the southeast of LZ Bird, and initiate search-and-destroy patrols there.[1] Documents found on the bodies of enemy KIA in the Go Chai Mountains on February 13, and on the morning of February 14, by troopers of Delta Troop, 1st Squadron, 9th Cavalry, indicated that two Viet Cong rifle companies were in the valley. They were believed to be part of a larger Viet Cong main force battalion that was operating somewhere in the valley complex or in the mountains surrounding it. A map found with the documents showed that the two companies were bivouacked about halfway down the valley at the base of Hon Mat Mountain, one of three mountains on the eastern side of the valley, the other two being Ho Trong Mountain to the north and Ong Cau Mountain to the south. The two companies were spread out over a distance of roughly 500 meters. Bravo Company was to attack and destroy the Viet Cong units.

Bravo Company had a solid reputation for professionalism under the command of 27-year-old Captain Diduryk, who had emigrated to America from Ukraine in 1950 with his parents and settled in the Jersey City, New Jersey, area. He attended St. Peter's Preparatory School and then Saint Peter's College, where he majored in physics and was a member of the National Society of Pershing Rifles, a military-oriented honor society for college-level students with an affiliation with the military, especially ROTC (the Reserve Officers' Training Corps). He graduated from Saint Peter's and was commissioned an army officer in 1960. He served tours of duty in Germany and at Fort Benning, and was given command of Bravo Company, 2/7th Cav. In November 1965, he played a key role in the battle of LZ X-Ray in the Ia Drang Valley. Under intense enemy fire, he led his unit into LZ X-Ray to reinforce the 1/7th Cav on the opening afternoon of the battle, moving his troops into positions

---

[1] Captain Myron Diduryk, U.S. Army Infantry, 1966–67, "Operations of Company B, 2nd Battalion, 7th Cavalry, 1st Cavalry Division (Airmobile), on a search-and-destroy operation on 15th February 1966 in Binh Dinh Province, Republic of Viet Nam. (Personal experience of a company commander).

on the perimeter to repel the attacking North Vietnamese. Captain Diduryk was described by Lieutenant General Moore in his book *We Were Soldiers Once ... and Young* as "the finest battlefield company commander I had ever seen, bar none."

On his second tour of duty in Vietnam as the Operations Officer of the 2/12th Cav, 1st Cav, Diduryk, then a major, was killed in an ambush. The helicopter he was riding in set down on the ground to check out a dead North Vietnamese soldier who had been killed by the door gunner, and he was hit in the stomach in the doorway of the helicopter by enemy fire and died outright.

Captain Diduryk and Bravo Company had been conducting saturation patrolling and search-and-destroy operations in the feeder valley directly north of LZ Bird since arriving in the Kim Son Valley on February 11.[2] Enemy resistance in the valley had been scattered and light, and the only significant contact occurred on the afternoon of February 13 when the lead element of Bravo Company encountered a seven-man North Vietnamese rifle squad. The Bravo Company troops engaged the enemy soldiers, resulting in an intense firefight. Bravo Company was unable to fix the enemy soldiers in position and they were able to break contact and flee into the jungle. The Bravo Company troops pursued them and attempted to reestablish contact, but were unable to do so. Bravo Company suffered several causalities in the encounter, including one KIA. The squad leader who led the assault on the enemy rifle squad received multiple gunshot wounds to the groin and stomach and died from the loss of blood before he could be evacuated to the 15th Med aid station at LZ English.

Since the start of operations in the Kim Son Valley on February 11, the units of the 3rd Brigade had conducted extensive search-and-destroy patrolling in the feeder valleys around LZ Bird. Enemy contact had been light, and with the exception of Captain Klein and Bravo Company, 1/12th Cav, in the Binh Son Valley south of Bird, there had been no decisive engagements. However, large quantities of weapons, ammunition, explosives, communications equipment, documents, and supplies had been found in the feeder valleys, indicating that the enemy was there in force but that it had adopted a strategy of lying low and avoiding contact.

The Suoi Run Valley was a small feeder valley located on the eastern side of the Kim Son Valley. It was roughly 3 kilometers long and slightly less than a kilometer wide at its widest point. It ran in a northwest–southeast direction, ending at the point where the Go Chai Mountains merged with the Ho Son Mountains. About halfway down the valley, it branched out to the east, creating a small side valley between Hon Mat Mountain and Ho Trong Mountain to the north. The side valley continued for about 2 kilometers before it ended at the base of the Go Chai Mountains where the village of Phu Huu was located. Just beyond Hon Mat Mountain, it again branched

---

[2] Description of the Kim Son Valley and the inland plains of Hoai An District based on maps of Binh Dinh Province, and Hoai An District, Interim Report of Operations, First Cavalry Division, July 1965 to December 1965, and author's recollection.

out to the east, creating a small side valley between Hon Mat Mountain and Ong Cau Mountain to the south. This side valley continued for about half a kilometer and ended at the base of the Go Chai Mountains where a small hamlet was located. The Suoi Run Valley had a narrow valley floor, and steep slopes and twisted ridges, both on the east and west sides, with flooded rice paddies alongside which ran the Suoi Run stream. The rice paddies had closely spaced bamboo thicket hedgerows marking the boundaries between them. The hedgerows overlooked the rice paddies and had only a limited number of paths through them. They provided the Viet Cong with positions from which automatic weapons fire could be directed at the Americans if they attempted to use the rice paddies as landing zones for their helicopters.

The slopes of the three mountains also overlooked the rice paddies and provided clear lines of fire into them, with good concealment. The slopes were covered with thick interwoven vines, bamboo thickets, rocks, and crevices camouflaged by elephant grass, and were loaded with leeches and snakes.

The majority of the people who inhabited the valley lived in the hamlet of Phu Huu, about halfway down the valley adjacent to the Suoi Run stream facing Hon Mat Mountain, or in one of the small hamlets at the eastern end of the two small side valleys. A small number of people also lived in the hamlet of Phu Ninh, located at the southern end of the valley on the high ground where the Go Chai and Ho Son mountains merged.

In its attack, Bravo Company would be supported by tube artillery at LZ Bird and Phu Xuan—an artillery position that had been established by the 3rd Brigade 1.5 kilometers east of Bird on the northern bank of the Kim Son River to support operations in the eastern side of the valley complex—an aerial reconnaissance team from Charlie Troop, 1/9th Cav, and aerial rocket gunships from Charlie Battery, 2/20th ARA. The battalion's reconnaissance platoon would be the immediate ready-reaction force and Charlie Company would be the reserve force. Both units would continue with their search-and-destroy patrols in the areas around LZ Bird but would be prepared to come to the assistance of Bravo Company on short notice should the need arise.

At 1530 hours on February 14, Bravo Company arrived by helicopter at the entrance to the Suoi Run Valley, 5 kilometers southeast of LZ Bird and 6 kilometers southwest of LZ Pony. The 1st Platoon was first in and secured the area for the rest of the company. The 2nd Platoon, 3rd Platoon, company Command Group, and Mortar Platoon followed in that order, and by 1730 hours, the airlift was complete and Bravo Company was on the ground and moving southward into the valley. Captain Diduryk's plan was to proceed halfway down the valley before sundown and establish night ambush positions on the eastern and western sides of the valley along trails leading to and from the base of Hon Mat Mountain, where the two rifle companies were reported to be located. Bravo Company would attack them at first light the following morning. The attack would follow on the heels of an extensive artillery barrage from the 105mm and 155mm batteries at Bird and Phu Xuan.

By 1900 hours, the 2nd Platoon reached a spot on the eastern side of the valley where an east–west stream emerged into the open valley from the small side valley that separated Ho Trong and Hon Mat mountains. It established its ambush position along the banks of the stream, adjacent to a heavily traveled trail. The position was approximately 300 meters northwest of the base of Hon Mat Mountain. The 3rd Platoon continued moving along the western side of the valley beyond the 2nd Platoon's position to a patch of dry ground 200 meters south of where the 2nd Platoon was located and 300 meters west of the base of Hon Mat Mountain. The 1st Platoon and Mortar Platoon moved to a spot on high ground west of the 3rd Platoon's position. The 1st Platoon was designated as the company reserve and could be maneuvered to either side of the 3rd Platoon, as needed. The company Command Group would remain with the 1st Platoon, while the Mortar Platoon would provide H&I fire in support of the three platoons, with priority of fire going to the platoon in contact. Bravo Company was in position by 1915 hours and the Mortar Platoon completed its registration fire by 1930 hours. The registration fire provided the platoons with accurate data for subsequent engagement of enemy soldiers with mortar fire if needed.

Shortly after Bravo Company established its night defensive position, the 3rd Brigade's direct support artillery battery at LZ Bird, the 1st Battalion, 21st Artillery, initiated volleys of H&I fire into the base of Hon Mat Mountain and onto the slopes above it with 105mm howitzers. The volleys lasted throughout the night and into the early morning. They consisted of no more than a few rounds fired at random intervals throughout the night, seeking to deny the Viet Cong freedom of movement and to destroy their morale.

At about the time that the H&I fire was initiated against the enemy's reported location, the battalion operations officer at LZ Bird radioed Captain Diduryk to inform him that the enemy Bravo Company was facing was actually a battalion, not just two rifle companies, and that it included a heavy weapons company. Enemy soldiers taken prisoner earlier that day by troopers of Delta Troop, 1/9th Cav, in the Go Chai Mountains south of LZ Pony, indicated that the formation was the 93rd Battalion of the 2nd Viet Cong Regiment. The battalion was also known as the 1st Battalion, and the 2nd Viet Cong Regiment was also known as the 2nd Main Force Regiment or 210th Viet Cong Regiment. Multiple unit designations were used by the North Vietnamese to identify their units. The battalion was believed to be spread out over a distance of roughly 1.5 kilometers northwest–southeast, along the base of Hot Mat and Ong Cau mountains. It was a much larger unit than the anticipated two rifle companies, and had significantly more firepower. Based on this information, Diduryk requested additional artillery support for Bravo Company's H&I requirement. However, due to the 3rd Brigade's priorities for artillery support, only two additional 105mm howitzers from LZ Bird were allocated to Bravo Company.

The 2nd Viet Cong Regiment was one of the original Viet Cong main force regiments formed in South Vietnam by the National Liberation Front in 1960.[3] It operated under the control of Central Office South Vietnam (COSVN), a Viet Cong military region, or front, which was the military wing of the National Liberation Front. It had been fighting government forces in the northern provinces of South Vietnam since its creation and was a battle-hardened unit. In 1965, COSVN was reorganized by the North Vietnamese command in the South and the regiment was assigned to the newly formed Sao Vang Division in Binh Dinh Province. The regiment consisted of three main force battalions, each of which had between 500 and 600 men organized into three rifle companies, supported by a fire support company with heavy weapons and mortar platoons, and reconnaissance, signaling, and logistics platoons. Artillery and sapper battalions also augmented the regiment.

The members of the 2nd Viet Cong Regiment were full-time professional soldiers who typically were born in the South and had migrated to the North sometime in the mid-1950s after the Geneva Convention, when Vietnam was partitioned into two countries, North Vietnam and South Vietnam. There, they were trained in the tactics of guerilla warfare and indoctrinated in Communism. They had re-infiltrated back into the South in the early 1960s. They were better trained than Viet Cong local force guerillas, who were farmers by day and fighters by night, and could operate in company, platoon, and squad-size units in the same fashion as local force guerillas. They were also better equipped than local force guerillas and typically were supplied with the same weapons as North Vietnamese Army regulars. They often wore khaki uniforms similar to those of the North Vietnamese regulars, along with pith helmets, earning them the nickname "hard hats."

Viet Cong main force units were known to be more deceptive and cunning in their tactics than the North Vietnamese, and were usually familiar with the local terrain, which gave them a big advantage in maneuvering on the battlefield. They were also better at camouflage than the North Vietnamese, and were adept at taking evasive action, often completely fragmenting and disappearing into the jungle.[4]

According to recent intelligence reports, the North Vietnamese command in the South had been mixing Viet Cong soldiers and NVA regulars in Viet Cong main force regiments in recent months in an apparent attempt to restore authorized strength

---

[3] A document provides a description of the history of the 2nd Viet Cong Regiment, which was one of the original Viet Cong main force regiments formed in the South by the National Liberation Front in 1960. Global Security, "North Vietnamese Army and Viet Cong Infantry/Artillery Regiments," www.globalsecurity.org.

[4] A document provides a description of Viet Cong main force units in South Vietnam. Viet Cong units were known to be deceptive and cunning in their tactics. Military Wiki, "Viet Cong Organization," https://military-history.fandom.com/wiki/Viet C.org.

levels to units that had been hurt in recent operations against government forces. In early 1966, it was believed that the 2nd Viet Cong Regiment was composed of both Viet Cong main force guerillas and NVA regulars.[5]

Captain Diduryk's plan for the attack on the morning of February 15 called for the 2nd and 3rd platoons to attack the enemy at the base of Hon Mat Mountain on signal, following a 15-minute artillery barrage from the batteries at Bird and Phu Xuan. The barrage would start at 0830 hours and end at 0845 hours, at which time the 2nd and 3rd platoons would attack. The Mortar Platoon would support their advance across the rice paddies by firing 81mm mortars into the bamboo thickets at the base of the mountain. Helicopter gunships from Charlie Troop, 1/9th Cav, and aerial rocket gunships from Charlie Battery, 2/20th ARA, would support the platoons' advance at the direction of Lieutenant Gauthier, the artillery forward observer assigned to Bravo Company.

The night passed without incident for the troops of Bravo Company. By 0730 hours on February 15, the fog in the valley started to lift and four helicopters from LZ English arrived at Bravo Company's position with a supply of small-arms ammunition, mortar rounds, medical supplies, and extra equipment, including PRC-25 radios and batteries. At 0830 hours, the 15-minute artillery barrage began. When it ended at 0845 hours, Captain Diduryk gave the signal by radio to Lieutenant John Particelli and his 2nd Platoon, and Lieutenant Hillyer and his 3rd Platoon, to attack. The platoons attacked in platoon wedge formation, the 2nd Platoon attacking to the southeast across the rice paddies toward the base of Hon Mat Mountain, while the 3rd Platoon attacked directly to the east across the Suoi Run stream and the rice paddies toward the base of Hon Mat Mountain, just north of Phu Huu. The Mortar Platoon fired multiple WP rounds at the bamboo thickets at the base to screen the platoons' movement across the rice paddies.

The 2nd Platoon crossed the east–west stream that separated Ho Trong and Hon Mat mountains and moved into the rice paddy complex bordering the base of Hon Mat Mountain. It had moved about 200 meters through the rice paddies, receiving only sporadic sniper fire, seemingly indicating that it was facing a small unit—possibly a multi-squad or platoon-sized unit—when suddenly the base of the mountain and the slope above it lit up with intense automatic weapons, small-arms, and mortar fire, fragmenting the platoon over a 150-meter-wide area. The troops took cover in the knee-deep water behind the rice paddy dikes and returned fire at the enemy positions, but not before they suffered a number of casualties. The casualties were forced to lie in the rice paddies against the dikes until they could be safely moved

---

[5] A document provides a description of Viet Cong and North Vietnamese forces operating in South Vietnam. Military Wiki, "NLF and PAVN Strategy, Organization, and Structure," http://military-history.fandom.com/wiki/Viet_Cong_and_ PAVN_strategy,_organization_and_structure.

back to the east–west stream for medical treatment or evacuation to the 15th Med aid station at LZ English. Lieutenant Particelli immediately called for and received mortar fire on the enemy positions in the bamboo thickets and trenches in front of his 2nd Platoon. The PRC-25 radio used by the artillery recon sergeant assigned to the 2nd Platoon was hit by enemy fire and damaged beyond use, so supporting artillery fire from LZ Bird for the 2nd Platoon was delayed.

The 3rd Platoon received multiple rounds of enemy mortar fire from the base of Hon Mat Mountain, but no automatic weapons or small-arms fire, suggesting that the enemy soldiers were located to the front of 2nd Platoon and north of the 3rd Platoon's line of attack. The 3rd Platoon suffered no casualties. This made it difficult for Captain Diduryk and his platoon leaders to accurately determine the strength and composition of the enemy force that Bravo Company was facing. The pilots of the aerial reconnaissance helicopters from Charlie Troop, 1/9th Cav, reported receiving enemy fire from the base and slope of Ong Cau Mountain, to the south of Hon Mat Mountain.

By 0930 hours, the attack had stalled. Captain Diduryk, Lieutenant Gauthier, their RTOs, and a rifle squad from the 1st Platoon moved northeast from the 1st Platoon's position on the western side of the valley through the rice paddies and across the Soui Run stream to the east–west stream north of the 2nd Platoon's position. They crossed the east–west stream and proceeded to move into the rice paddy complex to join Lieutenant Particelli and his 2nd Platoon. They immediately came under intense automatic weapons fire, resulting in the RTOs of both Diduryk and Gauthier being hit with small-arms fire. Both of their radios were also hit, one being damaged beyond repair. At that point, Diduryk radioed Lieutenant Colonel McDade to advise him that due to the loss of three of the company's radios, he was leaving the Battalion Command Network and switching to the Artillery Fire Direction Network. He also radioed Lieutenants Particelli and Hillyer to instruct them to switch frequencies on their radios to the Artillery Fire Direction Network. This arrangement allowed Gauthier and his artillery observers to communicate with the fire direction center at LZ Bird, while Diduryk and his platoon leaders could communicate with one another and with Lieutenant Colonel McDade.

The enemy to the 2nd Platoon's front was well dug in and concealed in the bamboo thickets and trenches overlooking the rice paddies, along a 300–400-meter front. Estimated to be a company-sized unit, it was equipped with automatic weapons, 40mm rockets, and 60mm mortars, and had excellent fields of fire into the rice paddies. Captain Diduryk again radioed Lieutenant Colonel McDade to advise him of Bravo Company's situation, and stated that it was preparing to resume its attack on the enemy position.

Captain Diduryk ordered the remaining three squads of the 1st Platoon, as well as the Mortar Platoon, to move from their position on the western side of the valley through the flooded rice paddies, across the Soui Run stream, and to the east–west stream north of the 2nd Platoon's position, and wait there for further instructions. The 2nd Platoon was ordered to reassemble at the east–west stream that it had crossed 30 minutes earlier by executing a fire-and-maneuver movement to its rear, utilizing covering artillery fire from LZ Bird. The 3rd Platoon was also ordered to move northward through the flooded rice paddies to the east–west stream and join the 1st, 2nd, and Mortar platoons there.

By 1045 hours, the four platoons were at the east–west stream in position to attack the enemy at the base of Hon Mat Mountain. The 3rd Platoon would lead the attack, while the 2nd Platoon provided a base of fire from the banks of the stream. The base of fire was intended to support the 3rd Platoon's assault and to prevent any enemy soldiers from escaping northward into the small side valley separating Ho Mat and Ho Trong mountains to the north, where they could take refuge in the small hamlet. The 1st Platoon was held in reserve behind the 2nd Platoon. The Mortar Platoon was to fire along the 3rd Platoon's right flank, shifting on order from Lieutenant Hillyer, as needed. Artillery from Charlie Battery, 1/21st Artillery, at Bird would fire immediately in front of the attacking troops, shifting east and south as the assault progressed. Helicopter gunships from Charlie Troop, 1/9th Cav, and aerial rocket gunships from Charlie Battery, 2/20th ARA, would attack enemy targets a kilometer southeast of Bravo Company's position to seal off enemy routes of withdrawal in that direction. The attack would commence on signal from Captain Diduryk following a tactical airstrike on the enemy position that had been requested from the USAF.

The USAF responded with a FAC in an O-1 Bird Dog and two Skyraiders, which made multiple passes over the enemy position. When the Skyraiders made their final pass, Captain Diduryk gave the order to attack. The 3rd Platoon, with bayonets fixed, assaulted on the heels of the attacking aircraft. It moved forward in bounds, utilizing the technique of fire-and-maneuver movement. About halfway across the rice paddies, it accelerated its movement to a dead run, "yelling like madmen." The aggressive assault startled the enemy soldiers and caused them to jump up from their trenches and concealed positions and flee north along the base of the mountain, in the direction of the east–west stream and into the supporting fire of the 2nd Platoon.

Seeing the success of the 3rd Platoon, Captain Diduryk ordered the 1st Platoon to attack through the right flank of the 2nd Platoon in a southeasterly direction, utilizing a wide-wedge formation. The 3rd Platoon was ordered to reorient the direction of its attack to the southeast along a wide trail through Phu Huu, using it as a guide. As the 3rd Platoon advanced, Lieutenant Hillyer changed the platoon's formation to a platoon line formation, with fire teams employing a fire-and-maneuver movement. The two platoons pushed the enemy to the southeast toward the small side valley that separated Ho Mat and Ong Cau mountains, shifting the supporting artillery and mortar fire as they advanced. The 2nd Platoon continued to block the escape of the enemy soldiers northward with suppressive fire and supporting artillery from aerial rocket gunships.

The 1st and 3rd platoons continued their attack southeast, encountering light-to-heavy, but disorganized, resistance. The enemy was on the run. Many of the enemy soldiers were wounded and were unable to evade the attacking troops. Those who were not wounded attempted to flee in small groups of three and four in the direction of the small side valley between Hon Mat and Ong Cau mountains and the small hamlet, or across the rice paddies to the southwest to the high ground where the hamlet of Phu Ninh was located. Aerial rocket gunships circled above the rice paddies and took the fleeing soldiers under fire as they attempted to cross, using the bamboo thicket hedgerows and rice paddy dikes as cover.

At 1200 hours, the Reconnaissance Platoon from Delta Company, 2/7th Cav, arrived at Bravo Company's command post at the east–west stream to provide security. At that point, Captain Diduryk ordered Lieutenant Particelli and his 2nd Platoon to move forward into the rice paddy complex and recover Bravo Company's wounded and dead. The casualties included multiple WIA and two KIA, both of whom received gunshot wounds to the upper body and bled to death in the rice paddies before they could be evacuated.

By 1450 hours, enemy resistance had ceased, and the 1st and 3rd platoons were ordered by Captain Diduryk to halt in place. At that point, the two platoons were resupplied with ammunition by hovering helicopters, and Lieutenant Colonel McDade, who had arrived at the east–west stream in his command-and-control helicopter shortly after the Reconnaissance Platoon had arrived, directed Diduryk and Bravo Company to continue their attack in the direction of Phu Ninh on the high ground to the southwest to exploit their success. He emphasized the need to take prisoners.

The platoons resumed their attack at 1500 hours in platoon wedge formation. The 1st Platoon was on the left and the 2nd Platoon on the right, anchored on the Soui Run stream, adjacent to Phu Huu. The 3rd Platoon was designated as the company reserve and was directed to sweep the area to the rear of the 1st and 2nd platoons and provide all-around security. The sweep was to focus on the stream, the streambed, and the hedgerows, which were riddled with fortifications. Upon completion of the sweep, the 3rd Platoon was to move forward and join the attacking platoons, on order.

At 1520 hours, contact was regained with the enemy. An enemy rifle squad of seven soldiers, who had hastily set up an ambush to the 2nd Platoon's front, was spotted by the point squad of the 2nd Platoon in time to allow the platoon to flank it and attack it from the rear, killing five enemy troops and capturing two. Simultaneous with this action, the 1st Platoon overran the command post of the enemy battalion, killing three enemy soldiers and capturing the battalion commander, who was wounded in the exchange. A number of documents and maps were also captured. The battalion commander and the documents were immediately loaded onto a helicopter and transported to LZ Bird, where the commander was interrogated by members of the division's military intelligence unit.

Approximately 20 meters beyond the ambush site, the 2nd Platoon discovered an abandoned mortar pit with unexpended mortar rounds, and U.S.-standard and field-expedient mortar bipods. The 2nd and 3rd platoons continued their advance, encountering diminishing resistance by enemy rear guard elements. The indications were that the fleeing enemy soldiers had withdrawn beyond Phu Ninh, seeking refuge in the rugged jungle mountains to the south.

In sweeping the battlefield, the bodies of 57 Viet Cong solders were found, and based on the number of body parts scattered around the battlefield, it was estimated that an additional 93 Viet Cong soldiers were killed and dragged away, either to the hamlet at the end of the small side valley or onto the high ground to the southwest leading to Phu Ninh. Four Viet Cong soldiers, including the battalion commander, were taken prisoner. The following enemy weapons and ammunition were found: nine crew-served weapons, two Chicom 12.7mm heavy machine guns, two 40mm rocket launchers, two American Thompson submachine guns, 10 American M-60 standard 7.62mm machine guns, 10 Type 56 assault rifles (one destroyed in place), two 45-caliber pistols, five American 40x46mm M-79 rifle grenades, 12 Chicom hand grenades (the potato masher type), 17 other grenades (destroyed in place), numerous pieces of many other weapons, 26 60mm mortar rounds, five U.S. standard bipods, four U.S. field-expedient mortar bipods, 400 rounds of 7.62mm linked machine-gun ammunition, and several thousand rounds of assorted small-arms ammunition

Along with the bodies of the Viet Cong soldiers, two escape routes leading away from the battlefield were discovered. The first one was found at the southern end of Phu Huu adjacent to the Soui Run stream. It ran to the small side valley to the east and ended in the vicinity of the hamlet at the end of the valley in thick jungle vegetation. It was a trench, 30 feet deep in spots, with overhanging jungle vegetation, including bamboo thickets, concealing it from aerial and ground observation. Foxholes and caves were located along it at approximately 5-meter intervals. Some of the foxholes contained hand grenades, while others contained enemy equipment and ammunition. The second escape route was discovered alongside a trail that led from one of the rice paddies in the vicinity of Phu Huu to the high ground to the southwest and to Phu Ninh. It ran in parallel to a rice paddy dike. It was 2 meters wide and was covered with overgrown jungle vegetation, including bamboo thickets. The two escape routes were littered with bloody bandages and enemy equipment covered in blood. In clearing the two routes, the troops of the 3rd Platoon encountered only light enemy resistance, which was quickly eliminated.

At this point, a second airstrike was ordered by Captain Diduryk, and a USAF FAC in an O-1 Bird Dog aircraft and two Skyraiders arrived over the battlefield at 1650 hours. Diduryk briefed the FAC and the two Skyraider pilots on the situation on the ground and requested airstrikes in the vicinity of the small hamlet in the side valley to the east separating Hot Mat and Ong Cau mountains, and in the vicinity of Phu Ninh on the high ground to the southwest. The two Skyraiders pounded the areas with a variety of ordnance, including napalm, WP and high-explosive bombs, and 20mm cannon fire.

At the completion of the airstrike, Captain Diduryk directed the platoons to make a rear sweep to the company command post at the east–west stream, with two platoons abreast policing the battlefield as they went. The platoons closed at the east–west stream at 1745 hours.

Bravo Company suffered two KIA and six WIA in the battle—one WIA by an Skyraider prior to the 3rd Platoon's attack across the rice paddy when the aircraft experienced a malfunction with its bomb-release mechanism and dropped a cluster bomb unit several seconds late, resulting in some of the bomblets landing within the 3rd Platoon's position and wounding the trooper.

Back at LZ Bird, the captured battalion commander spoke freely with his interrogators. His name was Lieutenant Colonel Dong Doan. He proudly announced that he was the commander of the 93rd Battalion, 2nd Viet Cong Regiment, and that his battalion was responsible for monitoring activities in the Soui Run Valley and surrounding mountains, extending from the head of the valley where the Go Chai and Ho Son mountains merged to the northern end of the Go Chai Mountains where LZ Pony was located. The area included the three mountains that overlooked the valley: Ho Trong, Hon Mat, and Ong Cau. The battalion's mission was to observe activities in the valley and ambush any American or ARVN forces that attempted to penetrate it either on the ground or by landing by helicopter in the rice paddies. He claimed that morale in the unit was good because the men had plenty to eat and many weapons with ammunition, and that they were sure they could defeat their enemy.

Lieutenant Colonel Doan estimated that he lost two platoons in the battle, but said that he had been unable to confirm this; he was unable to contact his company commanders for a report so he was not certain of the numbers. The battalion's rally point after the battle was the area where the east–west stream emerged into the open valley from the side valley that separated Ho Trong and Hon Mat mountains.

When the platoons reached Bravo Company's position at the east–west stream, Lieutenant Colonel McDade ordered Captain Diduryk and Bravo Company to return by helicopter to LZ Bird once all of the captured equipment and ammunition were loaded onto Chinook helicopters and transported to the 1st Cav's base camp at An Khe. There they would link up with Alpha, Charlie, and Delta companies, 2/7th Cav. Later that evening, Colonel Moore notified his battalion commanders that Colonel Elvy Roberts and the 1st Brigade would replace the 3rd Brigade in Phase III of Operation *Masher/White Wing* (*Eagle's Claw*) effective 1500 hours on February 17, and that the units of the 3rd Brigade would return to base camp on February 16 and 17 for rest and refit. The 2/7th Cav and 1/7th Cav would move by helicopter to An Khe on February 16 and 17 respectively, and together the two battalions would assume security for the base camp and surrounding area from the 1st Brigade. Charlie Troop, 1/9th Cav, would also return to base camp at that time. The 1st Battalion (Airborne), 12th Cavalry, which had been attached to the 3rd Brigade for Phases I and II and the start of Phase III, would remain in the field and rejoin its parent brigade, the 1st Brigade, and sister battalions, the 1st Battalion (Airborne), 8th Cavalry, and 2nd Battalion (Airborne), 8th Cavalry, when they arrived in the Kim Son Valley on February 17 and 18.

The 1st Brigade would continue with the division's plan to sweep the feeder valleys in an attempt to drive the enemy into escape routes at the heads of the feeder valleys, where they could be destroyed by infantry elements or tactical air power. The 1/8th Cav would work the high ground north of LZ Bird, while the 2/8th Cav worked the area southeast of Bird. The 1/12th Cav would continue sweeping the feeder valleys to the southwest of Bird. Apache Troop (Airborne), 1/9th Cav, with its observation helicopters, hunter-killer aerial teams, and Aero Rifle Platoon, would screen the areas east and west of Bird, and provide aerial reconnaissance support to the brigade's infantry battalions. Delta Troop, 1/9th Cav, would remain in the field and continue with its search-and-destroy patrols in the eastern Go Chai Mountains and in the vicinity of the 506 Valley and areas east toward Highway 1.

To simplify the changeover of the brigades and ease transportation requirements, the direct support artillery unit of the 1st Brigade, the 2nd Battalion (Airborne), 19th Artillery, would assume operational control of the firing elements of the direct support artillery unit of the 3rd Brigade, the 1st Battalion, 21st Artillery, in the Kim Son Valley. Likewise, the 1/21st Artillery would assume operational control of the firing elements of the 2/19th Artillery at the base camp in An Khe when it arrived there.

With the changeover of the 1st and 3rd Brigades, Major General Kinnard directed Colonel Lynch and the 2nd Brigade to move from the An Lao Valley to the Kim Son Valley and join the 1st Brigade in Phase III of Operation *Masher/White Wing* (*Eagle's Claw*). With that, Lynch closed down operations in the An Lao Valley and moved his command post to LZ Pony. He directed the 1st and 2nd Battalions, 5th Cavalry, along with their direct support artillery unit, the 1st Battalion, 77th Artillery, to move to LZ Duck, located on the high ground adjacent to Route 3A at the Hoai An District Headquarters, 5 kilometers north of LZ Pony. They were to move on the following morning, February 16. LZ Duck would serve as the jump-off point for the 2nd Brigade's infantry battalions to attack the Viet Cong and North Vietnamese in the Go Chai Mountains. The 2nd Battalion, 12th Cavalry, was to continue clearing operations in the area east of the An Lao Valley on the coastal plain and prepare to move by helicopter to LZ Pony on the afternoon of February 16. The 2/12th Cav would serve as the 2nd Brigade's reserve force, prepared to reinforce the two 5th Cav battalions should the need arise, and to provide security for the brigade forward base and artillery at LZ Pony.

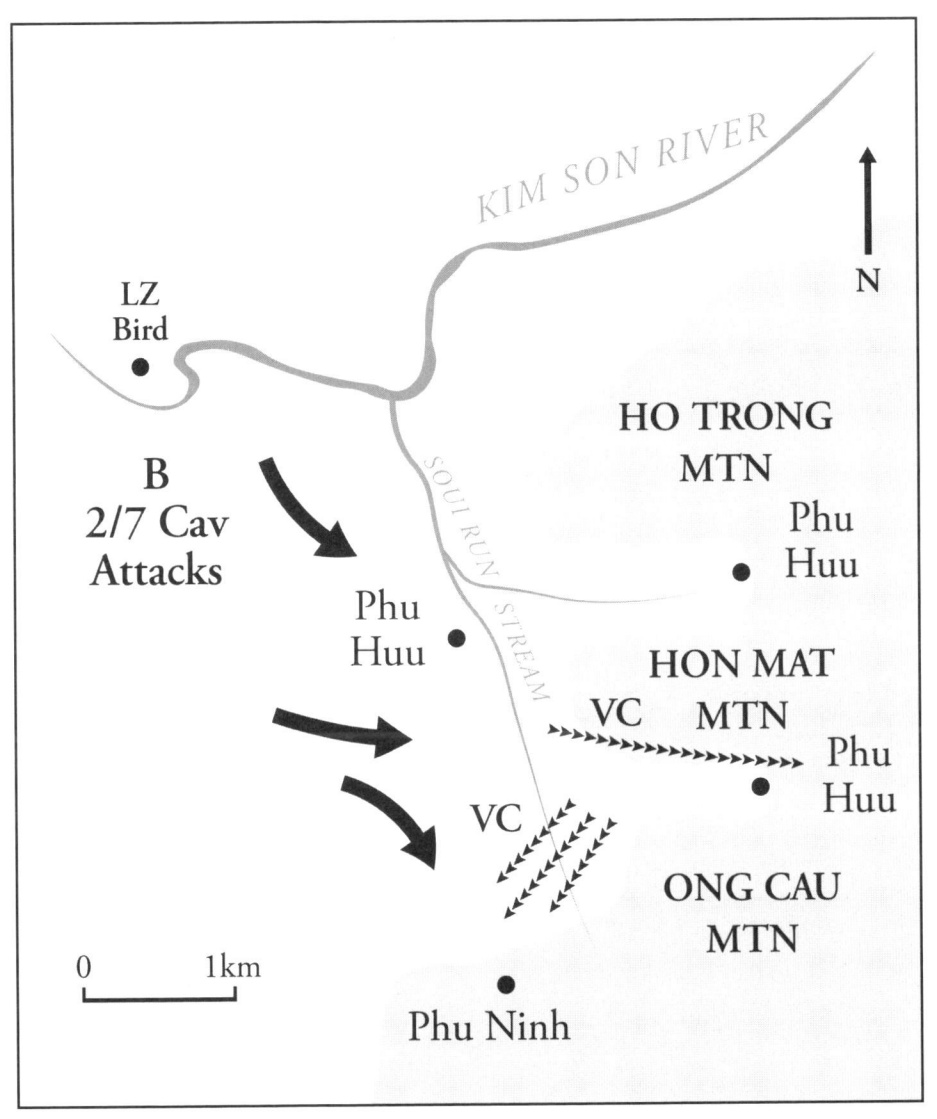

Map 9. 7th Cavalry Attacks the Viet Cong in the Suoi Run Valley, February 15, 1966

CHAPTER TEN

Death in a Narrow Place

The captured commander of the 93rd Battalion, 2nd Viet Cong Regiment, Lieutenant Colonel Doan, spoke freely with his interrogators at LZ Bird about his battalion's area of operation and its mission. The battalion was responsible for the Soui Run Valley and surrounding mountains, and its mission was to ambush any American or ARVN forces that attempted to penetrate the area. In speaking with his interrogators, Lieutenant Colonel Doan provided them with enough information so they had a pretty good idea of where his regiment and its headquarters were located—south of LZ Pony where the Go Chai Mountains merged with the Ho Son Mountains, approximately 2 kilometers south of where his command post was located and where he was captured by the troops of Bravo Company, 2nd Battalion, 7th Cavalry. To confirm this, his interrogators requested the division to conduct aerial surveillance of the suspected area utilizing a communications value-added network (VAN) that had been developed by the division's 13th Signal Battalion during the fighting in the Ia Drang Valley in November. The VAN consisted of a fixed-wing OV-1 Mohawk aircraft equipped with FM radios powerful enough to detect radio signals on the ground and special communications equipment that was capable of determining the location where the signals originated. The Mohawk would orbit over the suspected area at 10,000 feet, intercept any radio signals detected on the ground, and forward them to LZ Bird, where the special communications equipment was located.

By daybreak on February 16, the commanders in the 1st Cav had the information they needed on the location of the 2nd Viet Cong Regiment and its headquarters, based on the results of the aerial surveillance. The enemy regiment and its headquarters were in the Song Bien Valley, a small and narrow river valley in the extreme southeastern corner of the valley complex, 8 kilometers south-southwest of LZ Pony and 2 kilometers south of the hamlet of Phu Ninh, where the troops of Bravo Company, 2/7th Cav, captured Lieutenant Colonel Doan and his command post on the previous afternoon.

The Song Bien Valley was roughly 6 kilometers long and 1.5 kilometers wide at its widest point. It ran in a northeast–southwest direction, and like many of the valleys in the complex, it was characterized by steep mountain slopes that were covered with clumps of bamboo thickets, interwoven vines, rocks, and crevices, and were loaded with leeches and snakes.[1] The valley floor was covered with elephant grass 5–6 feet high and had a stream running down the middle of it. The area around the valley was so dense with jungle growth that potential landing zones for helicopters were extremely limited in size and number; the only suitable areas were on the mountain ridges to the east and south of the valley and in a clearing at the western end of the valley. The ridges were covered with huge boulders nestled in waist-high elephant grass, which made it extremely dangerous for infantry troopers to jump out of the helicopters without injuring themselves. The clearing at the western end of the valley as seen from a high-flying helicopter looked like a ready-made ambush site for Viet Cong soldiers lying in wait for the Americans if they attempted to use it as a landing zone for their helicopters. It consisted of a single rice paddy with a stream running alongside it. It was surrounded on all sides by thick jungle vegetation and was estimated to be large enough to accommodate only one helicopter at a time—barely enough to transport a squad of infantry. The stream adjacent to the rice paddy ran in a southwesterly direction and eventually emerged in the vicinity of Phu Ninh, where Captain Klein and Bravo Company, 1st Battalion, 12th Cavalry, had been working as a beater force. The eastern end of the valley consisted of a number of abandoned rice paddies and thatched-roof hootches in which the farmers and peasants who worked the rice paddy fields had lived. The rice paddies were scarred with large bomb craters from recent B-52 strikes. Thick jungle vegetation, 8 feet high or more, separated the clearing at the western end of the valley from its eastern end.

Shortly after receiving the information on the location of the enemy regiment and its headquarters, Colonel Lynch initiated a block-and-sweep of the Song Bien Valley. The companies of the 1st Battalion, 5th Cavalry, would air assault onto the high ground at the eastern end of the valley, seize and secure the position for follow-on artillery, and move down the slope into the valley and sweep to the southwest along the Song Bien stream, driving the enemy into a blocking position established by the 2nd Battalion, 5th Cavalry. The position was designated Objective Coil.

---

[1] In an unpublished manuscript, Captain Robert W. McMahon described the attack on the headquarters of the 2nd Viet Cong Main Force Regiment in the Song Bien Valley in the extreme southeastern corner of the Kim Son Valley complex by Bravo Company, 2nd Battalion, 5th Cav. Captain Robert W. McMahon, U.S. Army Infantry, "Operations of Company B, 2nd Battalion, 5th Cavalry, 1st Cavalry Division (Airmobile), in the attack upon a main force Viet Cong heavy weapons battalion in the vicinity of Bong Son, South Vietnam, 16–17 February 1966." Personal experiences of the Company Commander, dated 1966–67. U.S. Army Infantry School monograph. Description of the Kim Son Valley and the inland plains of Hoai An District, based on maps of Binh Dinh Province, and Hoai An District, and Interim Report of Operations, First Cavalry Division, July 1965 to December 1965.

The companies of the 2/5th Cav would air assault onto the high ground to the south of the valley, seize and secure the LZ as a blocking position, and move down the slope into the valley to establish a blocking position around the clearing at its western end. The clearing was designated LZ Pete. The position on the high ground where the 2/5th Cav would set down was designated Objective Recoil, which was roughly 2 kilometers south of Pete and 6 kilometers west of Coil. The 2/5th Cav would also seize and secure two additional positions on the high ground to the south: LZ Mike, 2 kilometers east of Pete and 2 kilometers north of Recoil, and Objective Joe, 3 kilometers south of Recoil. The three blocking positions would be company-sized positions, and together with that at LZ Pete in the valley would form a virtual north–south wall that would trap the Viet Cong if they attempted to maneuver up the southern slope away from LZ Pete to escape the 2/5th Cav's blocking position. The northern slope of the valley was very steep and nearly impossible to climb, with huge boulders, crevices, and thick jungle, so it was unlikely that the Viet Cong would attempt to evade to the north to avoid the blocking position at Pete.

The 2nd Battalion, 12th Cavalry, the designated brigade reserve force for the operation, would move by helicopter from the An Lao Valley to LZ Pony, where it would assume security of the LZ and be ready to come to the assistance of the 5th Cav battalions as needed.

Due to the volume of enemy ground fire that had been directed at the helicopters on air assaults in the Bong Son area, Colonel Lynch and Colonel Allen Burdett, Jr., Commanding Officer of the 11th Aviation Group, felt that a change of tactics was required as operations in Phase III progressed. From then on, air assaults would be made on the high ground to support a tactical plan of the troops sweeping down the slopes into the valley. Very little hostile ground fire had been encountered with air assaults onto the mountaintops in the An Lao Valley in Phase II, or onto the mountainous areas south of Bong Son in the deception operations, but aircraft accidents had increased with this tactical plan. Landings made on mountain peaks and ridges required a greater degree of pilot skill to overcome turbulence and density altitude problems. In one operation, a helicopter that attempted to land on a high peak pinnacle rolled over and slid down the mountain side, crashing into trees and becoming wedged between them. Unbelievably, no one was killed in the incident, but two infantry passengers were badly injured and had to be evacuated to a field hospital for medical treatment.

On the morning of February 16, Charlie Company, 1/5th Cav, air assaulted into Objective Coil at 0958 hours following a tactical airstrike and 20-minute artillery preparation with 930 105mm howitzer rounds from the batteries at LZs Pony and Duck. Charlie Company seized and secured the position, and by 1112 hours the entire battalion was on the ground at Coil. The landings were unopposed, and once a defensive perimeter had been established on the mountaintop, Alpha, Bravo, and Charlie companies moved out from Coil to clear the surrounding area. No enemy contact was made, but two dead Viet Cong soldiers were found, along with numerous 81mm mortar rounds that had been abandoned by the enemy. The dead soldiers were likely trying to flee the mountaintop when the airstrike and artillery barrage began earlier that morning, and were killed either by exploding bombs or artillery rounds. The 105mm howitzers of Bravo Battery, 1st Battalion, 77th Artillery, were then airlifted by sling load into Coil by Chinook helicopters to provide coverage for the area.

Following a 20-minute artillery preparation on the mountaintop to the south of the valley with 669 105mm howitzer rounds, the companies of the 2/5th Cav air assaulted into LZ Mike on the mountaintop to the south by 1352 hours and immediately proceeded to clear the surrounding area. Once Captain Robert W. McMahon and Bravo Company were on the ground, they moved west by southwest down the ridge in a wedge formation toward the clearing in the valley, where they would establish a blocking position at LZ Pete. When Bravo Company reached a spot on the slope where the valley below could be observed, McMahon directed it to halt and directed the artillery officer forward observer assigned to Bravo Company from Alpha Battery, 1st Battalion, 77th Field Artillery to register artillery fire in the valley, providing the company with a close-in defense. For more than an hour, the 155mm artillery batteries at LZ Pony and Phu Xuan fired high-angle rounds in support of Bravo Company but failed to get a single round over the 400-meter mountain north of the Song Bien Valley and into the valley. The artillery guns had the range to reach the valley but were unable to safely support the high-angle elevation required to get the rapid descents necessary to hit the target in the valley. The Mortar Platoon of Delta Company, however, had more success, demonstrating with a single marking round that it could hit the clearing at the western end of the valley from LZ Mike. Establishing an artillery position in the vicinity of Phu Ninh, west of the valley, would have allowed artillery to be fired directly into the valley from the west to support the blocking position at LZ Pete, if an artillery battery had been available.

Mel Gunderson from Black Hawk, South Dakota, a member of Delta Company's Mortar Platoon, remembered:

> We closed into LZ Mike late on the afternoon of February 16 and proceeded to move up a hill to the north of Mike along the ridge where we dug several mortar pits and set up our mortar tubes. The area was covered with elephant grass five-to-six feet high that blocked our view of the surrounding area so we had to be especially vigilant about guarding our section of the perimeter. We could see across the valley but we could not see down into it. The slopes were too steep and the valley too narrow. At about 1500 hours, our platoon leader provided us with the coordinates of the clearing at the western end of [the] valley and directed us to fire marking rounds into it on signal to demonstrate that we had the range and trajectory to reach it. We fired a marking round and hit the clearing on the first try. The 155mm artillery batteries at LZ Pony and Phu Xuan were unable to get any rounds over the mountain immediately north of the valley and down into it. The artillery rounds had to be "walked" slowly toward the target area because excessive adjustments in range could have caused rounds to overshoot the valley and land on the mountaintop to the south where we were located. We could see that high-angle

elevation firing from LZ Pony and Phu Xuan was going to be a problem in the eastern side of the valley complex where the valleys were very narrow.

While the Mortar Platoon was firing marking rounds into the clearing at the western end of the valley, two OH-13 observation helicopters from Bravo Troop, 1st Squadron, 9th Cavalry, entered the valley from the west and narrowly missed getting hit by a mortar round. The helicopters promptly exited the valley once the pilots realized what they had done, but not before they spotted several Viet Cong soldiers hiding in the jungle near the clearing at the western end of the valley and radioed this information to Lieutenant Colonel Meyer. With that, Meyer directed Captain McMahon and Bravo Company to proceed with the mission of moving down the slope into the valley and establishing a blocking position at Pete without the customary artillery support.

By 1700 hours, the 3rd Platoon of Bravo Company reached the valley and was at the Song Bien stream. The 1st Platoon had also reached the valley and was about 100 meters from a clearing, but was reporting hootches, bunkers, and signs of recent Viet Cong activity. The 2nd Platoon, Command Group, and Mortar Platoon were still moving down the slope and were roughly 1 kilometer from the bottom, carrying an 81mm mortar tube and 18 rounds of high-explosive ammunition. They would likely be unable to reach the clearing in the valley and establish a satisfactory defensive position there before darkness set in. The terrain was extremely rugged, with huge boulders, crevices, and thick jungle undergrowth that slowed their movement. At that point, Lieutenant Colonel Meyer directed Captain McMahon to pull back his two lead platoons and establish a night defensive position on the southern slope roughly 1 kilometer up from the valley.

While the 1st and 2nd battalions, 5th Cav, were busy moving into the Song Bien Valley, the 2/12th Cav continued with its clearing operations east of the An Lao Valley at the base of the Da Dan Mountains west of Bong Son. Shortly after midday, the battalion captured a North Vietnamese soldier who provided information on a large cave located in the area west of LZ Papa on the coastal plain. Acting on this information, the battalion dispatched Lieutenant Knox and Bravo Company to the area, and at 1445 hours they found the cave, which consisted of multiple chambers and was large enough to hold two companies of troops. After the demolition squad attached to the battalion from the 8th Engineer Battalion destroyed the cave, the battalion proceeded to move by helicopter to LZ Pony, where it assumed the brigade reserve role upon landing. It was on the ground at Pony by 2000 hours. Alpha Company, the first company to set down at Pony, immediately proceeded to move out of the LZ in the darkness into the Go Chai Mountains, 2 kilometers southeast of the LZ, to establish a suitable blocking position for the night.

Captain McMahon's plan for February 17 called for Bravo Company, 2/5th Cav, minus the 3rd Platoon, to move out of its night defensive position at first light and proceed down the slope on the right side of the ridge to the clearing, dig in, establish a perimeter defense around it, and prepare to defend it from all directions. The 3rd Platoon was to remain at the night defensive position on the southern slope until the empty water cans and extra mortar ammunition, which had been brought in the night before for added security, were loaded onto a supply helicopter for transport back to LZ Pony. It would then move down the left side of the ridge to the valley and sweep east to the clearing, where it would link up with the rest of Bravo Company.

At 0415 hours on February 17, all hell broke loose in the area southeast of LZ Pony in the Go Chai Mountains. Alpha Company, 2/12th Cav, in its blocking position 2 kilometers southeast of Pony, came under an intense ground attack, receiving small-arms, automatic weapons, and mortar fire from a large Viet Cong force estimated to be a reinforced platoon-sized unit. A three-man listening post from Alpha Company had been positioned along a creek bed several hundred meters south of the company's main perimeter when Viet Cong soldiers came down the creek toward them. The three troopers opened up on them with their M-16 rifles, resulting in several enemy KIA. The troopers, however, quickly realized that they had ambushed the lead element of a large enemy force and that they had to hightail it back through the jungle to Alpha Company's perimeter before the Viet Cong started chasing after them. The three troopers made it back to the perimeter with the Viet Cong hot on their trail. The enemy soldiers attacked Alpha Company's perimeter with numerous light machine guns and automatic weapons. Artillery fire from Pony and Duck was called in, and ground illumination was requested. The USAF responded with Smokey-the-Bear circling the battlefield and dropping flares to illuminate the ground and Puff-the-Magic-Dragon providing close-in air support with its 7.62mm mini-guns. Aerial rocket gunships from Bravo Battery, 2/20th ARA, were also called in to provide suppressive fire on the Viet Cong, allowing the Alpha Company troops to concentrate their firepower on two automatic weapons positions that were delivering devastating fire on their perimeter.

By 0700 hours, the Viet Cong had broken contact and withdrawn from the battlefield, leaving behind the bodies of 15 KIA by body count, another 17 estimated KIA based on blood trails and litter left on the battlefield, 17 WIA, and nine POW. The enemy WIA were so badly wounded that they were unable to flee and had been left for dead. The POWs were captured when the Alpha Company troops stormed their position and they were unable to escape-and-evade and were forced to surrender to the 2/12th Cav troopers. Also left behind on the battlefield were five AK-47 assault rifles, 35 SKS carbines, two RPD light machine guns, one BR40mm rocket launcher, 10 field packs, 38 grenades, and several thousand rounds of small-arms ammunition. In the attack, Alpha Company suffered one KIA. A member of the Mortar Platoon received a gunshot wound to the head while delivering mortar fire on the attacking enemy soldiers and died outright. Alpha Company also suffered four WIA.

While Alpha Company, 2/12th Cav, was battling the Viet Cong 2 kilometers southeast of Pony in the Go Chai Mountains, Alpha and Bravo companies, 1/5th Cav, were moving out of Coil down the eastern slope attacking west toward the blocking positions established by the 2/5th Cav at LZs Mike and Pete. The movement of the two companies followed an artillery barrage that pounded the area between Objectives Coil and Recoil, expending 431 105mm rounds. The companies moved on separate axes toward the two positions, but before they had gone far they were engulfed by enemy fire from the southern slope, being so heavily engaged that they could not advance or maneuver. It was estimated that the companies had encountered a multiple-company-sized force from the heavy weapons battalion of the 2nd Viet Cong Regiment.

Meanwhile, Captain McMahon and Bravo Company, 2/5th Cav, had moved out of their night defensive position on the southern slope at daybreak and had reached the valley. The company, however, was badly fragmented, the platoons having apparently reached different clearings. The 2nd Platoon had arrived at a clearing at the western end of the valley with a single rice paddy in it and a stream running alongside. The clearing was surrounded by thick jungle vegetation and was only large enough to accommodate a single helicopter at a time. The 1st Platoon, Command Group, and Mortar Platoon, meanwhile, had also reached a clearing in the valley, but it was not at the western end of the valley and was larger than a single rice paddy. It was scarred with four or five large bomb craters from recent B-52 strikes, each approximately 30 feet in diameter. Two of the craters were partially filled with water from recent rains. The clearing was large enough to accommodate four or more helicopters, enough to land an entire infantry platoon at a time. It backed up to thick jungle vegetation on its western side and faced a number of abandoned rice paddies on its eastern side. The 3rd Platoon was still at Bravo Company's night defensive position on the southern slope, loading empty water cans and extra mortar ammunition onto a supply helicopter to be lifted out.

The two clearings on the valley floor were separated by a kilometer of thick jungle vegetation, through which the Song Bien stream flowed. Once Captain McMahon discovered this, he decided to establish the company's blocking position in the larger clearing to the east, since the surrounding terrain was more conducive to defense and it was large enough to support a landing zone for the brigade reserve, if committed. He designated the larger clearing LZ Pete. The platoon leaders of the 2nd and 3rd platoons were directed to move their units to the larger clearing and dig in, while the Mortar Platoon was instructed to set up its mortar tubes in one or more of the dry bomb craters on the western side of the clearing. The bomb craters would serve as ready-made mortar pits.

No sooner had Captain McMahon issued the order to his platoon leaders to consolidate in the larger clearing than Bravo Company came under enemy fire. At 0915 hours, several Viet Cong soldiers opened up on the company with a machine gun and numerous automatic rifles from the southeast edge of the clearing. Thinking that the company was facing only a handful of enemy soldiers, McMahon directed Lieutenant Charles Clark and his 1st Platoon to move forward and attack and destroy the enemy force. With that, Clark and the 1st Platoon moved out, firing their rifles from the shoulder as they advanced. The advance, however, began to stall almost immediately due to enemy fire that was now being directed at the platoon from the slope to the southeast of the clearing. With that, McMahon ordered Lieutenant Keith Sherman and his 2nd Platoon, which was just getting to LZ Pete from the smaller clearing to the west, to move up on the right of the 1st Platoon and attack the enemy soldiers on the slope who were firing down on the 1st Platoon. He also attached the artillery forward observer assigned to Bravo Company, and his radio operator, to the 2nd Platoon so the artillery fire could be adjusted from the high ground and targeted close to the attacking platoon. The Mortar Platoon had by this time finished setting up its mortar tubes in one of the craters on the western side of the clearing, and under the direction of McMahon began delivering high-explosive rounds on the enemy position on the slope ahead of the attacking 2nd Platoon.

Upon hearing the gunfire in the valley, Lieutenant Donald O'Keefe, platoon leader of the 3rd Platoon, radioed McMahon for orders and was directed to move his unit directly to the area of the firefight and establish security to the west.

By 1000 hours, Lieutenant Sherman and the 2nd Platoon had succeeded in attacking up the southern slope and destroying the ground-level machine-gun bunkers from which the automatic weapons fire directed at the 1st Platoon had been coming. This came at the cost of one friendly KIA and several WIA. The artillery forward observer attached to the 2nd Platoon was hit in the chest with small-arms fire and died before he could be pulled off the slope and evacuated to the 15th Med aid station at the Special Forces camp. The 1st Platoon remained at the southeastern edge of the clearing, providing support for the 2nd Platoon. The platoon sergeant of the 1st Platoon was reporting that Lieutenant Clark had been hit with multiple gunshot wounds to the stomach, while several other troopers in the platoon had also been wounded. He also reported that the platoon was running low on ammunition. With that, Captain McMahon directed Lieutenant Charles H. Johnson, who had just rejoined the company after being in hospital with malaria, to go forward, take command of the 1st Platoon, and pull back the unit to the vicinity of the craters on the western side of the clearing under the cover of the 2nd Platoon. Johnson, along with volunteers from the Mortar Platoon, who by this time had fired all 18 of their mortar rounds in support of the 2nd Platoon, moved out across the rice paddies to the 1st Platoon's position at the southeastern edge of the clearing. At about 1030 hours, Johnson reported that they had carried all of the wounded, and the body of the artillery forward observer, back to the vicinity of the bomb craters. Ponchos had been used to carry the wounded troopers who could not walk and the body of the KIA, requiring four men per poncho. At the direction of Lieutenant Johnson, the platoon sergeant and a squad of men who were well dug in at the southeastern edge of the clearing were directed to remain there and provide covering fire for the 2nd Platoon as it withdrew off the slope.

By this time, the craters were filling up with wounded troopers and medics who were changing bandages and administering morphine. The craters provided protection from the enemy fire, but several of them were partially filled with water from the previous night's rain, and the wounded troopers in them had to be continuously checked to make sure they didn't slide down the side of the crater below the water level and drown.

At about 1045 hours, a platoon of Viet Cong soldiers came charging out of the jungle on the western side of the clearing, firing their AK-47 assault rifles and attacking the three-man demolition team from Bravo Company, 8th Engineering Battalion, which was attached to the 2/5th Cav, and the remaining members of the Mortar Platoon who were securing the position. The troopers aggressively returned fire with their M-16 rifles and M-79 grenade launchers, delivering deadly fire at the advancing enemy, halting the attack and forcing them to retreat back into the jungle. One of the engineers from the demolition team, however, was hit in the head with small-arms fire and died. When the enemy soldiers again charged out of the jungle to attack Bravo Company, the troopers put out another wall of fire at the advancing Viet Cong. A squad leader with the Mortar Platoon charged the enemy, firing his M-16 rifle while also throwing grenades at them. He stormed a machine-gun position that the Viet Cong were setting up and wiped out the three-man crew, as well as two other Viet Cong soldiers, and captured the machine gun. While attempting to maneuver back to the bomb crater for cover, he was struck down by enemy fire and died instantly. For his actions, he was posthumously awarded the Distinguished Service Cross for extraordinary heroism, the nation's second highest military award for heroism in combat.

Timed to coincide with the attack on the western side of the clearing, an enemy mortar concealed on the mountaintop to the northeast of LZ Pete opened up on the Bravo Company troops in the clearing, while another mortar on the mountaintop to the southeast of the clearing began firing on the 2nd Platoon as it withdrew off the slope. Meanwhile, intense automatic and small-arms enemy fire was being directed at the inside slopes of the bomb craters from Viet Cong soldiers on the southern slope.

While the tempo of the attack on Bravo Company was accelerating, Lieutenant O'Keefe and the 3rd Platoon were just reaching the clearing at the western end of the valley floor. Numerous Viet Cong soldiers were moving across the clearing into the jungle to the east that separated it from LZ Pete. Members of the 3rd Platoon immediately opened up on them, firing their M-16 rifles from the shoulder as they advanced. During the resulting firefight, several troopers in the 3rd Platoon were killed by enemy fire and several more were wounded, including O'Keefe, who was hit in the hand with multiple rounds of small-arms fire that almost severed his hand at the wrist. At that point, Captain McMahon directed the company's executive officer, Lieutenant Rufus Stephens, who was traveling with the 3rd Platoon, to take command of the platoon and keep it in the middle of the rice paddy, where the scouts in the observation helicopters and fixed-wing aircraft could more easily identify them. McMahon also radioed Lieutenant Sherman and directed him and his 2nd Platoon to pull back to the edge of the clearing under the cover of the 1st Platoon so that smoke grenades could be used to identify Bravo Company's friendly lines. He also directed his RTO to contact Lieutenant Colonel Meyer to request an airstrike on the southern slope, from where the mortar fire directed at the 2nd Platoon was coming, and on the mountaintop to the north of LZ Pete, source of the mortar fire being directed at the Bravo Company troops in LZ Pete.

Shortly afterwards, a USAF FAC in an O-1 Bird Dog aircraft and two Skyraiders arrived on station. Working with McMahon's RTO, the FAC was able to pinpoint the location on the southern slope from where the enemy mortar fire was coming, and also the source on the mountaintop to the north of LZ Pete of the other enemy mortar fire. Under the direction of the FAC, the Skyraiders dropped a variety of ordnance on the southern slope and on the mountaintop to the north, including high-explosive and white phosphorus bombs and napalm, to silence the mortars and enemy fire. The Skyraiders dropped some of their bombs so close to the Bravo Company troopers at the southeastern edge of the clearing that several of the troopers had to throw themselves into the mud in the rice paddy to douse their fatigue shirts which had caught fire from the WP bombs.

Captain McMahon remembered:

> By 1100 hours, the company was running extremely low on ammunition, and it appeared that half of the company was a casualty in some form. The company commander anticipated that the Viet Cong might try a mass assault so he ordered the company to move the wounded in the craters up to the edge of the craters, fix bayonets, and prepare for an assault.

While the troops of Bravo Company were preparing for an assault on their position by the Viet Cong, enemy soldiers had moved into the jungle on the southern slope above the clearings and were throwing grenades down at the elements of Bravo Company in the two clearings. Captain McMahon directed Lieutenant Sherman to send a fire team from his 2nd Platoon up the southern slope to attack and destroy the enemy soldiers.

At about this time, Lieutenant Colonel Meyer committed the remaining elements of his battalion to the battle. Captain Thomas Fincher and Alpha Company were directed to move from LZ Mike to the southwest and work their way down the southern slope to the valley and link up with Bravo Company in LZ Pete. Lieutenant George Long and Charlie Company were alerted to move by helicopter from LZ Mike to a ridge northeast of LZ Pete, then move down the northern slope parallel to the Song Bien stream toward Pete and link up with Bravo Company. Delta Company was to remain on the hill immediately north of LZ Mike, with its mortar platoon firing high-explosive rounds at the Viet Cong on the southern slope above Pete.

Shortly afterwards, a resupply helicopter from the 227th Assault Helicopter Battalion, flown by volunteer pilots, flew down the center of the valley on an east–west approach. Upon reaching LZ Pete, where the troops of Bravo Company were located, the pilot flared the helicopter only long enough to reduce its vertical and horizontal speed so the crew members onboard could push out crates of ammunition, medical supplies, food, and water into the clearing below. Several minutes later, a second resupply helicopter from the 227th, again piloted by volunteers, delivered ammunition and supplies to the 3rd Platoon troopers in the small clearing west of LZ Pete.

Captain McMahon recounted:

> Some of the crates of ammunition were spread out across the clearing but most of them landed in the craters. The helicopter was hit with more than one hundred rounds of automatic weapons fire from the Viet Cong, but miraculously it continued to fly and made it out of the valley and back to LZ English safely without any of its crew members being wounded. With the arrival of the supplies, the morale of the troops shot up 150 percent. Troops dashed out into the clearings to pull back the wounded who had been lying still in the middle of the rice paddies all morning so as not to attract the attention of the enemy soldiers on the slopes.

Captain Fincher and Alpha Company had moved out of LZ Mike and started to work their way down the southern slope toward LZ Pete, but before they had gone very far they came upon a Viet Cong main camp where they surprised a number of enemy soldiers who had returned to the camp to get heavy weapons to use against the Bravo Company troops in LZ Pete. The Alpha Company troops quickly dispatched the enemy soldiers before they were able to flee back into the jungle. The camp, which was being used by the Viet Cong as an ammunition camp, contained numerous recoilless rifles, a number of mortar rounds, communications equipment, and documents. The weapons and ammunition were destroyed in place by the Alpha Company troops and the company resumed its movement toward LZ Pete to link-up with Bravo Company.

Lieutenant Long and Charlie Company had moved by helicopter to the mountaintop northeast of LZ Pete, but had stalled in their attempt to move down the northern slope toward LZ Pete. Upon landing, the Charlie Company troops came under small-arms fire from what appeared to be a small enemy force. A brief yet intense firefight resulted before the Charlie Company troops were able to maneuver and overrun the Viet Cong position. The firefight resulted in multiple enemy KIA. Shortly afterwards, the Charlie Company troops started to receive automatic weapons and small-arms fire from an enemy force of unknown size on the high ground to the east. Helicopter gunships from Bravo Troop, 1/9th Cav, and aerial rocket gunships from Bravo Battery, 2/20th ARA, were called in to provide suppressive fire on the enemy position, allowing the Charlie Company troops to advance against it. Apparently, the landing of Charlie Company on the mountaintop had caught the Viet Cong soldiers off-guard and they were unprepared to launch a coordinated attack against the Americans when they first landed.

Meanwhile, Bravo Company at LZ Pete continued to defend the clearing. It was surrounded by the enemy, but was fighting back aggressively. When the Viet Cong directed automatic weapons and small-arms fire at the Bravo Company troops, the company responded by returning an even heavier volume of fire. The enemy attempted to probe the perimeter on the southeastern side, whereupon tactical airstrikes were called in and Skyraiders saturated the side of the clearing with 20mm cannon fire and high-explosive and WP bombs.

As the battle progressed, the regimental commander of the Viet Cong regiment, who was located somewhere in the valley, became so excited by the progress his troops were having against the Americans that he broke code and started giving orders to his subordinate commanders in clear Vietnamese on how to annihilate the Americans. The 1st Cav's military intelligence unit at LZ Bird, the 191st Military Intelligence Detachment, had been monitoring the Viet Cong's radio transmissions since the battle began earlier that day. The 13th Signal Battalion's communications VAN had been orbiting the battlefield and intercepting the Viet Cong's radio messages and forwarding them to Bird for decoding and interpretation by Vietnamese interpreters working there with the 1st Cav's military intelligence unit. However, the volume of communications activity in the valley by both the 1st Cav units and the Viet Cong made it virtually impossible to pinpoint the location of the commander of the Viet Cong regiment.

At about 1400 hours, Captain McMahon radioed the battalion operations officer at LZ Pony to report that the company was again running low on ammunition and that it needed to be resupplied. Shortly afterwards, two helicopters from the 227th Assault Helicopter Battalion arrived, using an east–west route into LZ Pete and the clearing to the west of Pete, where crew members onboard the helicopter pushed out ammunition and medical supplies to the Bravo Company troops on the ground. The helicopters were once again riddled with automatic weapons fire from the Viet Cong on the southern slope, and one crew member was hit with enemy small arms fire and badly wounded. The helicopters were able to continue flying and made it back to LZ English, where the wounded crew member was transported to the 15th Med aid station for treatment.

Shortly after Bravo Company was resupplied, Colonel Lynch attached Bravo Company, 2/12th Cav, to the 2/5th Cav, and alerted Lieutenant Knox and Bravo Company to move by helicopter from LZ Pony to the Song Bien Valley to reinforce Bravo Company, 2/5th Cav. At 1530 hours, the lead elements of Bravo Company, 2/12th Cav, lifted off from Pony for the flight to the Song Bien Valley, where Bravo Company, 2/5th Cav, was fighting for its life. As the helicopters approached the small clearing to the west of LZ Pete, the Viet Cong on the southern slope opened up on them with everything they had: recoilless rifles, machine guns, mortars, and small arms fire. The troopers of Bravo Company, 2/12th Cav, were able to jump out of the helicopters to the ground before they touched down, and the crew members pushed out the crates of ammunition that the 2/12th Cav had brought with them. The helicopters were riddled with bullets from enemy fire, but they kept flying, returning to pick up the remaining troops at Pony and transporting them to Pete. By 1700 hours, all of the troops of Bravo Company, 2/12th Cav, had landed at the small clearing west of LZ Pete. By 1730 hours, its lead elements had moved through the jungle area separating the clearing from LZ Pete and had linked up with Captain McMahon and Bravo Company, 2/5th Cav.

Rudy Jaramillo remembered:

> We were humping the jungle mountains south of LZ Pony in search of the Viet Cong unit that had attacked Alpha Company earlier that day when Lieutenant Knox told us that we had to return to Pony for transport to the Song Bien Valley to reinforce Bravo Company, 2/5th Cav. He said that Bravo Company, 2/5th Cav had encountered the regimental headquarters of a Viet Cong regiment and had been in contact with it all day. The Song Bien Valley was located about eight kilometers south of Pony so our helicopter flight was going to be quick.
>
> By the time we got back to Pony and loaded onto the helicopters, darkness was approaching. As we flew south over the mountains toward the Song Bien Valley, we could see the bright illumination straight ahead from flares being dropped by Smoky-the-Bear where Bravo Company, 2/5th Cav was in contact.
>
> Our helicopter approached the valley from the west. We could see the troops of Bravo Company, 2/5th Cav and those of Bravo Company, 2/12th Cav who had landed ahead of us in the clearing. Some of the troopers were engaged in hand-to-hand combat with Viet Cong soldiers on the southern side of the clearing. One trooper had wrestled an enemy soldier to the ground next to a creek that ran alongside the clearing and was attempting to force him into the creek to finish him off. As our helicopter flared to reduce its vertical and horizontal speed, we could hear the enemy bullets hitting the side of the helicopter. The door gunner on my side of the helicopter was hit with multiple enemy rounds and was bleeding badly. The pilot on my side was also hit with enemy fire and was also bleeding badly. The pilot on the left side of the helicopter could barely maintain control of the aircraft as he lowered it into the clearing. It was shaking violently, back-and-forth, and we slid out the door along with the crates of ammunition we had brought with us to the ground below before the helicopter had set down. The drop was about 10 feet, maybe a little more. We didn't know if the helicopter was going to come crashing down on us or not, but the pilot was able to hold on and fly the helicopter out of the clearing and out of the valley. I do not remember anyone getting hurt on the landing, but I remember that the guys already in the clearing were very happy to see us.[2]

---

[2] In an email to the author, Rudy Jaramillo described Bravo Company, 2nd Battalion, 12th Cav, moving from the area south of LZ Pony in the Go Chai Mountains to the Song Bien Valley in the extreme southeast corner of the Kim Son Valley to reinforce Bravo Company, 2/5th Cav. Bravo, 2/5th Cav, had been in contact with a heavy weapons battalion guarding the regimental headquarters of the 2nd Viet Cong regiment. Email from Rudy Jaramillo, dated July 9, 2021.

With Bravo Company, 2/12th Cav, on the ground and having linked up with Bravo Company, 2/5th Cav, in LZ Pete, the troops of the two Bravo companies set about to secure the area.

By 1635 hours, Charlie Company, 2/5th Cav, with the support of helicopter gunships from the 1/9th Cav, had overrun the enemy position on the high ground to the northeast of Pete. The Viet Cong soldiers broke contact and fled to the east, with the helicopter gunships chasing after them. Charlie Company reported 50 dead enemy on the battlefield. The unit then proceeded to move down the northern slope toward LZ Pete, where it encountered commo (communication) wire strung alongside the trail all the way down to the valley, which most likely indicated that a command group of some type had been positioned on the mountaintop and was directing the attacks against the Bravo Company troops in Pete using the commo wire for communications.

There was no additional enemy contact reported by Charlie Company as it moved down the northern slope until it reached the Song Bien stream in the valley and attempted to cross it and move southwest toward Pete. The Charlie Company troops then came under intense machine-gun fire from a position that had been set up on the northern slope at the base of a very steep hill to deliver fire on Pete. Charlie Company immediately started to take casualties and Lieutenant Long directed Lieutenant Jim Mullen and his platoon to attack and destroy the machine-gun position. The platoon members climbed the hill, slipping and sliding the whole way using rocks and vines to pull themselves up, and attacked and destroyed the machine gun and its crew. Charlie Company then moved along the Song Bien stream to Pete, where it joined the rest of the battalion, carrying its wounded and dead in ponchos. It suffered three KIA and multiple WIA in action that day.[3]

A member of Charlie Company recalled:

> We crawled up a steep hill just before we got to LZ Pete trying to take out a machine gun that had opened up on us as we attempted to cross the Song Bien Stream. We slipped as we climbed up the hill where we attacked and knocked-out the machine gun. One of the medics took a round to the shoulder trying to protect two troopers who had been hit with enemy fire.

By 1800 hours, the two Bravo companies in LZ Pete had halted the attack and the enemy broke contact and fled the battlefield. A sweep of the immediate area around the LZ turned up 54 Viet Cong KIA by body count, another estimated 100 KIA based on blood trails and litter left behind on the battlefield, and a number of Viet Cong WIA who were too badly wounded to flee and were left for dead on the battlefield.

---

[3] The document "Unit History, Charlie Company, 2/5th Cav, February 17, 1966" provided a description of Charlie Company, 2/5th Cav, moving down the northern slope of the Song Bien Valley to reinforce Bravo Company, 2/5th Cav, at LZ Pete. http://www.tallcomanche.org/February_1966.

A sweep of the slope southeast of LZ Pete revealed an additional 73 Viet Cong KIA, taking the total confirmed enemy dead to 127. Many of the bodies on the southern slope were severely burned from the airstrikes, many beyond recognition, indicating that the strikes had their desired effect. Equipment consisting of one 75mm recoilless rifle, four 57mm recoilless rifles with 10 rounds of ammunition, three 81mm mortar tubes, and 75 81mm mortar rounds was also found on the southern slope. Based on the type and quantities of equipment found, the volume of automatic weapons fire directed at the 2/5th Cav, the network of bunkers, the communications wire located in the area, and the number of telephones found on the trails, it was concluded that the 2/5th Cav had attacked and destroyed a heavy weapons company of the Heavy Weapons Battalion of the 2nd Viet Cong Regiment and the regiment's signal company.

By 1900 hours, the remaining elements of the 2/5th Cav had closed into LZ Pete and linked up with the two Bravo companies, and the battalion prepared to spend the night there. A resupply helicopter from the 227th Assault Helicopter Battalion, with helicopter gunship escorts from the 227th Battalion's Delta Company, brought in crates of ammunition, mortar rounds, medical supplies, food and water, and extra equipment including PRC-25 radios and batteries. The ammunition was distributed among the troops, while mortar tubes were set up in the craters on the western side of the LZ and mortar fire was registered all around the perimeter.

Chinook helicopters were brought in to evacuate the 55 wounded troopers of Bravo Company, 2/5th Cav, and the wounded troopers from the rest of the battalion. They were transported to the 15th Med aid station at the Special Forces camp for treatment. Another Chinook helicopter picked up the bodies of the friendly KIA and transported them to Graves Registration at LZ English. There were 13 in total, 10 from the 2/5th Cav, and one each from Bravo Battery, 1/77th Artillery, Bravo Company, 2/12th Cav, and Bravo Company, 8th Engineers. The bodies were transported to Graves Registration at LZ English.

Several kilometers east of LZ Pete, little had changed for the troops of Alpha and Bravo companies, 1/5th Cav. Their attacks west on separate axes toward blocking positions at LZs Pete and Mike earlier in the day had stalled, and they had been unable to advance or maneuver. They had encountered a large Viet Cong force on the southern slope less than a kilometer west of Objective Coil and were able to do little more than exchange small-arms fire with enemy snipers. The force was estimated to be a heavy weapons company from the Heavy Weapons Battalion of the 2nd Viet Cong Regiment. It was only under the cover of darkness that the two companies were able to pull back off the slope a safe distance and establish a night defensive position in the valley, where resupply helicopters brought in ammunition, medical supplies, and food and water. The wounded troopers were loaded onto the helicopters for evacuation to the 15th Med aid station at the Special Forces camp. The two companies spent the night in the valley 1 kilometer downslope from Coil and 5 kilometers east of LZ Pete.

The troops in both battalions were put on 100 percent alert for the night and were told to expect an attack. The M-60 machine gunners were given strict instructions not to fire unless ordered to do so, so as not to give away their positions. They could fire back at the enemy with their M-16 rifles and M-79 grenade launchers, and 45-caliber pistols, but the M-60 machine guns would be a dead giveaway of their location. The artillery batteries at Coil, LZ Bird, and Phu Xuan fired 105mm and 155mm rounds into the valley during the night along the Song Bien stream, on the trails leading into and out of the valley, on other avenues of escape from the area, and on the southern slope. Smokey-the-Bear provided illumination over the valley by dropping flares to further reduce enemy movement during the night, and Puff-the-Magic-Dragon provided suppressive fire along the perimeters of the two battalions with its 7.62mm mini-guns to discourage probes by the enemy.

The 2/12th Cav, minus Bravo Company, spent the night at LZ Pony securing the LZ as an artillery position for the 155mm howitzers, and as the 2nd Brigade's command post and forward operating base.

DEATH IN A NARROW PLACE • 141

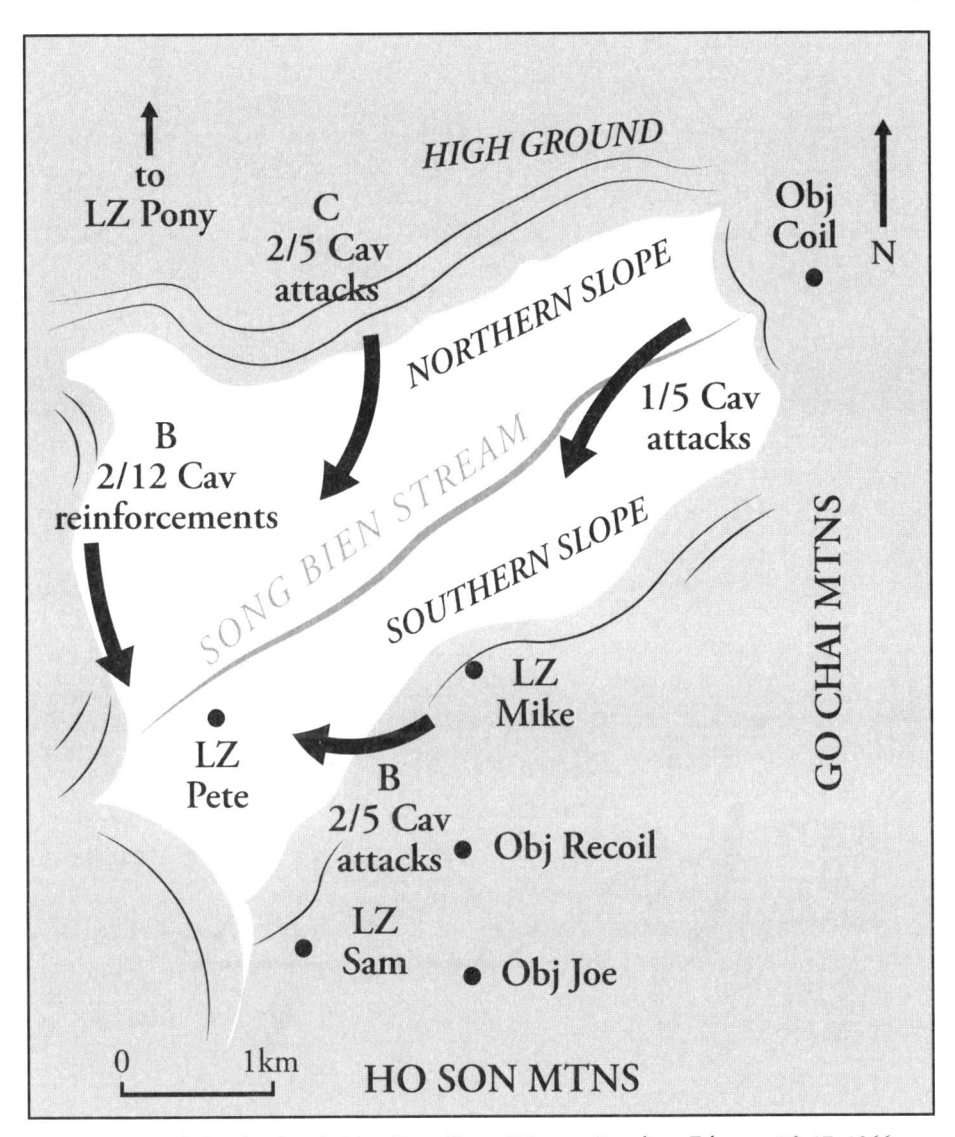

Map 10. 5th Cavalry Attacks Viet Cong Heavy Weapons Battalion, February 16–17, 1966

142 • THE BATTLE OF BONG SON

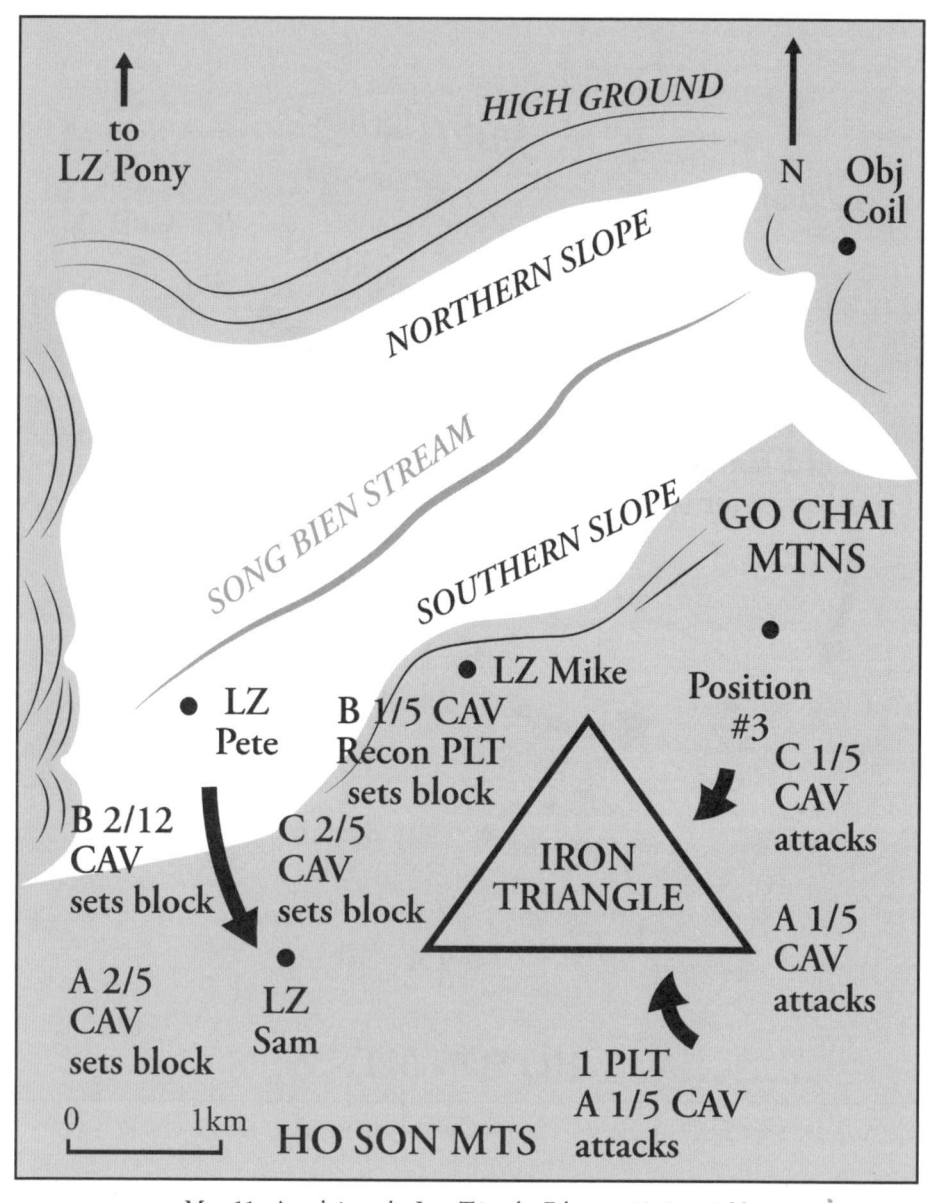

Map 11. Attack into the Iron Triangle, February 18–21, 1966

CHAPTER ELEVEN

The Iron Triangle

On the night of February 17, the troops of the 2nd Battalion, 5th Cavalry, spent a long and uneasy night at LZ Pete in the Song Bien Valley. Sniper fire was received throughout the night from enemy soldiers on the southern slope, and the troops were forced to fight off probes along the north, east, and south sides of the LZ. Artillery fire from LZ Bird and Phu Xuan was called in on the snipers, and when the enemy soldiers probed the perimeter in an attempt to determine if it was manned, Puff-the-Magic-Dragon raked the area with its 7.62mm mini-guns, allowing the troops to stay hidden in the darkness. Smokey-the-Bear remained on station throughout the night, dropping flares over the suspected enemy areas to expose the enemy positions and reduce enemy movement.

Shortly after daybreak on February 18, the fog started to lift and resupply helicopters from the 227th Assault Helicopter Battalion brought in ammunition, medical supplies, and food and water. With that, Lieutenant Colonel Meyer ordered his company commanders to send out clearing patrols in the areas around LZ Pete and the small clearing to the west of Pete. The areas were littered with the bodies of dead Viet Cong soldiers from the previous day's fighting, so it was not possible to determine if additional KIA were added during the night by Puff-the-Magic-Dragon or tube artillery.

The troops of the 2/5th Cav—and those of Bravo Company, 2nd Battalion, 12th Cavalry, which was still attached to Bravo Company, 2/5th Cav—spent the morning sweeping the areas around LZ Pete to locate and destroy enemy bunkers, trenches, and tunneling. Enemy contact was sporadic and light, but at one point, the 2nd Platoon of Bravo Company, 2/12th Cav, came upon a bunker on the southern slope that had enemy soldiers in it. A member of the lead squad walking point for the platoon was shot in the chest right in front of the bunker as he approached it. The other members of the squad attacked the bunker with small-arms fire and grenades, but the enemy soldiers were able to flee and disappear. They likely escaped via a tunnel that connected the bunker to others on the southern slope, permitting them to move freely within a large area. Aerial rocket gunships from the 2/20th ARA attempted to find the fleeing soldiers, but were unable to do so. The wounded trooper died from the loss of blood before he could be carried down the slope and transported by helicopter to the 15th Med aid station at the Special Forces camp.

In the sweep, the troops located and destroyed 2 tons of rice, five anti-tank mines, two M-14 mines, a large quantity of small-arms ammunition, one 82mm mortar with a bipod, four 82mm mortar rounds, a rocket launcher, and two containers of ammunition. After completing the sweep of the areas around LZ Pete, Lieutenant Colonel Meyer directed the companies of the 2/5th Cav to move up the southern slope to the high ground and establish company-sized blocking positions east and west of LZ Mike and south of the area to interdict the expected exfiltration of enemy soldiers from the valley as the 1/5th Cav worked its way down the valley.

The troops of the 1st Battalion, 5th Cavalry, also spent a long and uneasy night in the Song Bien Valley, 5 kilometers east of LZ Pete and 1 kilometer downslope from Coil. They also received sniper fire throughout the night from the Viet Cong and were forced to fight off enemy probes.

At daybreak on February 18, Lieutenant Colonel Ackerson directed the commanders of Alpha and Bravo companies, 1/5th Cav, to resume their attacks in the direction of LZs Pete and Mike. The two companies moved out of their night defensive position in a wide-front formation, Bravo Company on the left and Alpha Company on the right, supported by reconnaissance helicopters with helicopter gunship escorts from the 1st Squadron, 9th Cavalry, along with aerial rocket gunships from the 2/20th ARA. The companies encountered only sporadic fire from small groups of enemy soldiers as they moved along the Song Bien stream in a southwesterly direction. At one point, they came across the bodies of eight Viet Cong soldiers, and also found a rocket launcher and two metal containers of small-arms ammunition. The enemy soldiers were likely killed by artillery fire during the night.

At 0845 hours, Alpha Company located commo wire strung out along a north–south trail that crossed the stream, as well as two freshly dug graves with bodies in them. In one of the graves was a body dressed in a khaki uniform. The troopers were unable to determine if it was a Viet Cong main force soldier or a North Vietnamese regular. Whatever the case, the dead soldier was surely a member of the 2nd Viet Cong Regiment, which was known to consist of both Viet Cong main force soldiers and NVA regulars. In the other grave was a body dressed in typical jungle attire of black pajamas and sandals. The two were likely killed by Puff-the-Magic-Dragon with its 7.62mm mini-guns as they attempted to flee the area, being hastily buried by their fellow Viet Cong soldiers.

Shortly after coming upon the graves, the troops of Alpha Company encountered two Viet Cong soldiers to their front moving toward them. The enemy soldiers were dressed in black pajamas and were wearing scandals. The Alpha Company troops opened fire, killing one of them. The other enemy soldier managed to scatter to the southwest along the banks of the stream before the troops could engage him. The dead soldier was carrying a 9mm pistol, indicating that he was likely a high-ranking officer. They searched his body but didn't find any documents or maps on him that might be of value.

Midway down the valley, Bravo Company veered off to the south and started to move up the southern slope toward LZ Mike on the high ground, while Alpha Company continued its advance along the stream toward LZ Pete at the western end of the valley. As Bravo Company moved, it started to receive moderate enemy fire from the high ground. By 1200 hours, the 3rd Platoon of Bravo Company had reached the area southwest of LZ Mike, where it encountered an estimated company-sized unit. It was receiving automatic weapons and mortar fire from well-positioned bunkers and ground-level emplacements and was unable to maneuver. The 2nd Platoon of Alpha Company, which had been moving forward along the stream in close proximity to Bravo Company, was directed to move up the slope to the 3rd Platoon's location to help relieve the pressure on it. However, it too became heavily engaged as it moved and started to take casualties, and because of the intense enemy fire being directed at it, was forced to leave the casualties where they fell.

At 1455 hours, Lieutenant Colonel Ackerson requested the first airstrike of the day and the USAF responded with a FAC and eight Skyraiders. Working with the artillery forward observer assigned to Bravo Company, the FAC was able to pinpoint the location of the enemy soldiers on the southern slope and direct the Skyraiders to attack their position. The Skyraiders attacked in pairs, making multiple west–east runs along the ridge southwest of LZ Mike, from where the enemy fire was coming. The airstrike was followed by tube artillery from LZ Bird and Phu Xuan. The airstrike and artillery, however, failed to penetrate the enemy's defenses and appeared to be ineffective, and the 2nd Platoon's advance stalled. Meanwhile, the wounded troopers who had been unable to keep up with the platoon as it attempted to advance on the enemy position were forced to remain behind until reinforcements arrived to help them. They had to lie still in the jungle underbrush so as not to attract the attention of enemy snipers who might be in the trees searching for them.

At 1530 hours, the 2nd and 3rd platoons were still pinned down and unable to maneuver. Ackerson directed the remaining platoons of Alpha and Bravo companies to move up the slope to reinforce the two platoons, but they too became heavily engaged with the enemy as they moved and were unable to reach the high ground. It was only when darkness set in that the remaining platoons of Alpha and Bravo companies were able to maneuver onto the high ground to where the two pinned-down platoons were located. They reached the platoons at roughly 1737 hours and started to retrieve the wounded from under the enemy guns and pull them back a safe distance. Many of the wounded had been lying in the jungle underbrush all afternoon, with firing going on all around them, as the platoons of Alpha and Bravo companies made multiple attempts to advance up the slope on the enemy positions.

The troops of Alpha and Bravo companies were able to locate their wounded—six from Alpha Company and seven from Bravo Company—and pull them out of the contact area, but they were unable to bring out their dead. Darkness had set in, and with the enemy sniper fire that was being directed at them from upslope positions, they were forced to leave behind three KIA from Alpha Company and six from Bravo Company. Alpha Company withdrew to a position on the high ground east of the area of contact for the night. The position was designated Blocking Position 3. Bravo Company withdrew to LZ Mike. Resupply helicopters arrived and hovered over the two positions while the crew members pushed out crates of ammunition, medical supplies, stretchers, and food and water.

The wounded troopers had to be led down narrow jungle trails in the pitch dark to locations below the high ground where the helicopters could set down long enough for them to be loaded onboard for evacuation to the 15th Med aid station at the Special Forces camp. Many of the wounded were unable to walk and had to be carried on stretchers that the resupply helicopters brought in. Smokey-the-Bear circled over the valley and southern slope to provide illumination to reduce the risk of enemy soldiers moving into positions to ambush the troopers who were evacuating the wounded. By 2250 hours, all of the wounded requiring medical treatment had been loaded onto medevac helicopters and evacuated, and the 155mm artillery batteries at LZ Bird and Phu Xuan began their H&I fire into the contact area for the remainder of the night. From the volume of heavy automatic weapons fire received, and the disposition and elaborateness of the enemy defenses encountered, it was estimated that Alpha and Bravo companies had made contact with a heavy weapons battalion.

While the 1st and 2nd battalions, 5th Cav, were battling the Viet Cong in the Song Bien Valley, the 2nd Battalion, 12th Cavalry, was busy conducting hit-and-run raids in the vicinity of LZ Pony, 8 kilometers north of the Song Bien Valley, and LZ Duck, 13 kilometers north of the Song Bien Valley. The raids were intended to clear the areas of Viet Cong snipers who had been firing at aircraft. The raids netted one Viet Cong KIA, three Viet Cong suspects, and two weapons.

By the morning of February 19, Colonel Lynch knew that his brigade had stirred up a hornet's nest on the high ground above LZ Pete, and that he needed to move quickly to exploit the contact. He had the headquarters of the 2nd Viet Cong Regiment trapped, but the fighting was far from over. Consequently, he ordered a three-company block-and-sweep of the area. Lieutenant Knox and Bravo Company, 2/12th Cav, with Alpha Company, 2/5th Cav, attached, would conduct a sweep up the southern slope to a blocking position on the high ground 3 kilometers south of LZ Pete. The blocking position was designated LZ Sam. Lieutenant Long and Charlie Company, 2/5th Cav, would conduct a sweep up the southern slope in parallel to that of the 2/12th Cav. The line of movement would be roughly 2 kilometers west of the area where Alpha and Bravo companies, 1/5th Cav, battled the Viet Cong on the previous day.

In parallel to the three-company sweep up the southern slope, the 1/5th Cav's Reconnaissance Platoon would move by helicopter from Objective Coil to LZ Mike and link up with Bravo Company, 1/5th Cav. Charlie Company, 1/5th Cav, would move overland from Coil along the high ground to Blocking Position 3 and link up with Alpha Company, 1/5th Cav. The Reconnaissance Platoon and Bravo Company would set blocks to the north of the area to prevent enemy soldiers from escaping in that direction, and Alpha and Charlie companies would move into the area and attempt to reach the bodies of the nine KIA from the previous day's fighting and recover them. Due to the tenacity of the enemy, and to the disposition and elaborateness of its defenses, the troops nick named the area the "Iron Triangle," not to be confused with the Communist stronghold north of Saigon where the French battled the Viet Minh in the First Indochina War and South Vietnamese forces battled the Viet Cong in the postcolonial era.

At 0910 hours, Charlie Company, 2/5th Cav, made contact at the top of the southern slope with an enemy force estimated to be a platoon-sized unit. Bravo Company, 2/12th Cav—with Alpha Company, 2/5th Cav, attached—attempted to flank the enemy position, but it too encountered an enemy force that was estimated to be a platoon-sized unit. Based on this, Colonel Lynch directed the three companies to break contact with the enemy and pull back a sufficient distance to allow a tactical airstrike and tube artillery from LZ Bird to be employed. Two flights of Skyraiders dropped high-explosive and white phosphorus bombs, along with napalm, on the area and raked it with 20mm cannon fire. An artillery barrage followed on the heels of the airstrike. At the completion of the airstrike and barrage, the three companies maneuvered back onto the high ground and launched a coordinated attack against the Viet Cong positions. The enemy soldiers who were still alive had become disoriented and fled to the south in disarray. The action resulted in 36 Viet Cong KIA, with numerous rifles and miscellaneous equipment captured. In the encounter, Alpha Company suffered two KIA and Charlie Company also suffered two. The four bodies were recovered at the time and transported by helicopter to Graves Registration.

At 1500 hours, Alpha and Charlie companies, 1/5th Cav, had linked up in the vicinity of Blocking Position 3 and launched their attack into the Iron Triangle to the west, with Charlie Company leading. Roughly an hour into the attack, the two companies reported that they were receiving intense automatic weapons and mortar fire from well-prepared positions, and that the attack had stalled. They were receiving 50-caliber machine-gun fire from multiple positions on a nearby hill about 100–200 meters up from the base, and intense small-arms fire from positions along the base of the hill. The enemy was well dug in, with bunkers all around and a network of solid trenches. Enemy soldiers could be seen moving around in the trenches. It appeared that Alpha and Charlie companies had encountered a very large force, and they immediately started to take casualties.

The artillery forward observer assigned to Alpha Company from Bravo Battery, 1st Battalion, 77th Field Artillery, was hit in the chest with multiple metal fragments from enemy mortar rounds and died outright, leaving the company with no artillery support. Two members of a machine-gun crew with Charlie Company were also hit with enemy fire and killed, leaving the company with reduced automatic weapons support. Contact remained heavy and the wounded troopers were left where they fell.

At 1630 hours, Lieutenant Colonel Ackerson requested the second airstrike of the day and the USAF responded with a FAC and two Skyraiders. The Skyraiders made multiple west–east runs over the hill from which the 50-caliber machine-gun fire was being received and dropped high-explosive bombs, white phosphorus, and napalm, and raked the area with 20mm cannon fire. The airstrike was so close to Charlie Company's position that seven of its troopers were hit and wounded from the 20mm fire, several critically.

After the airstrike, Alpha and Charlie companies were still unable to maneuver and once again were only able to break contact with the enemy under the cover of darkness. The troops located and pulled back the 11 wounded and three KIA—the artillery forward observer assigned to Alpha Company and 2 troopers from Charlie Company—but were unable to recover the nine KIA from the previous day's fighting.

Alpha Company, minus its 1st Platoon, withdrew to Blocking Position 3 to the east of the contact area, while Charlie Company along with Alpha Company's 1st Platoon pulled back to a position south of the contact area. Shortly afterwards, a resupply helicopter arrived over Alpha Company's position and hovered above it long enough for the crew members to push out crates of ammunition, food, and water, but when a resupply helicopter approached Charlie Company's position from the west to deliver ammunition and supplies, and to pick up Charlie Company's wounded troops, it received small-arms fire from seemingly every direction and was forced to veer off to the south to avoid the fire. The 11 wounded troops would have to spend the night in the jungle, enduring the pain from their injuries, until they could be evacuated to the 15th Med aid station the next morning, if they survived that long. The 155mm artillery batteries at LZ Bird and Phu Xuan again resumed their H&I fire into the contact area once the helicopters had cleared the area.

At first light on February 20, a medevac helicopter from the 15th Med, accompanied by helicopter gunship escorts from Bravo Battery, 2/20th ARA, arrived at Charlie Company's position to evacuate the wounded troopers. Charlie Company now had just 10 WIA and three KIA—one of the wounded had died during the night. On its approach to Charlie Company's position, the medevac helicopter received automatic weapons fire from several directions, but the aerial rocket gunships from the 2/20th ARA quickly veered off in the directions of the enemy fire and raked the areas with their 2.75-inch rockets and silenced the gunfire. The medevac helicopter airlifted the wounded troopers to the 15th Med aid station in two separate flights. Shortly afterwards, a resupply helicopter arrived at Charlie Company's position and delivered crates of ammunition, medical supplies, and food and water, and picked up the bodies of the three KIA from the previous day's fighting for transport to Graves Registration.

At 0918 hours, following a 15-minute artillery prep with 155mm howitzer rounds from the batteries at LZs Pony and Duck, Charlie Company, along with Alpha Company's 1st Platoon, launched an attack into the Iron Triangle from the south. They attempted to reach the areas where the bodies of the nine dead troopers from the fighting on February 18 were located and retrieve them. The attack was supported by helicopter gunships from Bravo Troop, 1st Squadron, 9th Cav, and Bravo Battery, 2/20th ARA. Bravo Company remained in its blocking positions around LZ Mike to the north to prevent the enemy from escaping in that direction, and Alpha Company, minus its 1st Platoon, stayed at Blocking Position 3 to the east to prevent the enemy from withdrawing in that direction.

By 0939 hours, Alpha and Charlie companies made their way through the jungle and reached the base of the hill, where they encountered the enemy on the previous day. There was no enemy contact this time, and the two companies proceeded to sweep the hillside. They started to move up the slope toward the top of the hill when they came upon an estimated company-sized enemy force in trenches on the southeast side of the hill. The enemy had two 50-caliber and several M-60 machine guns. The two companies attacked the enemy from the hillside to the southeast and from the jungle area at the base of the hill to the northeast. At 1003 hours, Lieutenant Colonel Ackerson notified the company commanders of the two companies that he wanted to call in a tactical airstrike on the enemy position and that the two companies were to break contact with the enemy and pull back with their wounded a sufficient distance to allow the strike to be brought in.

Charlie Company reported no casualties in the brief encounter, but Alpha Company had suffered several WIA who required medical evacuation. However, there were no clearings in the area large enough for a helicopter to set down, so a demolition team had to be brought in to make one. Shortly afterwards, a Chinook helicopter with a squad of engineers onboard from Bravo Company, 8th Engineer Battalion, arrived over Alpha Company's position, and they rappelled down ropes to the ground carrying chainsaws and other tree-cutting equipment on their backs. By 1343 hours, an area large enough to allow the wounded troops to be hoisted up into a helicopter, one at a time, had been cleared. By 1423 hours, all of the wounded troops had been airlifted out of the area and transported to the 15th Med aid station at the Special Forces camp.

By 1510 hours, Charlie and Alpha companies had moved back to the area of engagement, with only sporadic contact with small enemy forces being encountered, and at the direction of Lieutenant Colonel Ackerson, Bravo Company moved south from its blocking positions around LZ Mike into the Iron Triangle and joined in the recovery of the nine KIA from the fighting on February 18. Alpha Company reported at 1559 hours that it had recovered the bodies of five of the KIA, and at 1704 hours, Bravo Company reported that it was within 25 meters of where the bodies of the remaining four were believed to be located. Bravo Company was in contact with what was estimated to be a small enemy force, but would be able to recover the bodies while maneuvering against it. By 1935 hours, the bodies of all nine KIA had been recovered and the three companies closed on positions to the north and east of the Iron Triangle. From there, the bodies were carried down jungle trails to waiting helicopters and loaded on board to be transported to Graves Registration. Once the helicopters had cleared the valley, the 155mm artillery batteries at LZ Bird and Phu Xuan resumed their H&I fire into the contact area.

While the companies of the 1/5th Cav were recovering the bodies of their dead from the Iron Triangle, the companies of the 2/5th Cav were conducting local patrols in the vicinity of LZ Pete in the valley below. There was only limited action, which included encountering a four-man Viet Cong rifle squad and one other Viet Cong in widely separated instances.

Alpha Company, 2/12th Cav, along with the battalion's Reconnaissance Platoon, had moved by helicopter to LZ Sam on the high ground west of the Iron Triangle and initiated local patrolling in that area. Initially, only light contact was experienced, but at 1050 hours, Alpha Company's command post at Sam began to receive sniper fire from an enemy force of unknown size. Shortly afterwards, the command post came under attack from an estimated Viet Cong company armed with an unusual number of automatic weapons, and Alpha Company's 1st Platoon, which was patrolling about 300 meters north of Sam, had to make a dash through the jungle to get back to Sam to help fight off the enemy. At 1900 hours, after three failed attempts to overrun the command post, the Viet Cong broke contact and fled the battlefield, leaving behind 23 dead in front of Alpha Company's position at Sam.

At 0650 hours on February 21, Colonel Lynch directed Lieutenant Colonel Ackerson to send a platoon back into the Iron Triangle to confirm that the enemy was still there. He did not want the platoon to become inextricably involved, but was looking for positive contact to be made with the enemy. He also wanted support to be ready to assist the platoon, if needed. On the past several nights, the 2/5th Cav at LZ Pete, and the 1/5th Cav at LZ Mike and Blocking Position 3, reported that enemy soldiers had been moving east–west past their night defensive positions at regular intervals throughout the night. Whenever the H&I artillery fire stopped, groups of three or four enemy soldiers would resume their movement past their positions. The two battalions had also reported that three-man listening posts positioned close to trails leading into and out of the area had been reporting the movement of enemy groups on the trails. Some of the groups were believed to have been as large as 15-strong. Vines with empty C-ration cans tied to them had been strung across other trails to detect movement, and they had been disturbed by the movement of enemy soldiers.

At 0746 hours, the 3rd Platoon of Charlie Company, 1/5th Cav, moved into the Iron Triangle from the south, and by 0815 hours it was reporting that it had reached the hill where it made contact on the previous afternoon. The 50-caliber machine guns were still there, but their crews apparently had not spotted them moving through the jungle toward the hill. The platoon, however, started receiving all kinds of fire from its right flank. It returned fire but was unable to continue moving forward due to the intensity of the fire directed at it. Lieutenant Colonel Ackerson ordered the platoon to disengage with the enemy and return to Charlie Company's perimeter to the south. The platoon successfully disengaged and pulled back to link up with the main body of Charlie Company at 0930 hours. It reported no causalities in the encounter.

Shortly afterwards, Colonel Lynch notified his battalion commanders that a B-52 strike had been requested and that the units of the 2nd Brigade were to withdraw from the Iron Triangle. Under the cover of artillery fire and tactical airstrikes, they were to move out of the area a distance of at least 1.5 kilometers. The companies in the valley and on the high ground to the north, east, and south of the Iron Triangle would move by helicopter to LZ Pony. The companies on the high ground to the west of the Iron Triangle were to move by foot to LZ Sam, 2.5 kilometers southwest of the Iron Triangle, or to Objective 22, 2 kilometers directly west of the Iron Triangle, and dig in. B-52s from Guam would be arriving mid-morning and in the early afternoon to drop deep-penetration bombs on the area in two separate airstrikes. The B-52 strikes would be followed by tactical airstrikes dropping hundreds of riot control agent CS gas grenades into the area.

Rudy Jaramillo recalled:

> Lieutenant Knox told us that we had to hike out of the Iron Triangle on short order because B-52s were on the way to attack it with deep penetration bombs and we had to move at least one-and-one-half kilometers to the west to be out of the strike zone. The area to the west of the Iron Triangle was covered with triple canopy jungle and was loaded with leeches and snakes, and wait-a-minute vines, and the going was slow. He told us that once we had gone a safe distance, we had to dig in and take cover to make sure that we didn't receive any backlash from the concussion of the bombs.[1]

At 1001 hours, the first flight of three B-52s arrived over the Iron Triangle and dropped their deep-penetration bombs, then a second flight of three B-52s arrived at 1607 hours and dropped more deep-penetration bombs on the area. Both of the

---

[1] In an email to the author, Rudy Jaramillo described the move of Bravo Company, 2nd Battalion, 12th Cavalry, from the area west of the Iron Triangle to an area a safe distance away in preparation for a B-52 strike on the Iron Triangle. Email from Rudy Jaramillo, dated July 9, 2021.

strikes were followed by tactical airstrikes that dropped hundreds of CS gas grenades into the area. At 1711 hours, a third tactical airstrike dropped more CS gas grenades. Colonel Lynch was airborne to observe the initial B-52 strike and witnessed the first bomb when it detonated. "That first explosion was right on the money, and the target coverage was fantastic," he stated.[2]

Following the airstrikes, the companies of the 1/5th Cav and 2/5th Cav returned by helicopter to the Iron Triangle. Bravo Company, 1/5th Cav, air assaulted into a clearing on the high ground to the east of the Iron Triangle in the vicinity of Blocking Position 3 after the area was prepped with artillery. The area was designated LZ Socker. Bravo Company secured the area for the rest of the battalion. By 1755 hours, the battalion had closed into Socker. In conjunction with the 1/5th Cav returning to the area, the 2/5th Cav air assaulted into LZ Pete in the valley, where it set up blocking positions. The 2/12th Cav, remained in the vicinity of LZ Sam and Objective 22 west of the Iron Triangle, where it too established blocking positions.

A new first in this operation was having the troops wear gas masks on air assaults into areas where riot control agent grenades had been dropped; this included the pilots and helicopter crew members.

Immediately after the 1/5th Cav was established at LZ Socker, Alpha and Charlie companies attacked west in the direction of the Iron Triangle, while Bravo Company set up blocking positions around LZ Socker and the battalion's Recon Platoon seized and secured Blocking Position 3. By dark, Alpha and Charlie companies had reached the eastern edge of the Iron Triangle, where they set up for the night. No enemy resistance was encountered. Smokey-the-Bear provided illumination throughout the night, while the 155mm howitzers at LZ Pony and Phu Xuan fired some 748 rounds into the area A Psy War loudspeaker ship flew over the area, urging any Viet Cong who might still be alive to surrender, and safe-conduct passes were dropped.

At daybreak on February 22, Alpha and Charlie companies, 1/5th Cav, along with the battalion's Reconnaissance Platoon, resumed their attack into the Iron Triangle. With the B-52 strikes on the previous day, the enemy's defenses had collapsed and the companies encountered no resistance. What they found was an area that had been totally destroyed. There were no trees standing or vegetation covering the ground. They found the bodies of 41 enemy soldiers scattered about, with numerous other bodies tangled together with the debris that resulted from the explosions. Several light machine guns and other weapons that were still intact were

---

[2] Quote from Colonel William R. Lynch, 2nd Brigade Commander, regarding USAF B-52 strike on Iron Triangle, February 21, 1966. 1st Lieutenant William E. Bates and Kenneth Sams, "Project CHECO; Operation Masher & White Wing, 25 January–6 March 1966, Report #150," dated September 9, 1966, page 22. Interview with Colonel William R. Lynch, Commander 2nd Brigade, March 10, 1966.

found throughout the area. They also located numerous bunkers, foxholes, trenches, and defensive positions that were now fully exposed, indicating that a large force had been housed in the area.

While Alpha and Charlie companies, 1/5th Cav, were sweeping westward through the Iron Triangle, the 2/5th Cav conducted a sweep from LZ Pete up the southern slope to LZ Sam. Its line of movement was through the western side of the Iron Triangle. In the sweep, Charlie Company, 2/5th Cav, in two separate incidents, encountered small groups of enemy soldiers moving through the area. It engaged them, resulting in eight enemy KIA. Charlie Company suffered one KIA in the encounters. A rifleman leading the attack received multiple fragmentation wounds to the face, stomach, and groin areas and died outright. Charlie Company also suffered one WIA who received shrapnel wounds, and required evacuation to the 15th Med aid station. In the sweep, the 2/5th Cav found bunkers with racks of cooking pots, a light machine gun that was still intact, a Browning automatic rifle (BAR) with a large quantity of ammunition, 16 grenades, 12 ponchos, web gear, and a hammock,

While the 2/5th Cav was sweeping up the southern slope toward LZ Sam, the 2/12th Cav was conducting search-and-destroy patrolling in the vicinity of Objective 22 west of the Iron Triangle on the high ground. There was no enemy contact encountered, but the battalion found a supply of 81mm mortar rounds and demolition equipment, which was destroyed in place. At 1300 hours, the 2/12th Cav returned to LZ Sam, being airlifted out of the area by Chinook helicopters and transported to LZ Pony. It closed into Pony at 1446 hours. The 2/5th Cav, upon reaching LZ Sam, was airlifted out by Chinook helicopters and transported to LZ Duck, and once the companies of the 1/5th Cav completed their sweep through the Iron Triangle and reached LZ Sam, they too were airlifted out by Chinook helicopters and transported to LZ Pony closing into Pony at 1610 hours. The battalions of the 2nd Brigade would remain at Pony and Duck for several days for rest and refit, include receiving replacements to fill the ranks left empty by the recent fighting.

For five days, from February 17–21, the battalions of the 2nd Brigade battled the 2nd Viet Cong Regiment, reinforced by a heavy weapons battalion, in the Song Bien Valley and in the Iron Triangle on the high ground above the valley. Attacks against the regiment resulted in heavy fighting as the enemy continued a stubborn defense of the area. The 1st Cav fired a total of 491 missions from conventional tube artillery, 10 ARA missions, and 43 TOT barrages (time on target, where the firing of artillery at different locations is synchronized so the rounds arrive at the target at roughly the same time), and the USAF put 39 tactical sorties into the target area. Friendly units conducted a total of 21 air movements into, around, and out of the objective area, and a total of 33 ground attacks against the regiment's positions, with units ranging in size from platoon to multiple company. The B-52 strike and a CS mission on the objective area at 1600 hours on February 21 resulted in cessation of the enemy's defense. Troops exploiting the B-52 strike encountered very light resistance, some bodies, and numerous weapons and items of personal equipment among the fortified positions. The following enemy equipment was captured during the engagement: seven Russian SKS carbines, six Chicom AK-47s, five light machine guns, five US M-1 carbines, five US M-1 rifles, one 60mm mortar, three 81mm mortars, one 82mm mortar, one 40mm rocket launcher, five 57mm recoilless rifles, three BARs, five small machine guns, and one 9mm pistol.

Colonel Lynch insisted that the operation would have been even more successful if the two B-52 strikes had been timed more closely together. The six-hour gap between the first strike at 1001 hours and the second one at 1607 hours prevented mopping-up operations that might have kept more of the enemy from escaping. Furthermore, because of the lateness of the second strike, there was insufficient daylight remaining for immediate sweeping of the target area. As a result, the enemy was afforded the opportunity to drag away its wounded and recover many of its dead. Evidence of many dead in the area was detected by the stench which covered the entire valley. The requirement to withdraw friendly troops several kilometers from the area during a B-52 strike also delayed mopping-up operations. It was also felt that many of the enemy soldiers left the area over a period of several nights in small groups, using little-used trails or moving across country. The suspected direction of movement was to the west.

In the five days of fighting, the 2nd Viet Cong Regiment suffered 339 KIA by body count, another estimated 409 KIA based on litter left on the battlefield, eight WIA, and another estimated 1,023 WIA. Forty-two Viet Cong soldiers and one NVA regular were captured, including a regimental headquarters' executive officer and a mortar company commander. Friendly losses were 46 KIA and 211 WIA.

CHAPTER TWELVE

No Rest for the Weary

While the 1st Cav was busy battling the North Vietnamese on the coastal plains of Bong Son in northeast Binh Dinh Province, the Viet Cong were busy preparing to attack its base camp at An Khe, deep in the Central Highlands in western Binh Dinh Province.[1] The North Vietnamese command in Binh Dinh Province had decided in late December 1965 "that an attack on the camp was needed in order to counter the Americans' efforts to defeat the Viet Cong in its political struggle, and to destroy key elements of the division, as well as create trouble in its rear area." The decision was apparently made in response to the success that the 1st Cav was having on the battlefield against the North Vietnamese and Viet Cong and because of the success of its civil affairs programs. To that end, the North Vietnamese command ordered the 407th Viet Cong Main Force Battalion with supporting units to attack the camp on the night of February 19. It aimed to destroy the communications equipment on top of Hon Cong Mountain and plant a Viet Cong flag there. The battalion was also to destroy the helicopters on the landing field in the center of the camp by mortar fire and create trouble for the Americans in the hospital area at the base of Hon Cong Mountain.

As luck would have it, Colonel Hal Moore and the units of the 3rd Brigade had returned to base camp from the Bong Son area only two days before the planned

---

[1] A document described in detail the preparation and attack by the 407th Viet Cong Regiment on the 1st Cav's base camp at An Khe on February 19, 1966. Commanding Officer, 407th Viet Cong Main Force Battalion, "Viet Cong After Action Report, An Khe, 2/66, Report on the Raid on 1st US Air Cavalry Division Base in An Khe on the night of 19 February 1966, Binh Dinh Sapper 502, No 10/L12," 1–13. History of the Vietnam War on Microfilm, https://jim4jet.webs.com/attacks1966.htm. Viet Cong and North Vietnamese documents captured by U.S. and allied forces in South Vietnam were forwarded to the Combined Document Exploitation Center (CDEC) in Saigon, where they were: a) microfilmed, b) translated and analyzed for intelligence purposes, and c) filed in the History of the Vietnam War on Microfilm Collection. The Collection was turned over to the National Archives in College Park, Maryland, in 1979 and declassified.

attack. The 3rd Brigade had been battling the North Vietnamese on the coastal plains in non-stop combat since January 24, a period of 24 straight days. On the evening of February 15, Major General Harry Kinnard directed Colonel Moore and the 3rd Brigade to return to base camp on February 16 and 17 for rest and refit and to receive replacements to fill the ranks left empty by the fighting in the Bong Son area. They were also to assume security for the base camp and surrounding area on February 17, effective 1830 hours. Colonel Roberts and the 1st Brigade would replace Moore and the 3rd Brigade in Phase III of Operation *Masher/White Wing* (*Eagle's Claw*) in the Kim Son Valley at that time. Unknown to Moore and the commanders of the 1st Cav, the changing of the brigades would occur little more than a day before the attack on the base camp by the Viet Cong, leaving little time for the troopers of the 3rd Brigade to set up their machine guns on the perimeter and register their mortars.

The site on top of Hon Cong Mountain was the main target of the attack. Hon Cong Mountain was a 2,750-foot-high jungle-covered peak that was located inside the perimeter of the camp in the southwest corner. The top of the mountain had been graded into a flat open area, roughly 40 meters square when the camp was built in September 1965, and a radio relay site had been established there. The site was a link in a communications network that extended from Qui Nhon to Phu Cat, to An Khe, to Pleiku. It was operated by a team of 40 signalmen from the 13th Signal Battalion, and the 54th and 586th Signal Companies. The 13th Signal Battalion was an organic part of the 1st Cav, while the 54th and 586th Signal Companies were independent units in the Army that operated under the control of I Field Force, Vietnam. The 54th and 586th Signal Companies had been assigned to the 1st Cav when they first arrived in Vietnam in September 1965 when the camp was being built.[2]

There was also a team of air traffic controllers at the site from the 17th Aviation Battalion, another independent unit in the Army that operated under the control of I Field Force, Vietnam. It controlled the helicopter and fixed-wing air traffic into and out of the area.

The radio relay site had a security fence around it that had been constructed by the 8th Engineers when the camp was built. Several three-man watchtowers were positioned along the security fence, with sandbagged bunkers inside the fence that could accommodate between four and six soldiers per bunker. It had a helipad on one side that was large enough for a single helicopter to set down for the offloading of troops or supplies. There were a number of sandbagged bunkers along another side of the site with communications equipment, including radio transmitters and receivers, located inside the bunkers with radio antennas positioned on top. Power generators with fuel tanks were located nearby. There was also a small Quonset hut on the site that contained the radar screens used by the air traffic controllers and sleeping quarters for

---

[2] Description of the 1st Cav's base camp at An Khe and surrounding area based on the topographic map of Vietnam, Highway 19 (QL19), An Tuc/An Khe, and author's recollection. Ray's Map Room, http://www.rjsmith.com/topo_map.html.

the troops. Because there were no roads up the mountain, supplies had to be delivered to the site entirely by helicopter. On the side of the mountain facing into the camp was a giant-sized replica of the 1st Cav's shoulder patch that had been constructed in full color, giving the site a landmark that was visible for many kilometers.[3]

The camp was the largest helipad in South Vietnam, and possibly the largest in the world at the time of its construction. It was capable of accommodating the division's 480-plus helicopters in addition to its trucks, jeeps, and tracked vehicles. It had a perimeter that was 26 kilometers around and had several large hill masses located within it, including Hon Cong Mountain. The hills provided visibility and control over the surrounding areas, as did an earthen berm located along the perimeter northwest of Hon Cong Mountain. The perimeter was protected by 12 layers of barbed wire of all patterns and types, the tricky barbed wire entanglements making it nearly impossible to penetrate the camp by creeping or climbing through them. Set back from the barbed wire on the inside of the perimeter were three-man watchtowers every 50 meters and sandbagged bunkers located 40–60 meters apart. Each bunker could accommodate four to six soldiers. Fixed searchlights were positioned along the barbed wire and on the hills in the camp to light up areas as far away as 5 kilometers. Outside the barbed wire, the jungle undergrowth had been cut back 25 meters or more, leaving an open dirt surface. At night, trucks equipped with powerful searchlights patrolled the perimeter to provide illumination for the crews manning the watchtowers and bunkers and to shed light on the hills inside the camp. The camp also had an airstrip next to it at the Special Forces Camp at An Tuc/An Khe that could accommodate USAF C-123 and C-130 aircraft. The airstrip was known as the An Khe Army Airfield.

Overall, the area around the camp was relatively flat and thinly wooded, and included numerous open areas that were covered with elephant grass, 4–5 feet high. The areas could be used as landing zones for helicopters to bring in troops if reinforcements were needed to defend the camp, and could also be used to insert troops onto the ground to conduct reconnaissance to detect possible enemy activity. The area also included the Song Ba River along the east and south sides of the camp. The river separated the camp from the Special Forces camp to the east and the village of An Khe to the southeast. The water in the river flowed very swiftly and in the monsoon season it ran deep, making it nearly impossible to cross it without using one of the wooden bridges that spanned the river in the vicinity of An Khe.

In the center of the camp was a large rectangular landing field for the division's helicopters. The jungle vegetation in the field had been cut to ground level, leaving only enough of it to reduce the helicopter dust in the dry season and the mud in the wet season, giving the field the name "the Golf Course." Between various sections of the field were areas for parking trucks, jeeps, and tracked vehicles, with a dirt

---

[3] Photo of Hon Cong Mountain and radio relay site on top, 1965–66, 1st Cavalry Division Association website, https://1cda.org/.

road running alongside the field. The road ran from the entrance of the camp to the northern end of the field. Tents housing troops were located around the field, as were tents for other purposes, such as processing centers for newly arrived recruits and outgoing veterans, battalion orderly rooms, and medical aid stations. Walkways built of PSP connected many of the tents, so it was unnecessary to trek through mud to get around the camp during much of the year.

Hon Cong Mountain itself was protected by two layers of barbed wire and stone walls. There were no trails leading up the mountain, but there was a dirt road that ran from the entrance of the camp to the base of the mountain and encircled it. The south side of the mountain was located adjacent to Highway 19 and was bordered by a cluster of hamlets, with strict security measures that provided no access to the area outside the camp. The villages of An Tuc and An Khe were located east of Hon Cong Mountain, adjacent to Highway 19, outside the camp and southeast of the Special Forces camp. They too had strict security measures that severely limited access to and from them from Highway 19.

The 407th Viet Cong Main Force Battalion would lead the attack on the camp, with other units providing support. The battalion was a main force sapper unit known to be operating in the Central Highlands Region in support of the Sao Vang Division. It would be supported by a mortar platoon with four 60mm mortars and four 82mm mortars, a local force Viet Cong company, militia, and provincial guerilla units. The battalion had recently moved to the Central Highlands Region from Khanh Hoa Province, north of Cam Ranh Bay on the South China Sea coast, and was unfamiliar with the roads or lines of communications in the highlands or with the terrain surrounding the camp, so its movement was expected to be difficult. It would require guidance from the Viet Cong local force companies in maneuvering around the area.

After an initial survey of the perimeter, the commanders of the 407th Battalion decided that the attack would be launched from the east and south sides of the camp: "The Americans had put emphasis on the protection of the west and north sides of the camp. The east and south sides of the camp from the Song Ba River northward were therefore more vulnerable to attack." The attackers would penetrate the perimeter at the point where the road leading from Highway 19 entered the camp. The point from where it veered off from Highway 19 to the camp was roughly 2 kilometers north of the Special Forces camp and 3 kilometers north of the village of An Khe. (The location of the entrance to the camp corresponded to the 3 o'clock position on the face of a time-of-day clock, where the perimeter of the camp formed the edge of the clock.) The entrance was protected by a wire mesh gate, with only a few layers of barbed wire positioned behind it and a guard station situated on the side of the roadway that was manned by military police. At daybreak, the barbed wire was routinely pulled back from behind the gate to the side of the roadway and the gate was opened to allow traffic into or out of the camp. At night, the gate was closed and the barbed wire was pulled back behind it. From the roadway, the Viet

Cong would cut their way through the wire mesh gate and barbed wire behind it and move into the interior of the camp. They would then maneuver to the west along one of the two roads in the camp toward their assigned target areas.

The attackers would also penetrate the perimeter from the south by southeast, along the Song Ba River in the vicinity of the hamlet of An Dan (2), adjacent to Highway 19. (The location corresponded to the 6 o'clock position on the face of a clock.) From there, they would maneuver across the interior of the camp to the north and west to their targets.

Finally, the attackers would move to the Special Forces camp located to the southeast of the camp, 1 kilometer north of the village of An Khe along the east side of the Song Ba River and east of the area known as Sin City.

The attackers would be organized into five groups, each roughly the size of a platoon, and each group would be assigned a specific target. Group 1 would enter the camp from the road leading to the entrance of the camp from Highway 19. It would cut its way through the gate and barbed wire behind it and maneuver along the southern portion of the camp toward Hon Cong Mountain. There, it would climb the mountain, attack and kill the defenders securing the site, destroy the sleeping quarters of the Americans using B-40 rockets, destroy the communications equipment inside the bunkers using satchel charges and rockets, and plant a Viet Cong flag at the site. After the battle, it would remain on the mountaintop to intercept and destroy reinforcements as they arrived. Then it would climb down the mountain and escape from the camp. The group would be armed with submachine guns, AK-47 assault rifles, two 40mm rocket launchers, multiple 40mm rockets, satchel charges, and grenades.

Groups 2 and 3 had slightly less ambitious assignments. Once they had penetrated the perimeter and entered the camp from the south by southeast, they would maneuver to the north into the landing field in the center of the camp, where they would destroy the helicopters and vehicles parked in the field with satchel charges and rockets, and attack and kill the American troops in the tents located around the landing field. They would also attack and kill the American troops in the hospital at the base of Hon Cong Mountain. These groups would be armed with AK-47 assault rifles, 40mm rocket launchers, multiple 40mm rockets, grenades, one fence-destruction tube, and pairs of scissors (i.e. wire cutters) to cut the barbed wire. They would also have 57mm recoilless rifles, which would be used to destroy the structures inside the camp.

Group 4 would not enter the base camp. Instead, it would slip undetected into the village of An Khe and move north into the Special Forces camp, remaining there for up to 10 days. There, it would identify targets for future attacks. The targets would likely include the airstrip at the Special Forces camp (where the camp's defenders would be killed), artillery positions situated in the areas to the east, southeast, and south of the base camp, and equipment depots and concentration points for American troops in the area. The attacks would be launched at the end of February after things had settled down in the camp following the attack on the night of February 19. The group would be armed with AK-47 assault rifles, submachine guns, explosive charges, and grenades.

The last group, Group 5, would enter the camp from the road leading into it from Highway 19 with the mission of supporting Group 1 in its attack on Hon Cong Mountain. It would attack and destroy any American elements that attempted to block Group 1's movement across the base camp to the mountain, or attempted to block its withdrawal from the mountain after the attack. As soon as Group 1 opened fire on the defenders on top of the mountain, it would initiate clearing operations in the areas along the road at the base of the mountain in an attempt to clear a path for Group 1's withdrawal, as well as establishing ambush positions to attack any ground relief forces that might be committed.

In the event that Group 1 was unable to reach the mountain, with or without the support of Group 5, it was to find concealment and wait until the Americans had moved past its position, even if this required an entire night of waiting, or even two or three nights. This would still ensure a surprise attack on the site, although the other groups would have already attacked their targets and escaped from the camp.

Combat support elements, including the local force mortar platoon, would support the attack by positioning themselves outside the perimeter along the northeast section of the camp and provide mortar fire in response to the attacking elements' direction. It would be equipped with multiple 60mm and 82mm mortar tubes and nearly 400 mortar rounds.

Several squads of infantry from the 407th Battalion would provide security for a medical aid station that would be set up in the jungle to the northeast of the camp to administer aid to any WIA resulting from the attack. They would also be available to evacuate the wounded from inside the camp along with any KIA.

Finally, members of the Viet Cong local force company, along with the local militia and provincial guerilla units, would deploy to open areas outside the perimeter to attack any American units attempting to land to reinforce the troops inside the camp. They would also protect the rear of the withdrawing groups after the attack. It was estimated by the commander of the battalion that it would take three days to fully withdraw from the area after the battle.

The 407th Battalion spent nearly two months planning and rehearsing the attack, starting on the night of December 20 and continuing to February 10, at which time it was ready along with the supporting units to carry out the attack on order from the North Vietnamese command in the province. Reconnaissance elements organized into groups of five or six Viet Cong soldiers per element would survey the perimeter, penetrate it at the two proposed spots (at the 4 o'clock and 6 o'clock positions), and move into the interior of the camp to become familiar with the terrain. This would include locating the battle positions they would likely encounter on the night of the attack as they moved across the camp. It would also include becoming familiar with the specific objectives on which the attacking elements would concentrate their heavy firepower and forces on the night of the attack, including the division headquarters, brigade command post, hospital, parking positions for trucks and other military vehicles on the landing field, and parking areas for the helicopters. For the element attacking the radio relay site on top of Hon Cong Mountain, this would include finding an avenue of approach up the mountain that would allow it to reach the top while it was still dark and there was still time left to carry out the attack in the darkness. The element attacking the Special Forces camp would have to find an alternative route into the camp from the village of An Khe to the north because of the difficulty of crossing the Song Be River in the monsoon season. This would have to be done in light of the fact that there were two companies of South Vietnamese Regional Popular Forces (local militia) garrisoned in the village.

At 0200 hours on February 19, the attack groups were ordered by the North Vietnamese command in the province to move to secure their positions on the perimeter of the camp and prepare to launch their attack into the camp later that night. This included cutting openings in the barbed wire entanglements that would allow them to climb through the wire to enter the camp. The groups would also have to find hiding places where they could spend the daylight hours waiting for the evening darkness to arrive. At 1130 hours, a number of helicopters from inside the camp arrived and set down alongside the road to the rear of where one of the attack groups was hiding. The troops onboard jumped off the helicopters and quietly went about their business of reconnoitering the area around the camp without ever spotting the attackers or their weapons or ammunition.

At 2250 hours that evening, the Viet Cong launched its attack. Groups 1 and 5 entered the camp through the barbed wire entanglements and covertly moved in the darkness across the southern portion of the camp along the road leading to Hon Cong Mountain. Groups 2 and 3 entered the camp and moved north and west along the other road toward the landing field where the helicopters and trucks were parked. The mortar platoon located outside the perimeter of the camp waited to receive targets for their mortars.

At roughly 0030 hours on February 20, the officer in charge of the radio relay site on top of Hon Cong Mountain reported to division headquarters that they were receiving fire from an unknown number of snipers and from an unknown number of directions, and illumination from Smokey-the-Bear was requested. No sooner had the request for illumination been made than one of the generators on top of the mountain was hit with a rocket or large-caliber round and exploded, along with several nearby cans of gasoline, lighting up the mountaintop. In parallel with the action on top of Hon Cong Mountain, mortar fire was now being received in the areas around the base of the mountain. The doctors at the 15th Med aid station and 2nd Surgical Hospital (Mobile Army) were reporting that they were under mortar attack, but that the rounds were falling mostly on unoccupied tents. Three members of the medical staff, however, were slightly wounded by metal fragments from the exploding rounds. The Air Ambulance Platoon located next to the aid station reported that its mess hall tent took a direct hit from a mortar round, but that the round turned out to be a dud and did not explode. The tent was empty at the time and no casualties were reported.

By now, the camp's ready-reaction force had been alerted and a platoon air assaulted onto the top of Hon Cong Mountain to help clear the area of enemy soldiers. The ready-reaction force was ironically the 3rd Platoon, Alpha Company, 2nd Battalion, 7th Cavalry. The 3rd Platoon was the platoon that was on the USAF C-123 aircraft that crashed shortly after takeoff from the An Khe airstrip on the morning of January 25, killing all onboard. The platoon had been reconstituted with a new platoon leader and fresh troops, and had only recently returned to action. Captain Joe Sugdinis was no longer the commander of Alpha Company. He was promoted to major when Alpha Company returned to camp on February 17 from the Bong Son area, and his replacement assumed command of Alpha Company at that time.

The ready-reaction force air assaulted into the radio relay site on top of the mountain only minutes after the initial report of sniper fire was received at division headquarters. At daybreak, the remaining platoons of Alpha Company, 2/7th Cav, started climbing up the mountain from its base, looking for enemy soldiers attempting to escape the area by climbing down the mountain. There were no casualties reported by Alpha Company, 2/7th Cav, either from the fighting on top of the mountain or from climbing up the mountain. Alpha Company, 13th Signal Battalion, was not so lucky, suffering two KIA in the attack, while four generators were damaged and had to be replaced. Helicopters delivered replacement generators to the site at first light so as to minimize the downtime of the communications network.

The attack on the radio relay site did not succeed in destroying any of the communications or transmission facilities, or air traffic control equipment on top of Hon Cong Mountain. Except for the destruction of the generators and nearby cans of gasoline, and the capture of one M-60 machine gun, there was very limited damage to the equipment at the site. The ready-reaction force from Alpha Company, 2/7th Cav, air assaulted onto the mountaintop by helicopter, thereby avoiding any possible ambushes that might have been set for it by Group 5 at the base of the mountain.

While the troops were battling the Viet Cong on top of Hon Cong Mountain, a Viet Cong rifle platoon from Group 5 attacked the 15th Med aid station at the base of the mountain with AK-47 assault rifles. The medical staff, together with bed-ridden patients in the aid station recovering from wounds received only days earlier in the fighting in the Song Bien Valley, were able to halt the attack and drive the enemy from the area. Shortly after the attack on the hospital was halted and the Viet Cong soldiers fled the area, the area came under mortar attack from the enemy. It was hit with 41 mortar rounds. The 15th Med aid station lost 10 tents from direct mortar hits, including the mess hall tent for the Air Ambulance Platoon located next to the aid station.

A number of mortar rounds also landed in other areas in the camp, but there were no reports of damage to any of the helicopters, trucks, jeeps, tracked vehicles, or tents lining the north side of the landing field. A total of 106 82mm mortar rounds landed in the western portion of the camp from a position to the northeast of it. What might explain why more mortar rounds were not fired into the center of the camp might be that Groups 2 and 3 never succeeded in breaching the perimeter and making it inside the camp, and were therefore unable to direct mortar fire at targets in the landing area. Members of the two groups were spotted as they attempted to climb through the barbed wire entanglements by the 7th Cav troopers manning the perimeter, and three of them were shot and killed in the wire. The remaining attackers from the two groups fled the area in disarray.

The continuous surveillance of the base camp by airborne helicopters on the lookout for enemy soldiers firing mortars into the camp was another factor that might have reduced the scope of the mortar attack. Aerial surveillance during nighttime hours, referred to as the Mortar Patrol, was a standard practice used by the 1st Cav as part of the security measures for the camp. The commanders of the 407th Battalion in their surveillance of the camp and surrounding areas failed to notice the aerial surveillance by the 1st Cav helicopters. It is possible that the flashes of light in the darkness from the firing of mortars were spotted by a helicopter crew and that the helicopter attacked the site, killing the enemy soldiers or at least forcing them to abandon their mortars and flee the area.

It was not clear from the 407th's after action report what happened to Group 4. It had the mission of slipping into the village of An Khe undetected and moving north to the area of the Special Forces camp to identify targets for future attacks. The group was supposed to remain in the area of the Special Forces camp for a period of 10 days, during which time it was to launch at least two attacks. The report only stated that "attacks from the east and south were not successfully launched." It was rumored that in spite of the South Vietnamese Regional Popular Force soldiers garrisoned in the village, the group made it into the village undetected but never reached the Special Forces camp. It got as far north as Sin City, where it decided to stay instead, looking for targets.

The commanders of the 407th Battalion claimed in their report, that the results of the attack on the camp were as follows: 497 American KIA, 97 aircraft of all types destroyed, 50 vehicles of all types destroyed, two artillery 105mm howitzers destroyed, 10 tents destroyed, and the hospital destroyed. The report also claimed that an M-60 machine gun was captured from the site on top of the mountain, which apparently was true. The report went on to say that the 407th Battalion suffered 11 KIA and seven WIA in the attack. It was estimated by the defenders of the radio relay site on top of Hon Cong Mountain that 20 enemy soldiers were killed in the fighting in the area and that their bodies were dragged off the mountaintop by the Viet Cong and down the side of the mountain, never to be found, before the defenders were able to fully secure the site.

The 1st Cav in its daily journal reports for February 19 and 20, reported that it suffered 10 KIA and 62 WIA in the attack. Two members of Alpha Company, 13th Signal Battalion died from gunshot wounds received defending the communications site on top of Hon Cong Mountain shortly before midnight on February 19. There were no reports of casualties from the 54th or 586th Signal Companies at the site, or from the 17th Aviation Battalion of air traffic controllers at the site. There were also no reports of casualties from the ready-reaction force that air assaulted onto the mountaintop—3rd Platoon, Alpha Company, 2/7th Cav—to help clear the area of enemy soldiers. Nor were there any reports of casualties from the remaining platoons of Alpha Company, 2/7th Cav that climbed up the mountain on the morning of February 20 in search of enemy soldiers climbing down the mountain fleeing the area.

The remaining 8 KIA died in the fighting at the 15th Med aid station at the base of the mountain helping to halt the attack on the hospital and drive the enemy from the area. All 8 of them were bed-ridden patients in the aid station recovering from wounds received only days earlier in the fighting in the Song Bien Valley. Also, several members of the medical staff were wounded in the fighting.

The daily journal reports stated that 1 OH-13S observation helicopter was hit by a mortar and destroyed, and 8 Chinook helicopters were hit with metal fragments or small-arms fire, but all were repairable. Ten tents were hit by mortars and destroyed, and 1 M-60 machine gun was captured on top of Hon Cong Mountain in the fighting. Also, 4 generators and several gas cans on top of the mountain were destroyed. There were no reports of damage to the communications or transmissions facilities, or to the radar equipment used to track helicopters and fixed-wing aircraft in the area.

Unrelated to the attack on the camp on the night of February 19, the camp was officially designated Camp Radcliffe on February 21, 1966, in honor of Maj. Donald G. Radcliffe, the division's first casualty in South Vietnam. Major Radcliffe was the executive officer of the 1st Squadron, 9th Cavalry, and a helicopter gunship pilot in the unit. He was also a member of the division's site selection team for the camp that had arrived in South Vietnam in early August 1965.

Although most of the division's troops were in the Bong Son area fighting the Viet Cong and North Vietnamese in Operation *Masher/White Wing* on February 21, Ambassador Henry Cabot Lodge, General Westmoreland, and Major General Kinnard participated in the dedication ceremony.

Major Donald Radcliffe was a warrior.[4] At the age of 15, he joined the Merchant Marines and saw action in both the Atlantic and Pacific during World War II. He later applied for Officer's Candidate School and was commissioned a Lieutenant

---

[4] Information on the death of Major Donald G. Radcliffe, Executive Officer of the 1st Squadron, 9th Cavalry, and helicopter pilot, was provided by the Vietnam Helicopter Pilots Association, http://www.vhpa.org. KIA Info by Name, description of Major Radcliffe's last mission.

just before his 19th birthday. In the Korean War, he commanded a tank platoon. In the late 1950s and early 1960s, he was involved in the development of the airmobile concept at Fort Benning along with Brigade General Kinnard where he was instrumental in the development of airmobile tactics.

In early August when Brigadier General John M. Wright, assistant division commander of the 1st Cav, and members of the base camp site selection party, learned of the III Marine Amphibious Force's (III MAF) plans to launch a preemptive attack against the 1st Viet Cong Main Force Regiment in the Chu Lai area, Major Radcliffe volunteered to pilot a helicopter gunship for the 6th Airlift Platoon tasked with providing gunship support for helicopter operations in I Corps. The 1st Viet Cong Regiment had partially surrounded the newly constructed airfield at Chu Lai north of the Binh Dinh–Quang Ngai provincial boundary. Several companies of Marines would air assault into the area and move to attack the Viet Cong in what was called Operation *Starlite*. The commanders of the III MAF and 2nd ARVN Infantry Division learned of the Viet Cong's plans to attack the airfield from Viet Cong soldiers taken prisoner in recent fighting with the ARVN. Major Radcliffe was fatally wounded by enemy fire as he delivered suppressive strikes at the enemy as the helicopters landed to offload the Marines.[5]

---

[5] Remembrances left for Major Donald G. Radcliffe, Executive Officer of the 1st Squadron, 9th Cavalry and helicopter pilot provided a detailed account of Major Radcliffe's death. Source: Vietnam Veterans Memorial Fund, The Wall of Faces, https://www.vvmf.org, posted on 12/13/1999, by Dan Fisher.

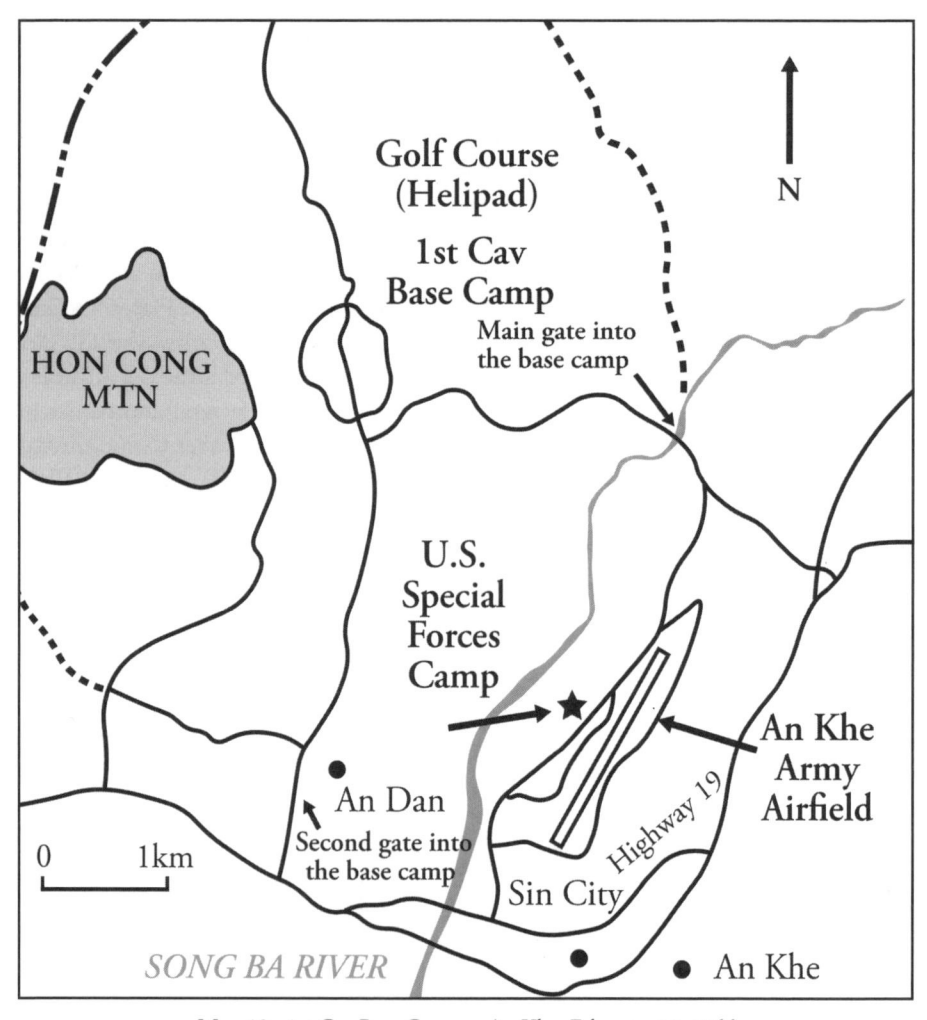

Map 12. 1st Cav Base Camp at An Khe, February 19, 1966

CHAPTER THIRTEEN

The Go Chai Mountains

Back in the Bong Son area, the battalions of the 1st Brigade had been conducting single- and multi-company search-and-destroy operations in the feeder valleys to the north, northwest, and south of LZ Bird in the Kim Son Valley, with blocking positions set along likely avenues of escape, but with little to show for it. Since the arrival of the 1st Cav in the Kim Son Valley on February 11, the enemy in the valley had adopted a pattern of avoiding contact and fighting only when it wished. The only significant contact for the 1st Brigade since replacing Colonel Moore and the 3rd Brigade on February 17 occurred on February 20. Charlie Company, 1st Battalion (Airborne), 8th Cavalry, had been pursuing an enemy unit estimated to be a squad-sized unit that attacked Bravo Company, 1/8th Cav, in its night defense position shortly after midnight. The enemy had attacked it with small-arms fire and grenades, and fled in the direction of Charlie Company in its night defensive position. At first light, Charlie Company initiated search-and-destroy patrolling in an attempt to catch the fleeing enemy if it was moving through the area. Charlie Company failed to make contact with the fleeing enemy, but it did capture a Viet Cong rallier (one who promotes the interests of the Viet Cong by conducting propaganda lectures, forming local guerilla units, collecting taxes, etc.,) who was moving across its front. The rallier said he was a member of the Lion Tinh Medical Battalion, a Viet Cong mobile field hospital. He added that the Viet Cong F106 Battalion was the defensive unit protecting the hospital, and that both battalions were commanded by the medical battalion commander, who was also a medical doctor. The rallier was taken on a helicopter flight of the area, during which he pointed out some of his unit's positions, including the possible location of the hospital.

At 1335 hours, Charlie Company encountered an estimated squad-sized unit in the area identified by the rallier as being the possible site of the hospital. The Charlie Company troops engaged the enemy unit, but were unable to fix it in position and the enemy fled into the jungle, leaving blood trails indicating that it suffered a number of casualties in the encounter. The Charlie Company troops pursued the enemy, and at 1453 hours regained contact with a force that was now estimated to be a platoon-sized unit. This time, Charlie Company succeeded in fixing the enemy in position with the help of the helicopter gunships providing overhead cover for its advance. Tactical air support was requested and the USAF responded with two Skyraiders that pounded the enemy position with high-explosive bombs and napalm, and raked the area with 20mm cannon fire. At the completion of the airstrike, the Charlie Company troops stormed the position, killing six enemy soldiers who survived the airstrike and capturing one other. There were also a number of enemy KBA, but the bodies were too badly burned and torn apart by the bomb explosions and napalm to allow a body count. Charlie Company reported no friendly casualties in the encounter.

Continuing with its search-and-destroy patrolling, Charlie Company discovered a 70-bed hospital as it moved through the area. The hospital had no patients or medical personnel, but bloody bandages and medical debris were scattered around, indicating that the hospital had been occupied recently. The hospital structure was destroyed.

On February 22, Major General Kinnard notified Colonel Roberts that the 1st Brigade was to expand its search area to include the Go Chai Mountains on the eastern side of the valley complex. Roberts then ordered Lieutenant Colonel Beard and the 1st Battalion (Airborne), 12th Cavalry, to move by helicopter to the Go Chai Mountains and initiate search-and-destroy operations there. Kinnand and Roberts believed that units of the 2nd Viet Cong Regiment were still in the mountains in force, based on the volume of enemy ground fire received by aircraft from the 1st Squadron, 9th Cavalry, reconnoitering the mountains. Recent contact made by the 2nd Battalion (Airborne), 8th Cavalry, on the western side of the mountains in recent days further indicated the presence of enemy forces in the area. The 40th (Mechanized) and 41st Regiments of the ARVN 22nd Infantry Division were conducting search-and-destroy operations in the 506 Valley immediately to the east of the Go Chai Mountains, so it was also an opportunity to act as a blocking force for the ARVN regiments by targeting trails leading into and out of the mountains from the 506 Valley.

By mid-morning on February 22, the companies of the 1/12th Cav had moved by helicopter to the Go Chai Mountains. At 0853 hours, Captain Donald McMillan and Charlie Company were first on the ground at a spot designated LZ 185, 2 kilometers southeast of LZ Pony. The Charlie Company troops seized and secured the position for follow-on infantry, and at 0923 hours, Captain Drake and Alpha Company closed into LZ 185. Captain Klein and Bravo Company were last on the ground at 1150 hours at a position designated LZ 184, 2 kilometers south of LZ 185 and 4 kilometers southeast of LZ Pony. The landings were unopposed and the companies immediately initiated search-and-destroy operations, Charlie Company to the west, Alpha Company to the southeast, and Bravo Company to the south. Almost immediately, Bravo Company started seeing signs of enemy activity, including commo wire strung along an east–west trail and freshly dug foxholes. At 1430 hours, Bravo Company reported that it was receiving sniper fire from what was estimated to be a squad-sized unit located several hundred meters to the south of its position. Captain Klein requested tactical air support and the USAF responded with a FAC and two Skyraiders. The Skyraiders dropped high-explosive bombs and napalm on the area where the enemy fire was coming from and raked it with 20mm cannon fire. At the end of the airstrike, Bravo Company followed up with a sweep of the area and found six enemy KBA. The Bravo Company troops encountered several enemy soldiers attempting to flee the area but were unable to fix them in position and the enemy soldiers fled into the jungle and escaped.

Bravo Company suffered one KIA and several WIA in the encounter. The KIA was a medic who was administering first aid to a wounded trooper in his platoon when he was hit and killed by enemy small-arms fire. Bravo Company pulled back with its WIA and KIA to a clearing that was large enough for a medevac helicopter to land and pick up the wounded. When the medevac arrived and set down in the clearing, enemy soldiers came charging out of the jungle, firing their rifles at the Bravo Company troops who were carrying the wounded to the helicopter. The Bravo Company troops drove the enemy away from the area, but not before they suffered further casualties, totaling two KIA and 10 WIA. The medevac successfully airlifted out the wounded troopers on multiple flights and transported them to the 15th Med aid station at LZ English for treatment. The KIA were transported to Graves Registration.

By 1850 hours, the companies of the 1/12th Cav had set up their night defensive positions and established ambush sites along trails leading into and out of the mountains from the 506 Valley. By 1930 hours, the mortar platoons completed their registration fire, and the direct support artillery battery at LZ Bird initiated volleys of H&I fire into the areas with its 105mm howitzers. The volleys continued throughout the night and into the early morning.

The companies of the 1/12th Cav reported no enemy contact during the night of February 22, but a clearing patrol sent out by Alpha Company at 0650 hours on February 23 encountered a group of enemy soldiers setting up a machine-gun position several hundred meters northeast of Alpha Company's perimeter. The Alpha Company troops quickly overran the position, resulting in one enemy KIA. They captured a Chicom machine gun, a 9mm pistol, and a pair of binoculars.

North of Alpha Company's position, a clearing patrol sent out by Charlie Company netted five enemy prisoners. The Charlie Company troops were moving along a trail north of the company perimeter when they came across the bodies of five North Vietnamese soldiers. The enemy soldiers were likely killed by artillery fire during the night. As the Charlie Company troops continued moving along the trail, they encountered a group of North Vietnamese soldiers sitting alongside the trail resting. Upon seeing the approaching troops, one of the enemy soldiers made a run for it, but was stopped dead in his tracks by the Charlie Company troops. The remaining five soldiers in the group surrendered. The Charlie Company troops captured several rucksacks but no weapons. The prisoners were taken back to Charlie Company's perimeter for transport to LZ Bird for interrogation by the division's military intelligence unit. It turned out that the prisoners were members of the 7th Battalion, 18th NVA Regiment. Their mission was to exfiltrate from the area east of Highway 1, where the 3rd Brigade had launched the deception operations preceding Phase I four weeks earlier, and move into the eastern Go Chai Mountains.

At 1050 hours, a clearing patrol from Bravo Company reported that it found the bodies of two North Vietnamese soldiers who were also likely killed by artillery fire during the night. The Bravo Company troops recovered five automatic rifles—two AK-47s and three Chicom SKS carbines. They also found a sign along a trail in Vietnamese indicating safe and unsafe ways to move through the area, according to the ARVN interpreter who was traveling with Bravo Company.

In the absence of any hard contact in the area southeast of LZ Pony, Lieutenant Colonel Beard alerted Captain McMillan and Charlie Company to move by helicopter to an area 6 kilometers southeast of LZ Pony on the eastern side of the mountains, and initiate search-and-destroy patrols along the trails leading to and from the 506 Valley. The area was northeast of the Song Bien Valley, where the battalions of the 2nd Brigade had battled the headquarters element of the 2nd Viet Cong Regiment and a heavy weapons battalion guarding it only days earlier. At 1150 hours, Charlie Company closed into the area. No sooner had it landed than it came under small-arms and mortar fire from a hill to its west. Based on the volume of fire received, the enemy force was estimated to be a platoon-sized unit. Tube artillery from LZ Pony was requested, and at the end of the artillery barrage, USAF Skyraiders dropped high-explosive bombs and hundreds of CS gas grenades on the hill. With aerial rocket gunships from Alpha Battery, 2nd Battalion, 20th ARA, providing aerial cover, the troops of Charlie Company attacked up the hillside. At 1515 hours, after advancing only a few hundred meters, the company reported that it was receiving intense automatic weapons and mortar fire and that it was unable to maneuver. It had sustained a number of casualties and was forced to leave them where they fell in the jungle underbrush. Charlie Company remained in contact until darkness set in, when it was able to break contact with the enemy and pull back a safe distance to a clearing where a medevac helicopter could be brought in to evacuate the wounded. Charlie Company reported, three KIA, two MIA, and three WIA.

While Charlie Company was battling the enemy 6 kilometers southeast of LZ Pony, Alpha Company was engaged in a heavy firefight with an enemy force 3 kilometers southeast of Pony. The enemy force was estimated to be a company-sized unit equipped with numerous heavy automatic weapons, including 50-caliber machine guns. Alpha Company had been moving in a southeasterly direction when at 1445 hours it encountered the enemy and immediately started taking casualties. Captain Drake requested an airstrike and shortly afterwards a USAF FAC in an O-1 Bird Dog and two Skyraiders arrived on station. Working with the artillery forward observer assigned to Alpha Company, the FAC was able to pinpoint the source of the automatic weapons fire. Under the direction of the FAC, the Skyraiders made multiple passes over the location, dropping high-explosive and WP bombs, along with napalm. On the heels of the airstrike, all available artillery from LZs Pony and Duck was called in on the enemy position. Alpha Company remained in contact until darkness set in, at which time it pulled back a safe distance to a clearing where a medevac helicopter was brought in to evacuate the wounded to the 15th Med aid station at LZ English. A Chinook helicopter was brought in to pick up the KIA and transport the bodies to Graves Registration at English. Alpha Company suffered 30 casualties in the firefight, with 6 KIA, 7 MIA, and 17 WIA.

The area of Alpha Company's contact was in the vicinity of where Alpha Company, 2nd Battalion, 12th Cavalry, came under an intense ground attack in the early hours of February 17 from an estimated reinforced platoon-sized unit. Artillery fire from LZs Pony and Duck along with gunship support from the 2/20th ARA had to be used to halt the attack and drive the enemy from the battlefield. The enemy left the bodies of 15 KIA behind in addition to 17 WIA. Numerous light machine guns, AK-47s, and SKS carbines were also left behind. The 2/12th Cav suffered one KIA and four WIA in the attack. At daybreak, the 2/12th Cav with support from observation helicopters from the 1/9th Cav, attempted to reestablish contact with the enemy force but was unable to do so. From information learned from the enemy WIA, the unit was part of a main force battalion from the 2nd Viet Cong Regiment. The regiment included a heavy weapons battalion in addition to its rifle companies. The unit that attacked the 2/12th Cav was believed to have been a heavy weapons platoon with multiple M-60 machine guns.

The attack on the 2/12th Cav on February 17, marked the first time that the 1st Cav battled a main force Viet Cong battalion since arriving in Vietnam. It quickly learned that main force battalions were well-equipped and well-trained like their North Vietnamese sister battalions. They were also familiar with the local terrain, something that gave them an advantage on the battlefield, which might have explained how the enemy unit was able to establish devastating lines of fire on the 2/12th Cav.

At 1730 hours on February 23, the 2nd Battalion, 8th Cav, was alerted to reinforce the 1/12th Cav with one company. Bravo Company, 2/8th Cav, commenced movement by helicopter to the vicinity of Alpha Company's position, closing at 1800 hours when it was attached to the 1/12th Cav. A platoon from Bravo Company, 2/8th Cav, was immediately dispatched by helicopter to a location 2 kilometers south of the position of Charlie Company, 1/12th Cav, to search for a helicopter that had been shot down earlier that afternoon by enemy ground fire. The position was on the high ground overlooking the Song Bien Valley in the vicinity of Objective Coil, where the 1/5th Cav had launched its attack against the headquarters unit of the 2nd Viet Cong Regiment only days earlier. Shortly after setting down, the platoon of Bravo Company located the helicopter, but in the process it encountered five enemy soldiers. It engaged the enemy but was unable to fix them in position, and they escaped into the jungle. Bravo Company sustained one WIA in the encounter. There was no report on the status of the helicopter or crew.

On February 24, Alpha and Charlie companies, 1/12th Cav, returned to the areas of the previous day's fighting to recover their MIA. Nine troopers had been unable to pull back with the companies on the previous evening and were forced to spend the night in the jungle, alone and wounded. Alpha Company found its seven MIA, five of whom were dead and two wounded. The KIA had died either in the fighting on the previous evening or during the night. The two WIA survived the night and were evacuated to the 15th Med aid station at English. Charlie Company found its two MIA, but one of them had been badly wounded and died during the night. The other MIA was wounded but still alive. He was evacuated to LZ English for medical treatment.

In the fighting on February 23, the companies of 1/12th Cav suffered a total of 21 KIA, as follows: Alpha Company, 12; Bravo Company, two; Charlie Company, five; and Headquarters Company, two. The two from Headquarters Company were medics who were assigned to the rifle companies. One of Alpha Company's KIA received a gunshot wound to the head but managed to live long enough to be evacuated to the U.S. military hospital at Clark Air Base in the Philippines for treatment, where he died 14 days later.

In policing the battlefields, Alpha Company found the bodies of 12 enemy KIA. Bravo Company also found the bodies of several North Vietnamese KIA and encountered three enemy snipers in bunkers who were firing at them. The Bravo Company troops attacked the snipers, killing all three of them. Charlie Company, in sweeping the battlefield, also made contact with the enemy, resulting in two KIA, and capturing four 75mm recoilless rifles, two SKS carbines, a Chicom AM radio, and several backpacks, along with other equipment. A wounded enemy soldier found on the battlefield with the radio said that the 1/12th Cav had battled two rifle companies and two heavy weapons companies from the 2nd Viet Cong Regiment over the previous two days.

While the companies of the 1/12th Cav were policing the battlefields on February 24, Alpha and Charlie companies, 2/8th Cav, were conducting a coordinated two-axis sweep west of the battlefields. At 1655 hours, the two companies became engaged with an estimated company-sized unit and an intense firefight resulted. Artillery fire from LZ Pony was requested, followed by aerial rocket gunships from the 2/20th ARA. Contact was broken by 1830 hours, and the two companies pulled back a safe distance to a clearing and consolidated their positions for the night. Alpha Company suffered five KIA in the encounter, which included a platoon leader who was hit in the head with enemy small-arms fire and died instantly. Charlie Company suffered one KIA. The bodies of the KIA were recovered at the time and transported by helicopter to Graves Registration at LZ English. No estimate of enemy casualties was provided.

For the next four days, from February 25–28, the companies of the 2/8th Cav continued to conduct search-and-destroy operations in the area where Alpha and Charlie companies, 2/8th Cav, had battled the enemy on the afternoon of February 24. Contact was limited, but at 1415 hours on February 26, Charlie Company engaged a group of five enemy soldiers who were spotted moving to its front. The group was fired at, resulting in two enemy KIA and two WIA. The fifth member of the group was later found dead in the jungle underbrush, with his body booby-trapped with grenades. Also on February 26, Charlie Company captured the commanding officer of the 17th Mortar Company (82mm), 18th NVA Regiment, who confirmed that units of the 18th NVA Regiment were in the 1st Brigade's area of operations.

The encounters that the companies of the 1/12th Cav and 2/8th Cav made in the southeastern Go Chai Mountains appeared to be random in nature. None of them appeared to be based on any intelligence collected by the enemy and none lasted longer than 12 hours. Although two company-sized units supported by heavy weapons companies were encountered, and hard fighting ensued, there appeared to be no pattern to the enemy's method of operations.

While the battalions of the 1st Brigade were battling the Viet Cong and North Vietnamese in the Go Chai Mountains south of LZ Pony, the battalions of the 2nd Brigade were at LZs Pony and Duck for rest and refit, which included filling the ranks left empty by the fighting in the Iron Triangle in the previous days. The battalions conducted local patrolling in the vicinities of Pony and Duck and along the Kim Son River where it ran through Hoai An District on its way to join the Bong Son River.[1] No significant contact was reported during the period, but at 1450 hours on February 23, the troops of the 2/5th Cav came under automatic weapons fire at a bathing point in the Kim Son River. Four troopers were hit with enemy small arms fire. Alpha Company was sent to the area to clear it, and on the way it encountered a small group of Viet Cong soldiers fleeing the area. The Alpha Company troops opened fire on them resulting in five enemy KIA. The Alpha Company troops captured a machine gun. No casualties were reported by Alpha Company.

On February 26, the 1/5th Cav returned to the Iron Triangle in an attempt to catch any Viet Cong who might have returned to the area to recover weapons or equipment. At 0745 hours, Bravo Company, 1/5th Cav, air assaulted into LZ Mike on the high ground above the Song Bien Valley after a 10-minute artillery preparation from the 155mm howitzers at LZ Pony. The Bravo Company troops seized and secured the area, and the remainder of the battalion closed into Mike by 0849 hours, with no enemy contact reported. Alpha and Charlie companies attacked to the south toward the Iron Triangle, with Bravo Company trailing. A special demolition team from Bravo Company, 8th Engineer Battalion, accompanied the 1/5th Cav into the area to aid in blowing up bunkers and fortifications. They found elaborate camp sites with underground stoves and bunkered huts, and freshly dug graves. They also found indications that the Viet Cong had been back in the area to police up lost equipment.

The 1/5th Cav returned to LZ Pony on February 27. On the morning of February 28, the 1st Platoon, Bravo Company, 1/5th Cav, was on patrol 1 kilometer

---

[1] Descriptions of the Kim Son Valley, inland plains of Hoai An District, and the Go Chai Mountains based on maps of Binh Dinh Province, and Hoai An District. Interim Report of Operations, First Cavalry Division, July 1965 to December 1965.

southeast of LZ Pony at the base of the Go Chai Mountains, when it started to receive sniper fire from the hamlet of Tan Thanh to its south. Due to the morning fog, the troopers were unable to pinpoint the source of the sniper fire, so the 1st Platoon moved into the hamlet. At 0740 hours, the platoon reported that it had one wounded trooper, but the location of the sniper had been identified and a squad was pushing deeper into the hamlet towards where the fire was coming from. At 0805 hours, the platoon reported that it was still receiving sniper fire and now had three WIA. Shortly afterwards, it reported that it was receiving automatic weapons and small-arms fire from multiple directions and was pinned down, and that it had five WIA, one of whom was very seriously wounded and required medical evacuation. Consequently, the company commander of Bravo Company directed the 3rd Platoon, which had been on patrol to the east of the hamlet, to move to the site to help the 1st Platoon pull back its wounded so that aerial rocket gunships from the 2/20th ARA could be brought in. He also ordered the battalion's Reconnaissance Platoon, which was attached to Bravo Company, to pick up stretchers at the company command post en route to the site and set up a perimeter north of the hamlet, where a medevac helicopter could be brought in to evacuate the WIA. At 0905 hours, the 3rd Platoon had arrived at the site and was sweeping the hamlet in search of the wounded. It had found two WIA, but was unable to locate the other three. At 0933 hours, the 3rd Platoon reported that it had found one WIA and eight KIA; the latter had been stripped of their weapons and ammunition.

At the perimeter that was set up by the Reconnaissance Platoon north of the hamlet, a wounded survivor of the ambush reported that the 1st Platoon had been moving deeper into the hamlet toward the location from where the sniper fire was believed to be coming when automatic weapon opened up on them from at least three different directions:

> We returned fire and we threw hand grenades, and with the help of several M-79 grenade launchers, we thought that we had knocked out the machine guns and we started to retrieve the wounded. Suddenly from our right flank, a group of about 15–20 Viet Cong emerged into the open from hiding in the brush firing their AK-47s while the enemy machine guns opened fire on us again from multiple directions. The fire was so intense that we tried to pull back letting the wounded lie where they had fallen. The Viet Cong overran our position and took the weapons and ammunition from the wounded who were now KIA.

Artillery fire from LZ Duck was called in on Tan Thanh and on the hamlet immediately to the east of it, followed by aerial rocket gunships from the 2/20th ARA. At 1020 hours, after the artillery preparation, the platoons of Bravo Company, together with the battalion recon platoon, conducted a coordinated assault through what remained of the two hamlets, with no enemy contact reported. The Viet Cong were believed to have escaped into the mountain to the south.

As a result of the contact at Tan Thanh, Alpha, Bravo, and Delta companies, 1/5th Cav, conducted a coordinated air assault into the Go Chai Mountains at positions roughly 3 kilometers south of Tan Thanh. From there they swept north back toward Tan Thanh in an attempt to catch the Viet Cong. The companies air assaulted into two positions along a north–south stream that ran down the center of low ground in the middle of the mountains. Bravo Company air assaulted into a position to the west of the stream, designated LZ Linda, while Alpha Company assaulted into a position to the east of the stream, designated LZ Lee. Delta Company followed Alpha Company into Lee.

The three companies closed into the LZs by 1230 hours with no enemy contact reported. Bravo Company immediately sent out two elements; one element was to move northward along a ridge and the other was to move to the northeast into the low ground that ran north–south the length of the mountain. Alpha Company moved to the northwest into the low ground and swept northward. The stream was the boundary between the two advancing companies; Bravo Company stayed to the west of the stream, while Alpha Company remained to the east of it. Delta Company remained at Lee to provide mortar support for the two advancing companies.

Although there was no enemy contact reported on the landings, an aerial reconnaissance helicopter from the 1st Squadron, 9th Cav, that was providing aerial scouting for Alpha Company, experienced a tail rotor failure at 1400 hours less than 100 meters north of LZ Lee, causing it to crash down into the jungle and start burning. The pilot and scout onboard were unhurt and were able to escape with their weapons and ammunition before it exploded. They then hiked through the jungle on foot back to LZ Lee to join the troops of Delta Company.

At 1620 hours, Alpha Company reported that it had come upon a group of six young kids, ages 5–18, hiding in the bushes. Apparently, they lived in a nearby cluster of hootches and were playing in the area. When they saw the troops of Alpha Company approaching, they quickly hid in the bushes. They had no weapons.

At 1720 hours, Alpha Company had advanced to within 1 kilometer of Tan Thanh when it started to receive sniper fire from a ridge to its west. At 1751 hours, Alpha Company reported that it had suffered one KIA. Aerial rocket gunships from the 2/20th ARA were called in to attack the enemy position, followed by an artillery barrage from LZs Pony and Duck. At 1825 hours, Alpha Company reported that it was still receiving sniper fire from the ridge and that it now had two men dead and one wounded. Aerial rocket gunships from the 2/20th ARA were again called in to attack the enemy position on the ridge, followed by more tube artillery fire from the batteries at Pony and Duck. The Viet Cong were believed to be well dug in and to have multiple M-60 machine guns. Because of the approaching darkness, Alpha Company would have to wait until morning to maneuver against the enemy position.

At 2055 hours, helicopters from LZ English arrived to resupply Alpha, Bravo, and Delta companies with ammunition, mortar rounds, medical supplies, and food and water. Alpha Company's WIA were evacuated to the 15th Med aid station at the Special Forces camp and the bodies of the two KIA were transported to Grave

Registration at LZ English. The mortar platoons for the two companies completed their registration fire around their perimeters, while the artillery batteries at Pony and Duck did the same for close-in defense to allow the companies to engage the enemy if observed. The plan for the next day was for the two companies to continue their attacks northward toward Tan Thanh.

On the evening of February 28, Major General Kinnard notified Colonel John Hennessey, who had replaced Colonel Roberts as commander of the 1st Brigade, and Colonel Lynch of the 2nd Brigade that he had ordered an end to Operation *Masher/White Wing* (*Eagle's Claw*), effective at 2400 hours, February 28. The two brigades would participate in the next and final phase of Operation *Masher/White Wing*, named *Black Horse*.

Major General Kinnard and his brigade commanders must have been pleased with the results of Phase III. All eight infantry battalions of the division, along with the 1st Squadron, 9th Cav, participated in Phase III. On February 15, friendly units attacked and destroyed two companies of the 93rd Battalion, 2nd Viet Cong Regiment, in the Soui Run Valley, on the eastern side of the Kim Son Valley, and overran the battalion command post. In the process, they captured the battalion commander, who had been wounded in the fighting. A number of documents and maps were also captured. In the interrogation process that followed at LZ Bird, the captured commander spoke freely with his interrogators and had inadvertently provided them with enough information so they had a pretty good idea of where the regimental headquarters was located—in the Song Bien Valley, in the extreme southeastern corner of the Kim Son Valley. The location was confirmed that night by aerial surveillance. Friendly units moved to the area and attacked and destroyed an enemy heavy weapons battalion that was guarding the regimental headquarters. Over the next five days, a total of 21 air movements into, around, and out of the objective area were carried out, and a total of 33 ground attacks were launched against the headquarters, with attacking units ranging in size from platoon to multi-company. On the fifth day, B-52 strikes dropped deep penetration bombs on the area, followed by tactical airstrikes that dropped hundreds of CS gas grenades, resulting in the cessation of the enemy's defense.

Friendly units also battled a number of squad- and platoon-sized units in the center of the Kim Son Valley. The latter were attempting to flee the area ahead of approaching forces that had been sent to drive them into blocking positions set along likely escape routes or into the open, where they could be destroyed by tactical air support.

The results of Phase III by the numbers were impressive: 709 enemy KIA by body count, another estimated 760 enemy KIA, 979 estimated enemy WIA, and 245 enemy captured. More than 140 individual weapons were captured, along with 46 crew-served weapons. A grenade making factory was found and destroyed, numerous weapons caches were unearthed, and three field hospitals were located and destroyed. Friendly losses were 101 KIA and 512 WIA.

CHAPTER FOURTEEN

Black Horse

The fourth and final phase of *Masher/White Wing* took place in the Cay Giep Mountains, southeast of Bong Son along the South China Sea coast. It was named Operation *Masher/White Wing/Black Horse* and was intended to find and destroy any North Vietnamese or Viet Cong forces operating in the mountains there. It was led by Colonel Lynch and the 2nd Brigade, supported by a regiment from the ARVN 22nd Infantry Division and a mechanized infantry troop from the ARVN 3rd Armored Cavalry Squadron. The operation started on March 1 and ended on March 5.

Based on information obtained from captured North Vietnamese soldiers, Major General Kinnard and his commanders believed that one or more battalions of the 18th NVA Regiment, and possibly the D21 Viet Cong Local Force Company, were operating in the Cay Giep Mountains. Information received from villagers in the area further indicated the presence of hostile forces there, as did the encounters experienced by the 1st Battalion, 7th Cavalry, with enemy elements in its deception operations from January 24–27.

The Cay Giep Mountains stretched south from the Bong Son River to just north of Dam Tra O-Lake, a distance of roughly 11 kilometers.[1] They were 8 kilometers wide at their widest point and were characterized by a series of mountain masses with steep slopes, gorges, and ravines, and were covered with double- and triple-canopy jungle that provided excellent concealment from aerial and ground observation. Bordering the mountains to the east were coastal lowlands and marshy areas of the South China Sea. To the north was the Bong Son River, and to the west was Highway 1. To the south were flatlands that extended south to Dam Tra O-Lake, with numerous small fishing villages located along inlets from the South China Sea. The inlets and wide sandy beaches provided excellent infiltration routes to Bong Son.

---

[1] A description of the Cay Giep Mountains was based on maps of Binh Dinh Province, and Hoai An District. Interim Report of Operations, First Cavalry Division, July 1965 to December 1966.

Interrogation of captured Viet Cong soldiers indicated that most of the villagers in the area had ties to the Viet Cong, as ralliers who were actively involved in promoting the interests of the Viet Cong, tax collectors collecting from the local populace, or recruiters organizing new guerilla elements at the hamlet and village levels. There were no indications that Viet Cong regular forces utilized the area on a permanent basis. However, it did appear that the beaches were used as rest areas for troops recuperating from wounds or injuries received in recent operations or sickness. The local villagers appeared to be prosperous and healthy, and when questioned by local government authorities they were cooperative. Many of them, however, displayed ignorance when questioned about ties to the Viet Cong. One captured Viet Cong soldier stated that his Viet Cong local force group of 40 men with six weapons fled to the Cay Giep Mountains after a brief encounter with government forces. There they disposed of their weapons and then returned to the villages and hid by mixing with the local populace. The local villagers appeared to be consistently used by the Viet Cong.

Colonel Lynch's plan for the operation called for the 2nd Brigade to attack into the Cay Giep Mountains with four battalions of infantry while holding one battalion in reserve. The operation would begin at 0630 hours on March 1, weather permitting, with an intense hour-long artillery bombardment of the areas where the infantry would be setting down. The bombardment would also include naval gunfire from the USS *Orleck*, a U.S. Navy destroyer offshore with the Navy's 7th Fleet. When the bombardment stopped, the battalions would air assault into landing zones on the eastern side of the mountains, roughly 5 kilometers south of the northernmost point of the mountains, and initiate search-and-destroy sweeps to the west. On March 2, the 2nd Brigade would continue with its search-and-destroy sweeps, while one battalion would air assault onto the northernmost part of the mountains and sweep south. On March 3 and 4, the battalions would continue with their east–west sweeps while also conducting north–south sweeps in attempts to catch enemy soldiers fleeing the mountains. On March 5, the battalions would be airlifted out of the mountains and transported to LZ English, where they would board USAF C-123 troop transport and CV-2 Caribou planes and return to the 1st Cav's base camp at An Khe for rest and refit.

The 2nd Brigade would lead the operation, supported by the 41st Regiment of the ARVN 22nd Infantry Division and the ARVN 3rd Troop, 3rd Armored Cavalry Squadron. The 2nd Brigade would consist of the 1st and 2nd battalions, 5th Cavalry; the 1st and 2nd battalions (Airborne), 8th Cavalry; the 2nd Battalion, 12th Cavalry; and Apache Troop (Airborne), 1st Squadron, 9th Cavalry, with its hunter-killer aerial teams and Aero Rifle Platoon. The ARVN 41st Regiment would surround the mountains by closing off escape routes to the north along the Bong Son River and to the west along Highway 1, while the ARVN 3/3rd Armored Cav would close off escape routes to the south to Dam Tra O-Lake and to the east to the

South China Sea. Searchlight ships would be positioned 3 kilometers offshore during the night in conjunction with the ARVN Junk Fleet to illuminate the shoreline and catch any Viet Cong who might be attempting to escape by sea.

At 0730 hours on March 1, after a one-hour weather delay, the 155mm artillery howitzers at LZs Pony and Duck, along with naval gunfire from the USS *Orleck*, initiated preparation firing into the mountains.[2] At 0845 hours, the Reconnaissance Platoon from the 2/5th Cav lifted off from LZ Duck and headed for the Cay Giep Mountains, but when the helicopters approached the eastern side of the mountain where they were to set down to offload the troops, the pilots discovered that the LZ preparatory fire had failed to clear an area large enough for the helicopters to land. Colonel Lynch requested a tactical airstrike to clear the landing zones and the USAF responded in less than 15 minutes with two Skyraiders. Because of the extremely dense jungle, multiple runs had to be made over the area by the Skyraiders, which dropped a variety of ordinance, including 500lb high-explosive and white phosphorus bombs, and napalm.

The airstrike cleared away enough of the jungle to allow the troopers of the Reconnaissance Platoon, along with a two-man team of pathfinders (also known as Black Hats) from the 11th Pathfinder Company (Airborne), to rappel down ropes to the ground from a height of 100 feet, one helicopter at a time. When the lead helicopter in the formation came to a hover over the clearing, the crew members threw out ropes and the four troopers onboard climbed out onto the skids to rappel down the ropes. Almost immediately, the helicopter started to experience turbulence and altitude density problems, and turned slightly to the left and then to the right. Suddenly, it descended down the mountainside, gaining speed as it went with troopers still hanging off the ropes. Several of the troopers went into the trees and were dragged off the ropes, with the ropes springing up toward the aircraft and into the controls of the helicopter. One of the pathfinders was still on one of the ropes when the helicopter crashed about two-thirds of the way down the mountainside. Unbelievably, no one was killed. Combat engineers from Bravo Company, 8th Engineer Battalion, were brought in on a Chinook helicopter with chainsaws to finish the job of clearing an area on the mountaintop for the remaining helicopters in the formation to land. The engineers were lowered into the clearing by climbing down a rope ladder. The clearing was designated LZ Bob East. There was no enemy contact reported, and the remainder of the Reconnaissance Platoon and a pathfinder were on the ground at Bob East by 1010 hours.

---

[2] Colonel Richard D. Gillem (Ret.), "11th Pathfinder Company (Airborne/Provisional). Vietnam," 168–76, provided a description of the air assault of the Reconnaissance Platoon, 2nd Battalion, 5th Cavalry, and the two-man Pathfinder team from the 11th Pathfinder Company (Airborne/Provisional), into the Cay Giep Mountains, March 1, 1966.

Corporal Bennie Matthews, a senior pathfinder, was on a rope when the helicopter crashed. He remembered his brush with death:

> LZ Bob was nothing more than a spot circled on a military map. It represented a jungle mountaintop covered with tall trees. I was in the lead helicopter in the formation of seven along with three troopers from the Reconnaissance Platoon, 2/5th Cav. Our helicopter approached the mountaintop from the north and slowly came to a hover over a small clearing on the eastern side of the mountaintop. On signal from the pilot, we dropped the ropes over the side of the helicopter, climbed out onto the skids, and started to rappel down the ropes to the ground. The aircraft started to turn to the left and then to right, and then it started to gain air speed with three of us dangling from the ropes below the helicopter. Next thing I know, I was being dragged through the trees and stripped of my helmet, my radio, my rucksack, and my M-16 rifle.
>
> While I was getting whacked by the trees, I watched the tail section of the aircraft break off from the back of the fuselage. I tried to reach around my body to get my knife so I could cut the rappelling rope and free myself from the aircraft, but before I was able to do that, the helicopter crashed into some trees down the mountainside.
>
> I'm woozy. I'm hanging upside down from a tree. At least the dragging through the trees is over. Then the real horror settles in. I'm going to get captured by enemy soldiers. I've heard all those stories from guys about what the Viet Cong do to American prisoners, like cut-off their testicles and stick them into their mouths for their buddies to later find. I have no knife, no rifle, no weapon at all.
>
> I kind of lose consciousness, like I'm in a twilight zone. I open my eyes to see this huge infantryman severing my rappelling harness and rope. I try to stand up, but my knees crumple. This giant of an infantryman, rifle pack, and all, lifts me up over his shoulder and carries me down the mountainside through the jungle to a clearing where a medevac helicopter is waiting.
>
> When I wake up, I'm in the hospital in Bong Son. I heard that one of the three guys from the 2/5th Cav who was in my helicopter is also there in the tent. Years later at a Pathfinder reunion, my company commander, now Colonel Richard Gillem, told me that they were still trying to find the names of the three guys from the 2/5th Cav who were in my helicopter.

According to Colonel Gillem, "Bennie was blessed with amazing grace. His back was not broken, and he was released to his 11th Pathfinder team at its forward base camp south of Bong Son. However, he was unable to walk without assistance, and he required another soldier to help him. Bennie was flown back to the 1st Cav's base camp at An Khe and given light duty while recuperating."

Corporal Matthews noted: "I never found out the name of the infantryman who carried me down the mountainside. He saved my life."

The helicopter crew chief, Carl McCall, also described the incident:

> We came to a hover over LZ Bob. Prior to take off, the pilot briefed the troopers not to drop their ropes until the helicopter came to a hover and he was sure of the aircraft power. He then would give the word to the troopers to rappel. He indicated that if the helicopter started to lose RPM, he would turn the aircraft nose into the wind.
>
> Upon arrival over the clearing, the pilot gave the troopers the signal to drop their ropes and rappel down. I moved forward in the passenger compartment to the wall behind the pilots in the cockpit and grabbed the bed rolls to throw out to the troopers rappelling down. I started to sense trouble. I whipped out my knife to cut the rappelling ropes to prevent them from getting tangled up in the tree branches and pulling the helicopter down causing

it to crash. At that moment, the door gunner shouted over the intercom that there was still one trooper on a rope.

I was then conscious of a different noise from the helicopter as it entered into a violent vertical vibration for a split second and then I heard a loud noise from the rear of the aircraft. The helicopter went into a flat spin. Next thing I remember, I was being taken out of the wreckage of the aircraft.

The pilot of the second helicopter in the formation, Captain William Cressall, also saw that the lead helicopter was having some difficulty when it made a "right pedal turn" to the north, and started descending down the mountainside, gaining air speed as it went, with the three troopers still hanging off the ropes. "I radioed the pilot of the aircraft to tell him that he still had infantry troopers dangling below!"

Captain Cressall remembered:

The aircraft seemed to be traveling at some 50 or 60 knots [58–69 miles per hour]. At that speed, the first infantryman hit the trees and was dragged off the rope. With that, I made a "May Day" call. The helicopter then started to make a right turn to the east toward a clearing as the second infantryman went into the trees and was dragged off the rope. The rope momentarily became snagged on the branches and then sprang up toward the aircraft appearing to go up into the controls of it.

At about that time the tail boom broke off from the aircraft about two feet behind the attaching points and hung at a 90-degree angle to the fuselage. The aircraft had turned to the north again and overshot the clearing area at about 100 feet altitude. One infantryman was still suspended upside down by his feet about 20 feet below the aircraft. The helicopter continued to fly toward the base of the mountain in what appeared to be a 50-knot speed and crashed about two thirds of the way down the mountainside.

The 15th Med aid station at the Special Forces camp was alerted to the crash and a Chinook helicopter with rescue personnel onboard was dispatched to the crash site. The rescuers climbed down a rope ladder to the wreckage. The aircraft commander, the pilot, the crew chief, and the door gunner were all injured but miraculously still alive. The rescuers found Corporal Bennie Matthews outside the aircraft dangling upside down from a tree. He was barely conscious but still alive. All of them were evacuated to the 15th Med aid station at the Special Forces camp.

By 1048 hours, Bravo and Charlie companies, 2/5th Cav, deployed into LZ Bob East, and Charlie Company, followed by Bravo Company, initiated search-and-destroy sweeps to the west across the mountains for 1 kilometer to a position designated LZ Bob West, with no enemy contact reported. By 1122 hours, Alpha Company, 2/5th Cav, closed into Bob East and initiated a search-and-destroy sweep to the southwest to a position designated Objective 3, which was 1.5 kilometers from Bob East. Again, there was no enemy contact reported.

In parallel with the 2/5th Cav's attacks, Alpha and Bravo companies, 2/8th Cav, air assaulted into a position on the eastern side of the mountains 5 kilometers directly south of LZ Bob East. The position was designated LZ John North. The troops of the 2/8th Cav, like those of the 2/5th Cav, were forced to rappel down ropes to the ground because the LZ preparatory fire had failed to clear an area large enough for the helicopters to land. Finally, Charlie Company, 2/8th Cav, air assaulted into a position 1.5 kilometers south of LZ John North, designated LZ John South, and proceeded to attack west across the mountains for 1.5 kilometers to a position designated Objective Kim. Alpha Company attacked northward 2 kilometers to a position designated Objective Amy, while Bravo Company secured John North. The 1/8th Cav then air assaulted into an area on the western side of the mountains, 7 kilometers west of Objective Amy, and initiated search-and-destroy sweeps to the south.

The Aero Rifle Platoon of Apache Troop, 1/9th Cav, the Apache Blues, also air assaulted into the northernmost point of the mountains and initiated search-and-destroy patrolling there. At 1135 hours, it encountered a group of military-age men dressed in black pajamas carrying 6-foot-long logs in the direction of the base of the mountains. The men were not carrying weapons. As it turned out, the logs were being taken to two separate tunnel entrances leading into the mountain. One of the entrances was under a hootch, the other under a pile of dried palm leaves. Combat engineers from the division's 8th Engineer Battalion were called in to destroy the entrances and tunnel.

The only contact that was reported by any of the battalions in their search-and-destroy patrolling was an encounter by Charlie Company, 2/8th Cav, shortly after it air assailed into LZ John South in the southeastern corner of the mountain. Charlie Company came upon two Viet Cong to its front, resulting in two enemy KIA. The Charlie Company troops also captured two rucksacks, one of which contained 41,000 Piasters—the standard monetary currency of South Vietnam at the time.

Shortly before midnight, Bravo Company, 1/8th Cav, came under attack in its night defensive position on the western side of the mountains by an enemy force estimated to be of multi-platoon size. Artillery fire from LZs Duck and Pony, followed by aerial rocket gunships from the 2/20th ARA, were used to halt the attack. Seven enemy KIA were left at Bravo Company's perimeter, and based on the debris left on the battlefield, there were an estimated five more enemy dead. The 1/8th Cav reported no casualties in the attack.

While the battalions of the 2nd Brigade had little to show for their efforts on the first day of the operation, the ARVN 3/3rd Armored Cav had better luck. With its American M-113 APCs, it conducted a search-and-destroy sweep from the southernmost point of the mountains to a blocking position established by the 2/8th Cav, south of LZ John South, a distance of roughly 3 kilometers. In the sweep, it encountered an enemy force estimated to consist of about 150 Viet Cong. It attacked the enemy and quickly overran it with its APCs. The encounter resulted in 50 enemy KIA, with another 30 captured. The captured soldiers were put on a Chinook helicopter and transported to the 1st Cav's base camp at An Khe for interrogation. They had been attempting to flee the area ahead of the search-and-destroy sweeps that were being conducted to the north by the units of the 2nd Brigade. An abandoned 100-bed hospital was also found in the sweep by the ARVN 3/3rd Armored Cav. There were no patients or medical personnel in the hospital, but there were numerous medical supplies, including bottles of plasma, penicillin, and other anti-serums, packages of surgical knives, a case of needles, thread, complete surgical kits, and a spectroscope. The supplies were loaded onto a Chinook and transported to the Bong Son Dispensary. The ARVN 3/3rd Armored Cav did not generally report its casualty figures to the 1st Cav, but it was believed to have suffered no friendly casualties in the encounter.

The ARVN 41st Regiment, which had been guarding the north and west sides of the mountains, reported six enemy KIA, with no friendly casualties in the day's operations.

On March 2, the battalions of the 2nd Brigade continued with their search-and-destroy patrols in the eastern and western portions of the Cay Giep Mountains. In its patrolling of the area between LZs Bob East and Bob West on the eastern side of the mountains, the 2/5th Cav reported at 1349 hours that it found a hospital located in a network of caves, and that it had captured two females believed to be doctors or nurses, along with 35 bed-ridden patients. In the process of capturing the hospital, the 2/5th Cav troopers engaged a number of Viet Cong soldiers who were guarding it, resulting in four enemy KIA and two WIA. Ponchos and medical supplies were also captured. The 2/5th Cav reported no friendly casualties in the encounter.

On the western side of the mountains, the 1/8th Cav had been receiving sniper fire and probes from an estimated 30–40 enemy soldiers in its night defensive position since shortly after midnight. The 1/8th Cav troopers engaged the enemy with artillery from LZs Duck and Pony and from the 2/20th ARA, resulting in six enemy KIA and 10 WIA. The wounded soldiers were too badly injured to flee and had been left in the jungle underbrush for dead. At 0205 hours, the 1/8th Cav troopers were again reporting probes by enemy soldiers. The 1/8th Cav troopers responded with small-arms and mortar fire, resulting in one enemy KIA. No friendly casualties were reported in either incident. At 1342 hours, Delta Company reported that it captured a number of automatic rifles and grenades, and found bunkers in the vicinity of a small village, and at 1730 hours, Delta Company reported that it was receiving fire from enemy snipers and was responding with small-arms and mortar fire. It suffered one KIA in the encounter. A trooper received gunshot wounds to the head, chest, and back and died from the loss of blood before he could be evacuated to the 15th Med aid station at the Special Forces camp for treatment.

The 2/8th Cav, in its search-and-destroy patrolling between LZs John North and John South in the southeastern corner of the mountains, made contact with a squad-sized enemy unit. The 2/8th Cav pinned down the enemy, who were only able to break contact and flee the area after two hours. The jungle vegetation was so thick that the 2/8th Cav troopers were unable to launch any coordinated attack against the enemy and fix them in position. The contact resulted in three enemy KIA and two WIA. The wounded had been left on the battlefield and had to be evacuated to the 15th Med aid station at the Special Forces camp for medical treatment.

In support of the 2nd Brigade's ongoing ground operations in the Go Chai Mountains south of LZ Pony, USAF B-52 strikes were conducted on the morning and early afternoon of March 2 in the eastern Go Chai Mountains, where the battalions of the 1st and 2nd brigades had battled elements of the 93rd Battalion, 2nd Viet Cong Regiment, and 7th Battalion, 18th NVA Regiment, in recent days.[3] A USAF O-1E Bird Dog aircraft with two USAF FACs onboard provided bomb damage assessments. In the course of assessing the damage, the aircraft—from the 21st Tactical Air Support Squadron, 505th Tactical Control Group, based at Pleiku—was hit by enemy ground fire and came crashing down into a ravine at roughly 1520 hours. It immediately started to burn.[4]

The crash site was located by aerial reconnaissance helicopters from Bravo Troop, 1/9th Cav, and a platoon from the 2/12th Cav was dispatched to the site in a rescue operation. The platoon arrived at the site at 1712 hours to find that the two pilots had not survived the crash. The bodies were burned beyond recognition and no dog tags were found. The name tags on the pilots' uniforms were still intact, however, and were used to identify the bodies, which were removed and transported to Graves Registration at LZ English. The recovery operation was completed at 2120 hours by the 2/12th Cav platoon and a team from Graves Registration.[5]

On March 3 and 4, the battalions of the 2nd Brigade continued with their search-and-destroy sweeps through the mountains with little to show for it. On the

---

[3] The document "Project CHECO; Operation Masher & White Wing, 25 January–6 March 1966, Report #150," dated September 9, 1966, provided a description of the USAF B-52 strike into the eastern Go Chai Mountains, south of LZ Pony, on March 2, 1966. It also provided a description of the crash of a USAF O-1E Birddog aircraft south of LZ Pony that was providing a bomb damage assessment following the B-52 strike. The aircraft was hit by enemy ground fire and crashed to the ground, killing the two FACs onboard, Captains William E. Bates and Kenneth Sams.

[4] The website "Vietnam Air Losses" provided the names of the two USAF FACs killed in the crash of the USAF O-1E Birddog aircraft providing bomb damage assessment following the B-52 strike in the eastern Go Chai Mountains, south of LZ Pony, on March 2, 1966, https://www.vietnamairlosses.com.

[5] Remembrances left for USAF FACs Captain Marshall M. Holt, Jr., Des Moines, Iowa, and Captain Paul A. Meiners, Kayesville, Utah, provided information about the mission of Holt and Meiners. Vietnam Veterans Memorial Fund, The Wall of Faces, https://www.vvmf.org, posting by WKillian@smjuhsd.org, July 1, 2021. Details of the incident and the attempted rescue and subsequent recovery of the bodies of Captains Holt and Meiners were provided by the Daily Journals, Headquarters, 1st Air Cav Div, March 1–5, 1966.

afternoon of March 5, Colonel Lynch alerted the battalions to move by helicopter back to the Special Forces camp. By midday on March 5, all of the battalions had been airlifted out of the Cay Giep Mountains by Chinook helicopters. The 1/8th Cav and 2/8th Cav, and Apache Troop, 1/9th Cav, were returned to the control of the 1st Brigade upon arrival at the camp.

Although Operation *Masher/White Wing/Black Horse* did not result in any decisive engagements with enemy forces, information gained concerning Viet Cong activities in the area would assist in future operations. It was learned from captured enemy soldiers that the Viet Cong had moved out of the area, probably to the south, one or two days before the operation commenced when they learned of the 1st Cav's plans to attack the mountains in force. There was no evidence that the area was being used by Viet Cong units on a recurring basis, nor was there any evidence of extensive supply caches. The area was, however, being used as a rest area for troops recuperating from wounds or injuries received in recent operations or sickness, and to support transient units moving through the area. A Viet Cong local force guerilla organization existed in the villages, as it did in most of the villages in the Bong Son area.

The results of the operation were as follows: two Viet Cong hospitals found, one with 35 bed-ridden patients and two female doctors or nurses (both hospital structures were destroyed); the 2nd Brigade reported 19 enemy KIA by body count, another 12 estimated KIA, and 15 enemy WIA; friendly losses were one KIA and six WIA.

CHAPTER FIFTEEN

Conclusion

By mid-March, the Sao Vang Division was no longer in the Bong Son area in any large numbers. The aerial reconnaissance helicopters of the 1st Squadron, 9th Cavalry, no longer received ground fire when reconnoitering the 1st Cav's areas of operations in northeast Binh Dinh Province, and intelligence reports from the police of Hoai Nhon and Hoai An districts, along with intelligence from ARVN sources, further indicated that the Sao Vang Division had withdrawn from the area. With that, Major General Kinnard terminated Operation *Masher/White Wing* and the units of the 1st Cav were extracted from the field and transported back to the division's base camp at An Khe, now known as Camp Radcliffe, for rest and refit. Security of LZ English was taken over by the ARVN 22nd Infantry Division as part of its security role for the Special Forces Camp at Bong Son, and security for LZ Hammond was assumed by the ROK Capital "Tiger" Mechanized Infantry Division as part of its security role for Highway 1. The 1st Cav subsequently redirected its efforts to the western Central Highlands along the Cambodian border in search of staging areas used by the Viet Cong and North Vietnamese to offload truck convoys arriving via the Ho Chi Minh Trail carrying supplies destined for units operating in Pleiku and Binh Dinh provinces.

Overall, General Westmoreland and his commanders at the MACV had to have been pleased with the results of Operation *Masher/White Wing*. In 41 days of sustained fighting—four days of deception operations, followed by 37 days of offensive operations—the 1st Cav battled each of the three regiments of the Sao Vang Division, resulting in enemy losses of more than 3,000 KIA (1,342 by body count, and another estimated 1,700, based on debris left on the battlefield). The 1st Cav inflicted known losses of 300 on the 7th Battalion and 200 on the 9th Battalion of the 22nd NVA Regiment, rendering the two battalions ineffective as fighting forces. The survivors of the two battalions split into small groups and fled the Bong Son area, seeking refuge in the jungle-covered mountains to the west. The 1st Cav drove the 8th Battalion of the 22nd NVA Regiment out of the An Lao Valley and returned control of the valley to the ARVN and South Vietnamese government authorities for them to secure and administer. The 8th Battalion had been garrisoned at the district headquarters at An Lao village since December 1964. The 1st Cav also inflicted heavy losses on two companies of the 93rd Battalion, 2nd Viet Cong Regiment, which included 57 KIA by body count and another estimated 93 KIA. This included capturing the battalion command post of the 93rd Battalion, along with the battalion commander, who was wounded in the fighting. Based on information obtained from the interrogation of the battalion commander, the 1st Cav was able to locate the headquarters of the 2nd Viet Cong Regiment in the extreme southeast corner of the Kim Son Valley complex and attack it with a multi-battalion force. It inflicted heavy losses on a heavy weapons battalion that was guarding the regimental headquarters, and dislodged the headquarters unit from the relative safety of its jungle sanctuary, forcing it to flee the area and seek refuge in the jungle-covered mountains to the south and west.

All this came at the cost of 199 Americans killed on the battlefield and 46 more who died in the crash of a USAF C-123 aircraft en route to the battlefield, making it one of the deadliest battles of the entire Vietnam War. The ARVN also paid a heavy price for its involvement in the fighting. It was estimated that between the ARVN Airborne Brigade, the ARVN 3rd Troop, 3rd Armored Cavalry Squadron, and the 40th (Mechanized) and 41st Regiments of the ARVN 22nd Infantry Division, it suffered at least as many KIA as did the Americans. This included several American advisors who were attached to the ARVN units. The ROK Capital "Tiger" Mechanized Infantry Division reported that it suffered 10 KIA. As for the U.S. Marines in Operation *Double Eagle/Lien Ket 22*, the companion operation to Operation *Masher/White Wing* in Quang Nghi Province to the north of Binh Dinh Province, and in the An Lao Valley in Phase II, the Marines reported several encounters with enemy forces but all of them were in areas well north of the Binh Dinh–Quang Ngai provincial boundary and were in direct support of Marine operations there.

Operation *Masher/White Wing* was a success. The 1st Cav, together with the USAF, the ARVN, the ROK, the U.S. Marines, and the U.S. Navy, demonstrated that it had the firepower, mobility, and leadership to find the enemy and deliver a severe blow to it in terms of personnel and equipment losses and in forced evacuation of formerly secure base areas.

However, within a few weeks of Operation *Masher/White Wing* being terminated and the 1st Cav returning to its base camp at An Khe, intelligence reports from the police of Hoai Nhon District indicated that North Vietnamese soldiers from the 22nd NVA Regiment were returning to the Bong Son area in small groups. By late April, intelligence indicated that the 22nd NVA Regiment was back in the area in force with at least two full battalions of infantry. It was hiding in the hamlets of Tuy Thanh and Tuong Son in the far northwestern corner of the coastal plain north of Bong Son, where the rice paddies started to give way to the foothills of the southern Quang Ngai Mountains at the Binh Dinh–Quang Ngai provincial boundary. The 22nd NVA Regiment had fled the Bong Son area in late January after it was attacked by the 1st Cav at Phung Du and was believed to have taken refuge in the mountains north and west of the An Lao Valley. After a short rest and refit, where it received fresh troops to fill the ranks left empty by the fighting and new equipment to replace that which was destroyed, it was back in the Bong Son area and ready for action.

Operation *Masher/White Wing* proved to be the start of a very long and deadly struggle between the 1st Cav and North Vietnamese for control of Binh Dinh Province. The 1st Cav continued to battle the regiments of the Sao Vang Division in the Bong Son area throughout 1966 with no end in sight. In early May, Colonel Moore and the 3rd Brigade returned to the area to battle the 22nd NVA Regiment in what was named Operation *Davy Crockett*, or *Bong Son II* as it was called by the troops, resulting in 345 enemy KIA and 82 detained, with 27 friendly KIA and 155 WIA. In late May, Colonel John J. Hennessey, who replaced Colonel Roberts, and the 1st Brigade battled the 2nd Viet Cong Regiment in the Vinh Thanh Mountains west of the Kim Son Valley and in the Suoi Ca Valley south of the Kim Son Valley, in what was named Operation *Crazy Horse*. This resulted in 507 enemy KIA and 27 captured, with friendly losses of 83 KIA, 356 WIA, and one MIA. Other major operations in the Bong Son area followed throughout the year, with one in late October, named *Operation Thayer II*, that continued into February 1967. It resulted in 1,757 enemy killed, with friendly losses of 184 KIA, 747 WIA, and two MIA.

In each operation, the story was the same. The 1st Cav conducted search-and-destroy operations to locate enemy forces in their jungle sanctuaries, attacked them when found, applying maximum American firepower and rendering them ineffective as a fighting force. Then the enemy, or those who survived, fled the battlefield, taking refuge in the mountains to the west of the coastal areas. There they received fresh troops to replace the casualties from the fighting and new equipment to replace that which was destroyed, and within a very short time returned to the coastal area fully reconstituted in terms of troop levels and equipment, ready for further action.

General Westmoreland's search-and-destroy strategy proved to be very successful at the tactical level, but without a complementing plan at the strategic level by President Johnson and his administration that would stop the unabated flow of Communist troops and supplies into South Vietnam from North Vietnam, it just wasn't clear just how General Westmoreland and the U.S. military could ever achieve victory in the Battle of Bong Son, or in the Vietnam War for that matter.

The Americans had been conducting bombing operations against North Vietnam since 1964, when they initiated bombing in retaliation to the Gulf of Tonkin incident. The bombing was intended to destroy North Vietnam's industrial base and its capability to wage war against South Vietnam, but most of the bombing against North Vietnam was not in the areas where its factories and military installations were located—Hanoi, Haiphong, and the area along the Chinese border. Instead, it was directed at the mostly rural areas north of the DMZ, far from Hanoi, Haiphong, or the Chinese border. President Johnson was apparently reluctant to approve bombing in the northern part of the country, where Hanoi and Haiphong were located, or close to the border with China, fearing that it might trigger direct intervention in the war by the Chinese. The result of this strategy was that the North Vietnamese were free to manufacture weapons and war materials in their factories, and prepare their troops for combat against the Americans in the South, without fear of being attacked by American bombers.

The Americans had also been conducting bombing operations over Laos since 1964 in an attempt to destroy the logistics bases built there by the North Vietnamese. The bases were used as staging areas for supplies destined for Communist troops operating in South Vietnam. The bombing was also intended to destroy the infiltration routes leading into South Vietnam from Laos, collectively known as the Ho Chi Minh Trail. However, in the absence of U.S. troops on the ground in Laos to identify targets for attacking aircraft, the bombing was considered of only limited value in terms of stopping the flow of troops and supplies into South Vietnam. President Johnson might have authorized the bombing against Laos, but he would not authorize the use of U.S. ground troops in Laos to support bombing operations there, choosing instead to respect the neutrality of Laos.

It was only in mid-January 1968, when General Westmoreland ordered the 1st Cav to terminate its operations in the Bong Son area and move north to the DMZ to reinforce the besieged U.S. Marines at the Marine Combat Base at Khe Sanh, that the Battle of Bong Son came to a close.

APPENDIX I

Book of Honor, Operation *Masher/White Wing*, January 24–March 5, 1966, in the Republic of Vietnam

Dedicated to the memory of those brave Skytroopers who gave their lives for their country and for the men who fought beside them in Operation *Masher/White Wing*, January 24–March 5, 1966, in the Republic of Vietnam.

USAF C-123 Aircraft Crash

2nd Battalion, 7th Cavalry
Alpha Company
ALSTON, CHARLES EDWARD, Raleigh, North Carolina
ASHLEY, CHARLES R. JR., Barney, Georgia
BELL, PAUL M., Centerville, Tennessee
BOWMAN, ROBERT CARLOSS, St Petersburg, Florida
BROOKS, MONTE D., Norfolk, Virginia
BROWN, JOHNNIE LEE, Natchez, Mississippi
BRYANT, GARY RAY, Greenville, South Carolina
BURKES, DAVID E., Waukegan, Illinois
COATS, JAMES PRESTON, Canton, Ohio
DEWEESE, BILLY CLARENCE, Barberton, Ohio
DOLLAR, EUGENE DOYCE SP4, Milwaukee, Wisconsin
ELICHKO, DEAN JOSEPH, Cranford, New Jersey
ESCHBACH, CHARLES LINWOOD, Detroit, Michigan
GIFFARD, SAMUEL POOKEAOKAL, Honolulu, Hawaii
GRIBLER, DONALD ROSS, Ft Wayne, Indiana
HERRINGTON, JEROME, Sardis, Georgia

HETTERLY, JOHN DONALD SR., Orlando, Florida
HICKS, WOODIE LEE, Cordova, Alabama
HOGAN, RADFORD DOUGLAS, Denver, Colorado
HUNTER, DAVID, Chicago, Illinois
JAMES, JOSEPH, Wilmington, North Carolina
JOHNSON, WALTER BOYCE, Des Moines, Iowa
KIM, EDWARD Y C., Wahiawa, Hawaii
KING, WOODROW WILSON JR., Baltimore, Maryland
KUILAN, WENCESLEO, Bayamon, Puerto Rico
LEDFORD, RAY DOUGLAS, Old Fort, North Carolina
LEONARD, EDWARD N., Richmond, California
MARSH, RONALD ALTON, Charlotte, Texas
MECHLING, DANIEL GARY, Kittanning, Pennsylvania
MITCHELL, DONALD THOMAS, Spartanburg, South Carolina
NOLEN, BOBBIE ELDON, Little Rock, Arkansas
O'DONNELL, JAMES PATRICK, Nashville, Tennessee
PASHMAN, STEPHEN MARK, Santa Cruz, California
PASLEY, HENRY, Columbus, Georgia
PHILLIPS, WILLIAM JOSEPH, Pasadena, California
SACKETT, ERIC, Austin, Texas
SMITH, EDWARD BRUCE, New York, New York
SUMMERS, EUGENE C., Fairmont, West Virginia
VENABLE, WESTOVEL, Newark, New Jersey
WILLIAMS, FRANK WAYNE JR, Jacksonville, Florida
WILLIS, HAROLD EUGENE, Bishop, California

Headquarters Company
TILLER, ROBERT, North Birmingham, Alabama

United States Air Force, 311th Air Commando Squadron, 315th Air Commando Group, 13th Air Force
CRUMLEY, HARRY R., Des Moines, Iowa
HANDLY, EDWARD C., Shelbyville, Indiana
WILLIAMS, LEONARD, Walterboro, South Carolina
YOUTSEY, RICHARD D., Manitou Beach, Michigan

Operation *Masher*—Bong Son Plain

1st Battalion, 7th Cavalry
Alpha Company
ALGARIN-RIVERA, RAFAEL ANGEL, Juncos, Puerto Rico
BABBAGE, EWING COTTRELL, Hopkinsville, Kentucky
BURNLEY, DILLARD REED, Shipman, Virginia
FUQUA, JOHN EDWARD, Nashville, Tennessee
HARSANYI, JIMMY ROGER, Allen Junction, West Virginia
WELLER, TERRY LEE, Ligonier, Pennsylvania
WILLIAMS, GENRETT, Jupiter, Florida
ZIEGLER, DAVID BARTELS, Baltimore, Maryland

Bravo Company
HILL, RAYMOND LEE, Knoxville, Tennessee
LAMBERT, GARY RAMOND, Lockport, New York
LEE, PAUL RICHARD, Bristol, Massachusetts
SEMLER, STANLEY KENTON, Stockton, California
TRAVIS, JON PAUL, Corning, New York

Charlie Company
DRAKE, GLENN FRANKLIN, Roaring Spring, Pennsylvania
FAIRCHILD, DAVID ACEL, Buhl, Idaho
FORRESTER, CARL JAMES, Mercer, Pennsylvania
FREDERICK, CHARLES EMMETT, Bellevue, Ohio
TOLLEY, CALVIN COOLIDGE JR., Pamplin, Virginia

2nd Battalion, 7th Cavalry
Alpha Company
BROPHY, DENNIS JAMES, Trenton, New Jersey
LAWSON, THOMAS ANDREW, Persia, Tennessee
LAY, JOHN EARL, Jellico, Tennessee
MIRANDA-PEREZ, NOE, Juana Diaz, Puerto Rico
PARKER, BENNIE FRANK, Bakersfield, California
ROSS, SAMUEL, Tams, West Virginia

TATSUNO, ALBERT HIROSHI, Aiea, Hawaii
WHITE, JAMES DARRELL JR., Decatur, Illinois

Charlie Company
BEARDEN, RICHARD DEWAYNE, Gadsden, Alabama
CRIBB, FLOYD ALLEN, Hemingway, South Carolina
DOMIAN, EDWARD THOMAS JR., Pittsburgh, Pennsylvania
DRAZER, THOMAS STEPHEN, Kouts, Indiana
DUTHU, ROY ANTHONY, Houma, Louisiana
FOX, CARL JAMES, Minter, Alabama
GRANT, THOMAS RICHARD, Conneaut, Ohio
GUYER, WILLIAM HARRIS, St Mary's, Ohio
LAGRAND, ROBERT HENRY, Bessemer, Alabama
MERONEY, RAPHNELL J., Chattanooga, Tennessee
QUIROZ, JOSEPH ALBERT, Chicago, Illinois
REEVE, DAVID LEO, Hurricane, Utah
RIVERA-REYES, JOSE ALBERTO, New York, New York
SHOCKLEY, THURMAN B. JR., Sparta, Tennessee
WEBSTER, RICHARD, Akron, Ohio

1st Squadron, 9th Cavalry
Charlie Troop
GEIS, WILLIAM CHARLES, Evergreen Park, Illinois

Delta Troop
GRIFFITH, JOHN HOWARD, Mount Vernon, New York
WETMORE, DOUGLAS MCARTHUR, Williamsburg, Kentucky

1st Battalion (Airborne), 12th Cavalry
Charlie Company
JOHNSON, JACK, New York, New York
QUINN, JOHN MICHAEL, New York, New York

2nd Battalion, 12th Cavalry
Alpha Company
AUGUSTINAS, WALTER PETER, New York, New York

BENNETT, MELVIN LESLIE, Cordova, Alabama
HAYES, NELSON LLOYD, Highland Park, Michigan
KELLER, DODD CLIFTON, Duluth, Minnesota
MC GRAW, THOMAS EDWARD, North Syracuse, New York
OLSON, RODNEY JAMES, Eau Claire, Wisconsin
WILLIAMSON, THOMAS DARRELL, Palestine, Texas

Bravo Company
GENSEMER, DAVID DANIEL III, Little Rock, Arkansas
LINDLEY, MARVIN LEROY, Spanish Fork, Utah
MC COY, EUGENE TAYLOR, Moulton, Iowa
PETEET, CHARLES LEONARD, Kaufman, Texas
SMITH, ROBERT LEE, Welch, West Virginia
ROGOFF, JAMES BILL, Kerman, California
THOMAS, JACK JR., Jackson, South Carolina
WAIT, BERNARD JOSEPH, Troy, New York

Charlie Company
DAVENPORT, RICHARD, New York, New York
DELGADO, RUBEN, Chicago, Illinois
NEGRON-RODRIGUEZ, JOSE, Morovis, Puerto Rico

Delta Company
ANDERSON, VICTOR EDWARD, Stone, Idaho

Headquarters Company
DONALDSON, ROBERT D., Dickerson, Maryland

2nd Battalion, 17th Field Artillery
STRICKLAND, HIRAM DILLARD, Graham, North Carolina

1st Battalion, 21st Artillery
GILMORE, KENNETH DEE, Austin, Texas

1st Battalion, 77th Field Artillery
PARKER, RICHARD DENNIS, Salt Lake City, Utah

11th Pathfinder Detachment, 11th Aviation Group
TAYLOR, JAMES ROBERT, Fort Lauderdale, Florida

227th Assault Helicopter Battalion
Charlie Company
HUNT, CLARENCE JR., Tucson, Arizona
JOHNSON, CLIFFORD CURTIS, Fairfax, Oklahoma
STOCKDALE, MELVIN JAMES, Moorhead, Minnesota
ST PETER, ROBERT EUGENE, Gilman, Illinois

228th Assault Support Helicopter Battalion
Bravo Company
ARNOLD, RICHARD EARL, Larned, Kansas
BAIR, CHARLES JACOB, Hollywood, Florida
HARDIN, WILLIAM RICHARD, Westfield, New Jersey
JOHNSON, TAYLOR DOUGLAS, Joaquin, Texas
LUNA, FORTUNATO JR., Alice, Texas
ROOP, FRANK, Fruitland, Florida
TURNER, CLAUDE TYLER, Wilmer, Alabama

229th Assault Helicopter Battalion
Bravo Company
PHILLIPS, HOWARD EDWARD, Scottsboro, Alabama

Charlie Company
ZAMORA, CARLOS JR., Carrizozo, New Mexico

United States Army, Special Forces Detachment B-52, Project Delta, 5th Special Forces Group (Airborne)
Team 2 (Capital)
COOK, MARLIN C., Vernon, Alabama
DOTSON, DONALD L., Alcoa, Tennessee
HANCOCK, JESSE L., Seattle, Washington
HOAGLUND III, GEORGE A., Phoenix, Arizona

Team 3 (Roadrunner)
BADOLATI, FRANK N., Goffstown, New Hampshire
HODGSON, CECIL J., Greenville, Texas
TERRY, RONALD T., Niagara Falls, New York

Operation *Masher/White Wing*—An Lao Valley

1st Battalion, 5th Cavalry
Bravo Company
BEERES, GEORGE KEVIN, Union City, New Jersey
CANLAS, SEBASTIAN PIADOCHE, Murcia, Philippines
CANTRELL, LESLIE HOWARD, Copperhill, Tennessee
COTTON, MOSES M., Porterville, Mississippi
HOBBS, RONALD WAYNE, Kalamazoo, Michigan
TAYLOR, THEODORE F. JR., Chance, Maryland

2nd Battalion, 12th Cavalry
Bravo Company
HOAR, JOHN MICHAEL, Belleville, New Jersey

Operation *Masher/White Wing* (*Eagle's Claw*)—Kim Son Valley

1st Battalion, 5th Cavalry

Alpha Company

CLEGG, LESTER HOWARD, Washington, D.C.
GREENE, PAUL HARISON, Cincinnati, Ohio
ARRIS, PATRICK JAMES, Waukegan, Illinois
PATZWALL, JAMES GEORGE, Baltimore, Maryland
PREIRA, DOMINIC J. JR., Burlington, Connecticut
TERLECKI, WALTER ALEXANDER, Hartford, Connecticut

Bravo Company

BARNES, RICHARD FRANK, Elmira, New York
BRUMLEY, BOB GENE, Lincoln, Nebraska
DAVIS, WILLIE EDWARD, Houston, Texas
GRAZIANO, ANDREW ALBERT, New York, New York
JESSIE, MARSHALL, New York, New York
MCCLELLAN, BRENT A., Clarksville, Pennsylvania
MCGRIFF, DANNY JAY, Fresno, California
MIDDLETON, KENNETH DALE, Port Huron, Michigan
MIZE, JAMES WESLEY JR., Palm Beach, Florida
PLISKA, MICHAEL DENNIS, McKeesport, Pennsylvania
RIGG, WILLIAM CECIL, Los Angeles, California
TART, CLIFTON LEE, New York, New York
WILLIAMS, CARTER LEE JR., Winona, Mississippi
YOUNG, CHARLIE M., Riviera Beach, Florida

Charlie Company

ALLEN, JAMES OTIS, Indianapolis, Indiana
GREEN, FREDDIE WALLACE, Charlotte, North Carolina
KENNY, RONALD MICHAEL, Mount Airy, Maryland

2nd Battalion, 5th Cavalry

Alpha Company

JAMES, JACK LLEWELLYN, Mason City, Iowa
LOPEZ-COLON, JUAN ANTONIO, Loiza, Puerto Rico
NAYLOR, RAYMOND LUKE, Lancaster, Kentucky

Bravo Company
BROWN, DAVID PETER, Flat Rock, Michigan
GORTON, GARY BRUCE, New York, New York
PETERSON, JESSE EARL, Barberton, Ohio
SMITH, ROBERT LINDO, Sanford, North Carolina
WEIAND, RAYMOND D., Mifflintown, Pennsylvania
WHITTEN, DAVID ELGA, Los Angeles, California

Charlie Company
BENKE, RONALD JOHN III, White Hall, Maryland
CARR, LEN E., New York, New York
FONGER, LYNDSEY FRANK, Tooele, Utah
LILLY, ROBERT C., Nimitz, West Virginia
RICE, THOMAS EVERETT, Howard Lake, Minnesota
WADE, DOUGLAS JOHN, Idaho Falls, Idaho

Delta Company
BOWEN, HARVEY LEWIS JR., Atlanta, Georgia
LOVE, HUGH ALLEN, Knoxville, Tennessee

1st Battalion, 7th Cavalry
Charlie Company
DINGER, JAMES ROBERT, Thompsonville, Michigan

2nd Battalion, 7th Cavalry
Alpha Company
TULLER, DENNIS J., Martinez, California

Bravo Company
FISHER, DAVID LUTHER, Mitchell, Illinois
FRASURE, HURSHEL, Bainbridge, Ohio
POSTON, RAYMOND ROGER, Kilgore, Texas
WORLEY, ROBERT KEITH, Saltville, Virginia

2nd Battalion (Airborne), 8th Cavalry
Alpha Company
ANDERSON, LEE DAVID, Lincoln, Nebraska

DETRIXHE, JAMES B. W., Bethlehem, Pennsylvania
MARSHALL, RICHARD ALLAN, Glen Avon, California
MERRELL, ROBERT DELL, Tiptonville, Tennessee
ROBINSON, JOSEPH LUTHER, Newport News, Virginia

Bravo Company
CAVAZOS, REYNALDO ROY, Quincy, Washington
CURRY, GLENN VERNARD, Detroit, Michigan

Charlie Company
NEMCHICK, MICHAEL JOSEPH, McKeesport, Pennsylvania
OGLETHORPE, THOMAS JAY, Petaluma, California

1st Squadron, 9th Cavalry
Alpha Troop (Airborne)
LANTER, KENNETH WAYNE, Cincinnati, Ohio
STEPHENSON, WILLIAM JAMES, Bound Brook, New Jersey
STEWART, JERRY DEAN, Lanagan, Missouri

Delta Troop
BISE, ROGER ALLEN, Morgantown, West Virginia
HOUSTON, JOHN WESLEY, Little Rock, Arkansas
RICHTMYRE, CHARLES LAWRENCE, Winnetta, Illinois

1st Battalion (Airborne), 12th Cavalry
Alpha Company
COBURN, WILLIAM H., Chesapeake, Virginia
DALE, CHARLES RICHARD, Gaithersburg, Maryland
DYSON, CHARLES E. JR., Philadelphia, Pennsylvania
HOUGH, MATTHEW, Bethune, South Carolina
JAMES, JOE NEAL, Oakland, California
LONG, ELDON DALE, Liberty, Kansas
MORRIS, WINSTON, Chicago, Illinois
RANGEL, RICHARD, San Bernardino, California
SANCHEZ, FRANKIE, Dodge City, Kansas
SEXTON, JIMMY CLYDE, Blountstown, Florida

SMITH, MARSHALL R., Lakewood, California
STOCHAJ, PAUL JOHN, Webster, Massachusetts

Bravo Company
ADAMSON, DONALD BRUCE, Grand Rapids, Michigan
MCDONALD, MICHAEL WILLIAM, Carmel, New York
NEVIN, PATRICK CHRISTOPHER, East Chicago, Indiana

Charlie Company
JUREK, DALMER DOLAN, Caldwell, Texas
MULWEE, ISAIAH JR., Bridgeport, Connecticut
NICHOLAS, TOMMY L., Decatur, Alabama
REYNOLDS, KENNETH ALDERSON, Washington, D.C.
THOMAS, RICHARD GEORGE, Cleveland Heights, Ohio
WILSON, MARVIN JAMES, Crosby, Minnesota

Headquarters Company
EL HONDAH, DOVE, Chicago, Illinois
MACK, ROBERT LEWIS, Cleveland, Ohio
WATSON, WILLIAM B. JR., Durham, North Carolina

2nd Battalion, 12th Cavalry
Alpha Company
DELA TORRE, LUIS, Los Angeles, California
HARRIS, JERRY BRUCE, Black Mountain, North Carolina
MCCORMICK, JEROME LOMAC, Rafford, North Carolina
MEDLEY, CLARENCE, Cleveland, Ohio
SANTOS-PINEDO, PEDRO, Ponce, Puerto Rico
STICE LARRY, DOUGLAS, Lakewood, Colorado

Bravo Company
DAVISON, WILLIAM A. JR., Montrose, Pennsylvania
JOHNSON, BOBBY GENE, Hammond, Louisiana
ROBINSON, SHEPPARD JR., Miami, Florida

Delta Company
FORD, RAYMOND SYLVESTER, Bardstown, Kentucky

1st Battalion, 77th Field Artillery
COLLINS, ELZIE J. JR SGT 19660219, Bravo Battery, Williamsport, Kentucky
ZELDES, MARK HILLARY 2LT 19660217, Alpha Battery, New York, New York

2nd Battalion, 20th Aerial Rocket Artillery
CONDY, LADD ROBERT, Boulder, Colorado

8th Engineers
SAMPT, JOHN FRANCIS, Bravo Co., Waterbury, Connecticut

United States Air Force, 21st Tactical Air Support Squadron (Forward Air Controller), 505th Tactical Control Group, 2nd Air Division
HOLT, MARSHALL M., Des Moines, Iowa
MEINERS, PAUL A., Kaysville, Utah

Operation *Masher/White Wing* (*Black Horse*)—Cay Giep Mountains

1st Battalion (Airborne), 8th Cavalry
Delta Company
HATCHER, CARLOS RANDALL, Norcross, Georgia

Sources
1st Cavalry Division Association, https://www.1cda.org, Book of Honor
Vietnam Air Losses: https://www.vietnamairlosses.com
The Coffelt Database of Vietnam Casualties, http://www.coffeltdatabase.org
Vietnam Veterans Memorial Fund, The Wall of Faces, https://www.vvmf.org

APPENDIX II

Memorandum Requesting Name Change

Memorandum from General Earle "Bus" Wheeler, Chairman of the Joint Chiefs of Staff, to General William C. Westmoreland, Commander of the MACV, requesting a name change for Operation *Masher*.

Source: COPY LBJ LIBRARY

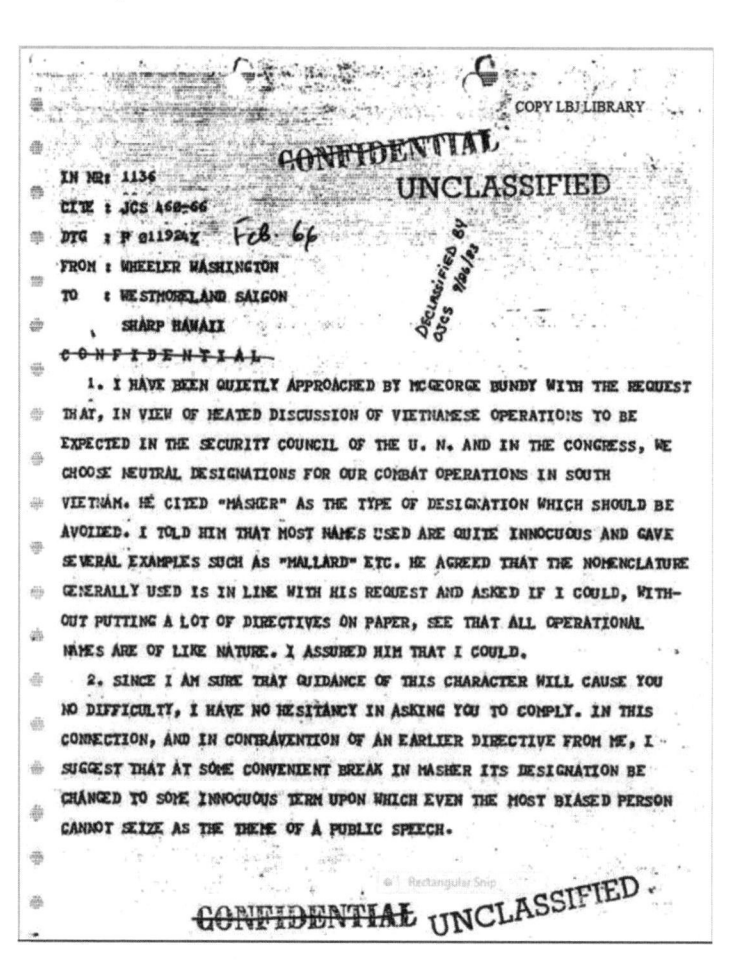

```
IN NR: 1136
CITE : JCS 468-66
DTG : P 011924Z Feb 66
FROM : WHEELER WASHINGTON
TO   : WESTMORELAND SAIGON
       SHARP HAWAII

CONFIDENTIAL

1. I HAVE BEEN QUIETLY APPROACHED BY MCGEORGE BUNDY WITH THE REQUEST
THAT, IN VIEW OF HEATED DISCUSSION OF VIETNAMESE OPERATIONS TO BE
EXPECTED IN THE SECURITY COUNCIL OF THE U. N. AND IN THE CONGRESS, WE
CHOOSE NEUTRAL DESIGNATIONS FOR OUR COMBAT OPERATIONS IN SOUTH
VIETNAM. HE CITED "MASHER" AS THE TYPE OF DESIGNATION WHICH SHOULD BE
AVOIDED. I TOLD HIM THAT MOST NAMES USED ARE QUITE INNOCUOUS AND GAVE
SEVERAL EXAMPLES SUCH AS "MALLARD" ETC. HE AGREED THAT THE NOMENCLATURE
GENERALLY USED IS IN LINE WITH HIS REQUEST AND ASKED IF I COULD, WITH-
OUT PUTTING A LOT OF DIRECTIVES ON PAPER, SEE THAT ALL OPERATIONAL
NAMES ARE OF LIKE NATURE. I ASSURED HIM THAT I COULD.

2. SINCE I AM SURE THAT GUIDANCE OF THIS CHARACTER WILL CAUSE YOU
NO DIFFICULTY, I HAVE NO HESITANCY IN ASKING YOU TO COMPLY. IN THIS
CONNECTION, AND IN CONTRAVENTION OF AN EARLIER DIRECTIVE FROM ME, I
SUGGEST THAT AT SOME CONVENIENT BREAK IN MASHER ITS DESIGNATION BE
CHANGED TO SOME INNOCUOUS TERM UPON WHICH EVEN THE MOST BIASED PERSON
CANNOT SEIZE AS THE THEME OF A PUBLIC SPEECH.
```

APPENDIX III

Citations

Sgt. Gary B. Gorton
DISTINGUISHED SERVICE CROSS CITATION
Awarded for actions during the Vietnam War

Citation:

The President of the United States takes pride in presenting the Distinguished Service Cross (Posthumously) to Gary Bruce Gorton (RA51447475), Sergeant, U.S. Army, for extraordinary heroism in connection with military operations involving conflict with an armed hostile force in the Republic of Vietnam, while serving with Company B, 2d Battalion, 5th Cavalry, 1st Cavalry Division. On 17 February 1966, Sergeant Gorton, serving as mortar squad leader, was accompanying his unit to establish a blocking position when they contacted and attacked a Viet Cong heavy weapons battalion. Moving his squad to some nearby shell craters, Sergeant Gorton immediately engaged the insurgents and delivered deadly and accurate mortar support to his company until his ammunition was expended. Under his direction he employed his squad as riflemen and successfully averted the Viet Cong assault against their sector defenses. The insurgents regrouped and again charged the American perimeter. With compete disregard for his own personal safety, Sergeant Gorton, exposed himself to an intense hail of automatic and small arms fire, throwing grenades and firing his weapon at the advancing Viet Cong forces. Sergeant Gorton killed five of the insurgents and personally captured a machine gun. His extraordinary heroism and devotion to duty, at the cost of his life, were in keeping with the highest traditions of the military service and reflect great credit upon himself, his unit, and the United States Army.

Headquarters, US Army, Pacific, General Orders No. 158 (July 14, 1966)

Home Town: New York, New York

Action Date: 17-Feb-66

Service: Army

Rank: Sergeant

Company: Company B

Battalion: 2d Battalion
Regiment: 5th Cavalry Regiment
Division: 1st Cavalry Division

Source: 1st Cavalry Division Association website, http://www.1cda.org

1st Lt. Stephens, Rufus

DISTINGUISHED SERVICE CROSS CITATION

Awarded for actions during the Vietnam War

Citation:

The President of the United States takes pleasure in presenting the Distinguished Service Cross to Rufus Stephens (0-5321191), First Lieutenant (Infantry), U.S. Army, for extraordinary heroism in connection with military operations involving conflict with an armed hostile force in the Republic of Vietnam. On 17 February 1966, First Lieutenant Stephens was serving as Executive Officer, Company B, 2d Battalion, 5th Cavalry Division (Airmobile), 1st Cavalry Division. He was accompanying the 3d Platoon in screening the high ground to Company B's flank. As the main force entered the Song Bien Valley, they were engaged by a Viet Cong force estimated to be a reinforced heavy weapons battalion which forced them to take defensive positions in three large bomb craters in the valley floor. The 3d Platoon, in spite of being at a numerical disadvantage, launched an attack at the Viet Cong perimeter trying desperately to help the friendly defenders. As they came to within 100 meters of the company, they came under a heavy barrage of machine gun fire which seriously wounded the platoon leader. Lieutenant Stephens immediately took charge and began regrouping the platoon to prevent their positions from being overrun. Without regard for his own personal safety, he exposed himself to the continuous machine gun fire in order to direct the medical evacuation crafts to his location. After successfully evacuating the wounded, he returned to his platoon and readied his men for an attempt to join the besieged company. The first attempt was unsuccessful. The volume of fire was increasing all the time and caused Company B to lose contact with outside fire support. Noting the problem, Lieutenant Stephens again braved the hostile fire in order to get to a position from which he could better control the oncoming fire support for the friendly defenders. He was wounded in the arm but refused medical attention so that he could continue controlling fire support against the insurgent attackers. Realizing that one of the friendly aircraft was preparing for a bomb-run that would endanger the friendly positions, Lieutenant Stephens once again braved the barrage of insurgent fire and waved off the plane averting certain disaster for the friendly defenders. By increasing the rate of fire, a rifle company was able to air-assault into Lieutenant Stephens' position and by joining forces they were able to make contact with the besieged company. By directing close-in tactical air strikes at the insurgents, the attacks were stopped. Lieutenant Stephens' sustained performance during this period of actual combat was a source of inspiration to the men of the 3d Platoon. First Lieutenant Stephens' extraordinary heroism and devotion to duty were in keeping with the highest traditions of the military service and reflect great credit upon himself, his unit, and the United States Army.

Headquarters, US Army, Pacific, General Orders No. 176 (July 29, 1966)
Action Date: 17-Feb-66
Service: Army
Rank: 1st Lieutenant
Company: Company B
Battalion: 2d Battalion
Regiment: 5th Cavalry Regiment
Division: 1st Cavalry Division

Source: 1st Cavalry Division Association website, http://www.1cda.org

Glossary

A-1E Skyraider	U.S. Air Force single-engine propeller driven dive bomber attack aircraft equipped with four wing-mounted 20mm cannons; had a weapons capacity that could be varied among high-explosive or white phosphorus bombs, napalm, and rockets; deployed in pairs
AK-47	Soviet-made 7.62mm assault rifle used by North Vietnamese and Viet Cong soldiers
APC	armored personnel carrier, military vehicle designed and equipped to transport personnel and equipment into battle
ARA	aerial rocket artillery, a UH-1 helicopter armed with 48 2¾-inch folding fin rockets carried in two pods of 24 each
ARVN	Army of the Republic of (South) Vietnam
C-123	U.S. Air Force Provider aircraft
C-130	U.S. Air Force Hercules aircraft, the larger four-engine brother to the C-123 Provider aircraft
CH-47 Chinook	twin-engine, large cargo-type helicopter
CH-54 Flying Cane	twin-engine heavy-lift helicopter designed to hold its cargo tight against its center spine to lessen drag and eliminate the pendulum effect in forward flight
Chicom Grenade	Chinese-manufactured grenade with a short wooden handle similar to a German potato-masher style grenade of World War II, with steel casing serrated (i.e., notched pineapple style) and smaller in size than the German grenade
CIDG	Civilian Irregular Defense Group, a South Vietnamese irregular military unit developed by the U.S. government from minority populations, such as the Montagnards, Nungs, and Cao Dai
CV-2 Caribou	Canadian-designed and produced tactical cargo aircraft with a short takeoff and landing capability; capable of carrying 32 troops or two Jeeps or similar light vehicles; had a rear loading ramp that could also be used for parachute dropping
FAC	U.S. Air Force forward air controller
Gunship	UH-1B helicopter armed with 30-caliber (7.62mm) mini-guns and automatic (40mm) grenade launcher placed in powered nose turret
H&I fire	harassing and interdiction fire
Hootch	a hut in which farmers and peasants in rural areas in Vietnam lived, typically constructed of a thatched roof and upright bamboo posts

Huey	UH-1D helicopter used for carrying infantry troops into battle, had two door gunners each with a 60-caliber machine gun; also used for command & control purposes and medical evacuation of wounded and injured troopers
KBA	killed by air (i.e., killed by helicopter gunship or tactical air support)
KIA	killed in action
Local Militia	South Vietnamese Regional Popular Force soldiers
Landing Zone (LZ)	an area where one or more helicopters can land or set down, allowing soldiers to climb onboard or jump off, or for equipment or ammunition to be loaded onboard or taken off; frequently an LZ is surrounded by artillery howitzers supporting infantry operations
M-16	lightweight 5.56mm assault rifle used by the U.S. Army's infantry soldiers
M-60	standard 7.62mm machine gun used by the U.S. Army's infantry soldiers
M-79	single-shot, shoulder-fired grenade launcher used by the U.S. Army's infantry soldiers, utilizing 40x46mm rounds
M-101 howitzer	105mm (4-inch) light field howitzer used by the U.S. Army
M-110 howitzer	8-inch (203mm) self-propelled howitzer installed on a purpose-built chassis used by the U.S. Army
M-113	fully tracked armored personnel carrier (APC) fitted with a 50-caliber machine gun used by the U.S. Army, nicknamed the "Green Dragon"
M-114 howitzer	155mm (6-inch) towed howitzer used by the U.S. Army
Medevac	UH-1D Huey helicopter configured for transport of wounded soldiers from the battlefield to field hospital
MIA	Missing in Action
NVA	North Vietnamese Army
OH-13	observation helicopter
Poncho	large square sheet of watertight material with slit in middle for soldier's head to stick out, designed as outerwear to keep the body dry from rain
PRC-25	lightweight infantry field radio
PSP	perforated (or pierced) steel planking material used for the construction of temporary runways, landing strips, and walkways
Puff-the-Magic-Dragon	U.S. Air Force C-47 aircraft equipped as a gunship with three 7.62mm mini-guns, providing close-in tactical air support to ground troops, nicknamed "Spooky"
RTO	radio telephone operator
Rucksack	bag with a metal frame that is strapped to the back with two shoulder straps, used by U.S. Army infantry soldiers for carrying ammunition, food, and water; typically made of strong waterproof material
Sapper	expert in demolitions and breaching fortifications
Slick	helicopter used to carry infantry troops into battle (see Huey)
Sling Load	cargo, such as an artillery howitzer, suspended beneath the underside of a Chinook helicopter by a long cable or line
SKS	Soviet-made semi-automatic carbine rifle used by North Vietnamese and Viet Cong soldiers
Smokey-the-Bear	U.S. Air Force C-123 aircraft used to drop magnesium-based flares to illuminate the ground at night, while circling over battlefield

Spider Hole	one-man fighting position dug into the ground used by North Vietnamese and Viet Cong soldiers, typically well camouflaged
Type 56	Chinese-made 7.62mm assault rifle used by North Vietnamese and Viet Cong soldiers, a variant of the Soviet-designed AK-47 assault rifle; also known as an AK-56
USAF	United States Air Force
VNAF	(South) Vietnam Air Force
Web Gear	belt around the waist with two harness straps, or suspenders, one over each shoulder, that connect to the belt both in the front and back; small equipment items, such as ammunition pouches, grenades, water canteen covers, entrenching tool carriers, first aid dressing cases, etc., can be attached to belt and straps
WIA	wounded in action
WP	white phosphorus bomb (a.k.a. Willey Pete)

Bibliography

The most used and most useful historical documents in my research were as follows:

1st Cavalry Division (Airmobile), "Combat Operations After Action Report (RCS MACV J3/32), Operation Masher 25 Jan–3 Feb 66, Operation White Wing 4 Feb–6 Mar 66," April 28, 1966.

1st Cavalry Division (Airmobile), "Operational Report on Lessons Learned for Quarterly Period Ending 30 April 66," May 5, 1966.

1st Cavalry Division (Airmobile), "Interim Report of Operations, July 1, 1965 to December 31, 1966."

1st Cavalry Division Association. *The 1st Air Cavalry Division, Vietnam, August 1965–December 1969.* Paducah, Kentucky: Turner Publishing Company, 1995.

1st Cavalry Division (Airmobile), "Quarterly Command Report for Second Fiscal Quarter, FY 1966, 1 Oct–31 Dec 65," January 10, 1966.

3rd Brigade, 1st Air Cavalry Division, "Combat Operations After Action Report (MACV/RCS/J3/32), Operation Masher, 24 Jan–4 Feb 66, Operation White Wing (Eagles Claw) 4 Feb–17 Feb 66," March 10, 1966.

2nd Brigade, 1st Air Cavalry Division, "Combat Operations After Action Report, White Wing, Search-and-Destroy, 2 Feb–15 Feb 66," March 16, 1966.

2nd Brigade, 1st Air Cavalry Division, "Combat Operations After Action Report, White Wing (Eagle's Claw), Search-and-Destroy, 16 Feb–27 Feb 66," March 16, 1966.

1st Brigade (Airborne), 1st Air Cavalry Division, "Combat Operations After Action Report (MACV/RCS/J3/32), Operation White Wing (Eagle's Claw), 17–27 February 1966," March 4, 1966.

2nd Brigade, 1st Air Cavalry Division, "Combat Operations After Action Report, Black Horse, Search-and-Destroy, 01 March–05 March 1966," March 16, 1966.

1st Battalion, 7th Cavalry, 1st Air Cavalry Division, "Combat Operations After Action Report, 24 Jan 66–4 Feb 66 and 5 Feb–16 Feb 1966," February 22, 1966.

2nd Battalion, 7th Cavalry, 3rd Brigade, 1st Air Cavalry Division, "After Action Report, 25 Jan 66–16 Feb 66," February 19, 1966.

"History of the 2nd Battalion, 12th Cavalry, Chapter II, 1 January to 4 March 1966, Operation Masher, Operation White Wing."

Daily Journals, Headquarters, 1st Air Cav Div, 28 Jan 66–4 Feb 66.

Daily Journals, Headquarters, 1st Air Cav Div, 7 Feb 66–15 Feb 66.

Daily Journals, Headquarters, 1st Air Cav Div, 16 Feb 66–28 Feb 66 (only available through a Freedom of Information Act request).

Daily Journals, Headquarters, 2nd Battalion, 12th Cavalry, 1st Air Cavalry Division, 27 Jan 66–4 Feb 66.

Daily Journals, Headquarters, 1st Battalion (Abn), 12th Cavalry, 1st Air Cavalry Division, 29 Jan 66–4 Feb 66.

Daily Journals, Headquarters, 1st Battalion (Abn), 12th Cavalry, 1st Air Cavalry Division, 11 Feb 66–28 Feb 66.

Daily Journals, Headquarters, 1st Battalion (Abn), 8th Cavalry, 1st Air Cavalry Division, 18 Feb 66–28 Feb 66.

Daily Journals, Headquarters, 2nd Battalion (Abn), 8th Cavalry, 1st Air Cavalry Division, 18 Feb 66–28 Feb 66.

Daily Journals, Headquarters, 1st Battalion, 5th Cavalry, 1st Air Cavalry Division, 18 Feb–28 Feb 66.
Daily Journals, Headquarters, 1st Air Cav Div, 1 Mar 66–5 Mar 66.
Topographic Maps of Vietnam, Binh Dinh Province, Hoai Nhon District, Hoai An District, Areas of Operation, Digital Map Images.
Topographic Maps of Vietnam, QL1/South of Tam Quan, LZ North English, LZ Tom, Truong Lam—Map Sheet 6838-3 Tam Quan, Digital Map Images.
Porter, Captain Melvin F., USAF SE Asia Team, Project CHECO, "Project CHECO, The Siege at Plei Me, 19–29 October 1965," Report #160, February 24, 1966.
Bates, 1st Lieutenant William E., and Sams, Mr Kenneth, USAF SE Asia Team, Project CHECO, "Operation Masher & White Wing, 25 January–6 March, 1966," Report #150, September 9, 1966.
Commanding Officer, 407th Viet Cong Main Force Battalion, "Viet Cong After Action Report, An Khe, 2/66, Report on the Raid on 1st US Air Cavalry Division Base in An Khe on the night of 19 February 1966, Binh Dinh Sapper 502, No 10/L12." Translation of captured Viet Cong document.
Westmoreland, General William C., COMUSMACV (Commander, U.S. Military Assistance Command, Vietnam), "Military Estimate of the Situation in Vietnam, 5–12 March 1965."
Wright, Captain Robert E., ADA Adjutant, "4th PSYOP Group Special Report—Effect of Malaria on Combat Effectiveness of Viet Cong and North Vietnamese Army Forces (U)." Translation of captured Viet Cong document.

Other Books and Articles

Albertson, Roger L. "'The Last Survivor,' A Memorial Day Tribute." http://www.projectdelta.net.
Anonymous, Fort Benning, U.S. Army. "In Memoriam: LTG Harold G. 'Hal' Moore." https://www.benning.army.mil/armor/eARMOR/content/issues/2017/Winter/1InMemoriamMoore17.pdf.
Aviation Safety Network. "ASN Aircraft accident Fairchild C-123K Provider 54–702, An Khe." https://aviation-safety.net/database/record.php?id=19660125-0.
Beene, Wallace. "Camp Honors Cav's 1st Killed in Action." *Pacific Stars & Stripes*, Wednesday, Feb 23, 1966.
Burns, Ken, and Lynn Novick. *Vietnam War, An Intimate History*. New York: Alfred A. Knopf, 2017.
Carland, John M. *Combat Operations, Stemming the Tide, May 1965 to October 1966*. Washington, D.C.: Center of Military History, United States Army, 2000.
Davidson, Phillip B. *Vietnam at War: The History, 1945–1975*. Novato, CA: Presidio Press, 1988.
Davidson, Ray. "A Man is Not Dead Until He is Forgotten, The Story of Frank N. Badolati." http://www.projectdelta.net.
Diduryk, Captain Myron, Infantry. "Operations of Company B, 2nd Battalion, 7th Cavalry, 1st Cavalry Division (Airmobile), in a search-and-destroy operation on 15 February 66 during Operation Masher/White Wing (Eagle's Claw), in Binh Dinh Province, Republic of Vietnam, Personal Experience of a Company Commander, dated 7 February 1967." U.S. Army Infantry School monograph.
Flames of War. "B3 Front in Vietnam." https://fliphtml5.com/miqg/vmeh.
Gibbons, William Conrad. *U.S. Government and the Vietnam War, Executive and Legislative Roles and Relationships,* Part IV. Princeton, NJ: Princeton University Press, 1995.
Global Security. "North Vietnamese Army and Viet Cong Infantry / Artillery Regiments." www.globalsecurity.org.
Goldstein, Richard. "Harry W.O. Kinnard, Who Said One Word Would Do, Dies at 93." The New York Times, January 10, 2009. https://www.nytimes.com/2009/01/11/us/11kinnard.html.
Hackett, Jim "Doc". Email to author dated June 2, 2011, with attachment entitled "LZ 4."
Hayes III, Major General Thomas J. "The Military Engineer: TME Looks Back: Vietnam, Army Engineers in Vietnam." *USA*, January–February 1966 issue.

Jaramillo, Rudy Email to author dated July 9, 2021.
Karnow, Stanley. *Vietnam: A History*. New York: Penguin Books, 1983.
Klein, Captain Stephen, Infantry. "Operations of Company B, 1st Battalion (Airborne), 12th Cavalry, 1st Cavalry Division (Airmobile), on a search-and-destroy operation on 12–13 February 1966, in Binh Dinh Province, Republic of Vietnam, Personal Experience of a Company Commander, dated 6 February 1967." U.S. Army Infantry School monograph.
Mason, Robert. *Chickenhawk*. New York: Viking Press, 1983.
McMahon, Captain Robert W., Infantry. "Operations of Company B, 2nd Battalion, 5th Cavalry, 1st Cavalry Division (Airmobile), in the attack upon a main force Viet Cong heavy weapons battalion in the vicinity of Bong Son, South Vietnam, 16–17 February 1966, dated 6 February 1967." U.S. Army Infantry School monograph.
Mertel, Colonel Kenneth D. (Ret.). *Year of the Horse: Vietnam, 1st Air Cavalry in the Highlands, 1965–1967*. Atglen, PA: Schiffer Publishing Ltd, 1997.
Military wiki. "United States Air Force in South Vietnam." https://military-history.fandom.com/wiki/United_States_Air_Force_in_South_Vietnam.
Moore, LTG Harold G., and Joseph L. Galloway. We Were Soldiers Once ... *and Young; Ia Drang: the battle that changed the war in Vietnam*. New York, New York: Random House, 1992. ISBN 978-0-679-41158-1.
Moutin-Luyat, Stephane. *Vietnam Combat Operations, A Chronology of Allied Combat Operations in Vietnam, 1965*. Stephane Moutin-Luyat, 2009.
"National Security Action Memorandum 328, 6 April 65." *Pentagon Papers* (Gravel Edition).
Skelly, Gerry. Email to author dated May 11, 2011, with attachment entitled "Regarding LZ 4 (Graveyard) January 28th 1966."
Sugdinis, Captain Joel E., Infantry. "Operations of Company A, 2nd Battalion, 7th Cavalry, 1st Air Cavalry Division, Near Bong Son, An Thi, Republic of Vietnam, 25–29 January 1966, Operation Masher, Personal Experience of a Company Commander, dated 1966–1967." U.S. Army Infantry School monograph.
Tolson, Lieutenant General John J. *Vietnam Studies, Airmobility 1961–1971*. Washinton, DC: Center of Military History, United States Army, 1999. CMH Pub. 90–4, 1973.
U.S. Army. "Bruce F. Crandall, Medal of Honor, Profile." https://www.army.mil.
USMCCCAOnline. "Bob Poos, AP correspondent dies after a lengthy illness." https://www.usmcc-caonline.com/cc-bob-poos-ap-correspondent-dies-after-a-lengthy-illness/.
Vietnam Helicopter Pilots Association. http://www.vhpa.org.
Vietnam Veterans Memorial Fund (VVMF) Wall of Faces, http://www.vvmf.org.
Vincent, Duane D. "An Lao Valley Incident." https://www.281st.com/281Remembrance/stories/an_lao_valley_incident_duane_vincent.htm.
Wagner, Jack. Email to author dated January 25, 2017, describing Alpha Company, 2nd Battalion, 7th Cavalry's move to Phung Du on January 28, 1966.
Wikipedia. "Ambush at the Mang Yang Pass." https://en.wikipedia.org/wiki/Battle_of_Mang_Yang_Pass.
Wikipedia. "Henri Huet, AP photographer." https://en.wikipedia.org/wiki/Henri_Huet.
Wikipedia. "Myron F. Diduryk." https://en.wikipedia.org.
Wikipedia. "Project Delta." https://en.wikipedia.org/wiki/Project_DELTA.
Wikipedia. "Robert McDade." https://en.wikipedia.org.
Wilensky, Robert J, MD, PhD. "The Medical Civic Action Program in Vietnam: Success or Failure?" Military Medicine, October 2001.
Wong, Daniel Jun Yi, University of Melbourne, Australia. "Hookworm Infections." https://dermnetnz.org/, dated 2013.
Zeller, Al. Email to author dated November 11, 2019, describing 2nd Battalion, 12th Cav's move to Phung Du on January 29, 1966.

Index

Reference to maps are in *italics*.

2nd Surgical Hospital (Mobile Army), 27, 28, 161
6th Airlift Platoon, 165
11th Air Assault Division (Test), 5, 6; *see also* U.S. Army (units): 1st Cavalry Division (Airmobile)
11th Aviation Group, 17, 24, 127
85th Evacuation Hospital, 27
145th Airlift Platoon, 29, 44, 45
506 Valley, 96–97, 102, 122, 168–70

Ackerson, Lt. Col. Frederick, 72, 90, 144, 145, 148–51
aerial rocket artillery (ARA) helicopter, 17, 24, 26, 28, 63, 66, 72, 77, 90–91, 98, 101–7, 113, 116, 118, 130, 135, 182–83
 and Go Chai Mountains, 170, 172, 174–75
 and Iron Triangle, 143–44, 148–49, 153
 and Phung Du, 38–39, 47, 52, 59
aircraft:
 A-1E Skyraider, 25–26, 29, 43, 47–48, 50, 52, 55, 60, 63, 69, 76, 90, 98, 100, 103, 118, 120–21, 134, 136, 145, 147–48, 168–70, 179
 B-52 bomber, 80, 126, 131, 151–54, 176, 184
 B-57 bomber, 59, 79
 C-47 suppressive fire (Puff-the-Magic-Dragon), 26, 55, 70, 76, 90, 130, 140, 143–44
 C-123 flare ship (Smokey-the-Bear), 2, 8, 9, 13–14, 18–21, 23, 29, 33, 80–81, 83, 157, 162, 178, 188
 CH-47 Chinook helicopter, 26
 CH-54 Flying Crane helicopter, 13
 CV-2 Caribou transport plane, 8, 9, 13–14, 18–19, 27, 29, 178
 O-1 Bird Dog, 25, 42, 118, 120, 134, 170, 184
 OH-13 Scout helicopter, 28, 39, 105, 129, 164
 UH-1 helicopter (Huey), 42
An Khe (village), 157–59, 161, 163
An Khe Army Airfield, 18–19, 157, 162
An Khe base camp, 3, 7, 8, 13, 17, 26, 27, 54, 65, 72, 121–22, 155–56, 178, 180, 182, 187, 188
 and *Black Horse*, 178, 180, 182
 and *Eagle's Claw*, 81, 83, 101, 104
 map, *166*
An Khe Pass, 10, 21–23, 33, 96
An Lao Valley, 2, 4, 5, 10–11, 13, 24, 29, 75, 83–93, 122, 127, 129, 187–89
 and *Eagle's Claw*, 97, 101–2
 and Phung Du, 31, 42, 44–45, 47, 53, 55
An Tuc/An Khe Special Forces Camp, 18–19, 157
Anderson, 2nd Lt. Lewis, 107, 108
anti-malaria pills, 7
Army of the Republic of Vietnam (ARVN):
 2nd Infantry Division, 84, 93
 22nd Infantry Division, 2, 9–10, 13, 24, 51, 56, 73, 81, 84, 93, 168, 177–78, 187–88
 Airborne Brigade, 9–10, 13, 31, 40, 55–56, 72–73, 81, 188
 4th Regiment, 3rd Battalion, 29, 84, 93
 40th (Mechanized) Regiment, 10, 56, 73, 81, 84, 93, 168, 188
 41st Regiment, 10, 73, 81, 84, 93, 168, 178, 183, 188
 3rd Troop, 3rd Armored Cavalry Squadron, 51, 67, 178, 188
 Junk Fleet, 179

B-3 Front (NVA), 3, 11
B-52s *see* aircraft
Baker, 1st Lt. Roger, 103, 105, 107–8
Battle of the Bulge, 4
Beard, Lt. Col. Rutland D., Jr., 17, 71, 77, 107, 109, 168, 170
Beckwith, Maj. Charles, 11–12, 29, 44–47, 83
Bin Dinh Provincial Hospital, 42
Bin Sonh Valley, 102–4, 109, 110, 112
Binh Tri Thien Division (NVA), 18, 95
Bong Son (town), 2, 12, 56, 65, 71, 82, 93
Bong Son Dispensary, 42, 49, 57, 88, 92, 183
Bong Son Plain, 3–5, 9, 10, 12, 13, 23, 43, 72, 78, 81
Bong Son Special Forces Camp, 2, 8, 9–10, 18–21, 23–24, 187
Brewer, Sgt. Forrest, 69
Bundy, McGeorge, xi, xii, 86
Burdett, Col. Allen, Jr., 127

Cambodia, xiv, xv, 2, 3, 8, 187
Camp Radcliffe, 164, 187
Cay Giep Mountains, 17, 177–79, 183, 185
Central Highlands, xiii–xiv, xv, 1, 2, 12, 18, 51, 54, 95, 99, 155, 158, 187
Chew Mountains, 96, 100
Chu Lai, 12, 165
Civilian Irregular Defense Group (CIDG), 2
Clark, 2nd Lt. Charles J., 132
Clark Air Base, 172
Coleman, J. D., 3
Crandall, Maj. Bruce, 64
crashes:
  C-123 aircraft tail #40702, 21–23
  Cessna O-1E Bird Dog tail #56-2529, 184
  CH-54 Flying Crane tail #64-14204, 13
Custer, Lt. Col. George Armstrong, 6

Da Dan Mountains, 13, 23, 25, 28, 31, 52, 53, 60–62, 65, 75, 79–80, 83, 89–90, 92, 129
Da Nang, xii, 10, 12
Dam Tra O-Lake, 3, 18, 27, 177, 178
Diduryk, Capt. Myron, 25, 31, 38, 100, 111–14, 116–21
Distinguished Service Cross, 5, 6, 133, 205–7
Doan, Lt. Col. Dong (Viet Cong), 121, 125

Eagle's Claw, 92, 95–110, 121, 122, 156, 176
English, SP5 Carver J., 13, 80

Fesmire, Capt. John, 25, 32–33, 40–41, 49, 100, 101
Forrest, Capt. George, 90
Fort Benning, xiii, 5, 6, 111, 165
forward air controller (FAC), 25, 60, 63, 69, 76, 90, 103, 118, 120, 134, 170, 184
  and Iron Triangle, 145, 148
  and Phung Du, 43, 47, 52
French Groupement Mobile 100, 19
Fritz, Capt. Ed, 110

Galloway, Joseph L., 3
Gauthier, Lt., 116, 117
Gillem, Col. Richard (Dick), 180
Go Chai Mountains, 111, 112–14, 121–22, 125, 129–31, 167–77, 184
  and *Eagle's Claw*, 96, 97, 101–2, 104, 109
Golf Course, 157
Graves Registration, 22, 60, 63, 72, 76, 88, 139, 147, 149, 150, 184
  and Go Chai, 169, 171, 172
  and Phung Du, 52, 54, 55
Ground Reconnaissance Team (GRIT), 28
Guam, 80, 151
Gunderson, Mel, 128–29

Hackett, PFC Jim "Doc," 18–19, 35, 41, 49
Hammond, SFC Russell E., 14
harassment & interdiction (H&I) fire, 65, 76, 114, 146, 148, 150, 169
Highway 1, 1, 2, 3, 9, 10, 12, 13, 17, 24–26, 28, 31, 65, 72–73, 77, 81, 122, 169–70, 187
  and *Black Horse*, 177, 178
  and *Eagle's Claw*, 93, 97
  and Phung Du, 40, 52, 55–57
Hillyer, Lt., 116, 117, 118
Ho Chi Minh, 2
Ho Chi Minh Trail, 2, 18, 21, 95, 187, 190
Ho Son Mountains, 95, 102–3, 105, 112, 113, 121, 125
Hon Cong Mountain, 155–64
Huet, Henri, 21, 41

Ia Drang Valley, xiv–xv, 3, 6–7, 9, 11, 14, 90, 99, 111, 125
Ingram, Lt. Col. Earl, 43, 51, 65–70, 76–78, 81
Iron Triangle, 143–54, 173
    map, *142*

Jaramillo, Raul (Rudy), 50–51, 67, 78, 80, 137, 151
Johnson, Lt. Charles H., 132–33
Johnson, Lyndon B., xi, xii–xiii, 3, 5, 10, 86, 189–90

Kampe, Lt. Col. Raymond L., 17, 34, 52, 54, 59, 60, 63, 65
Kelly, 1st Lt. Jim "Lurch," 20, 36–37
Kim Son Valley, 18, 89, 92, 112–13, 122, 126, 137, 156, 167, 173, 176, 188–89
    and *Eagle's Claw*, 95–99, 102–5
    map, *94*
Kinnard, Maj. Gen. Harry W. O., xiv, 4–6, 81, 89, 92–93, 122, 156, 164–65, 168, 176, 177, 187
Klein, Capt. Stephen, 102–10, 112, 126, 168
Knox, 1st Lt. Dean, 50–51, 66, 68–69, 76–78, 91, 129, 136–37, 146, 151
Korean War, 6, 9, 21, 165

Landing Zones (LZ):
    2: 28, 31, 33
    4: 31–32, 34–5, 39–40, 43–44, 46, 48–56, 59, 60, 62, 63, 65, 68, 73–73, 75, 79, 81, 91
    Albany, 9, 90, 99
    Bird, 100–4, 107, 111, 112–14, 117–19, 121–22, 125, 136, 140, 143, 145–48, 150, 167, 169, 176
    Brass, 47, 55, 84–85
    Duck, 98–100, 122, 146, 153, 174, 179
    English, 13, 80, 83, 86, 88, 90–91, 98, 102, 106, 109, 112, 116–17, 135–36, 139, 169, 171–72, 175–76, 178, 184, 187
    Hammond, 8, 10, 14, 17, 47, 71–72, 187
    Jim, 91, 102
    Mike, 127–28, 134–35, 144–47, 149–50, 173
    Papa, 34, 39, 52, 61, 63–64, 73, 75–76, 129
    Pete, 127–28, 131–39, 143–46, 150, 152–53
    Pony, 98–101, 104–5, 109, 113–14, 121–22, 125, 127–30, 136–37, 140, 146, 151–53, 168, 170–74, 184
    Quebec, 61–62
    Romeo, 52, 54, 59, 61, 71–72, 91
    Saber, 102, 104, 105
    Sam, 146, 150–53
    Steel, 31, 34
    Tom, 71, 72
    Two Bits, 24
    X-Ray, 6, 9, 64, 99, 111
long-range patrol (LRP), 71–72
Lynch, Col. William R., Jr., 6, 83, 122, 126, 127, 136, 176
    and *Black Horse*, 177–79, 185
    and Iron Triangle, 146–47, 150–52, 154

McDade, Lt. Col. Robert, 8–9, 25, 99–101, 111, 117, 119, 121
    and Phung Du, 35, 38–41, 43, 49
McMahon, Capt. Robert W., 126, 128–32, 134–37
malaria, 7–8, 27, 132
Masher/White Wing, 164, 187–89, 191–92, 197
    Phase I, 99
    Phase II, 92
    Phase III (*Eagle's Claw*), 89, 96, 100, 121, 122, 156, 176
    Phase IV (*Black Horse*), 177–85
Matthews, CPL Bennie, 180–81
Mertel, Col. Kenneth D., 22–23
Meyer, Lt. Col. Edward "Shy," 89, 92, 129, 134, 143–44
Military Assistance Command, Vietnam (MACV), xi–xii, 4, 11, 26, 29, 80, 83, 187
Moore, Col. Harold, 6, 8–9, 12, 29, 61, 66, 72, 80–81, 83, 89, 112, 121, 155–56, 189
    and *Eagle's Claw*, 97, 99, 109
    and Phung Du, 31, 34, 43–44, 46–48

National Liberation Front, 2, 4, 115
North Vietnamese Army (NVA):
    Binh Tri Thien Division (325th Division), 18, 95
    18th NVA Regiment, 3, 17–18, 27, 93, 97, 169–70, 173, 177, 184
    22nd NVA Regiment, 3, 11, 34, 49, 72, 81, 83, 92, 99, 187–89

7th Battalion, 49, 169–70, 184, 187
8th Battalion, 9, 11, 83, 92, 187–88
9th Battalion, 34, 81, 99, 187

Objectives:
  Coil, 126–28, 131, 139–40, 144, 147, 171
  Recoil, 127, 131
O'Keefe, Lt. Donald, 132, 133–34
Operations:
  Clean House, 3
  Double Eagle, 10, 81, 93, 188
  Flying Tiger, 10, 17
  Masher, 4, 5, 9–10, 21, 56, 81, 83, 86, 193–96
  Thang Phong II, 10
  see also Masher/White Wing

Particelli, Lt. John, 116–17, 119
Pathfinders, 32, 179–80
Phu Cat, 2, 8, 97, 156
Phung Du, 3, 5, 10, 12, 21, 25–26, 28, 31, 33, 189
  cemetery, 37, 39, 43–57
  maps, *30, 74*
  Position Dog, 9, 13–14, 25, 27, 34–35, 37, 44, 47, 48, 50, 52–53, 55, 59, 61, 65, 76, 80
  Position George, 17
Pickup Zone Tango, 17–18
Piper, 2nd Lt. John, 107–8
Plei Me Special Forces Camp, xiv, 3, 11
Pleiku Campaign, 1–3, 11–13, 18–19, 51
Pleiku provinces, xiii–xiv, 1, 8, 18, 79, 95
Poos, Bob, 20–21, 41
Project Delta, 10–11, 29, 44–47, 83, 85, 87–88

Qui Nhon, xiii–xiv, 1–2, 5, 10, 24, 27, 42, 81, 156
Quigley, 1st Lt. George, 103, 106, 107, 108

Radcliffe, Maj. Donald G., 164–65
Republic of Korea (ROK) Capital "Tiger"
  Mechanized Infantry Division:
  3rd Battalion, 1st Regiment, xiii, 9, 187, 188
Roberts, Col. Elvy B., 121, 156, 168, 176, 189

Sanford, 1st Lt. Teddy, Jr., 79, 109, 110
Sao Vang (Yellow Star) Division (NVA) see
  North Vietnamese Army: 18th Regiment;
  22nd Regiment; Viet Cong: 2nd Regiment

Sherman, Lt. Keith, 132, 134
Skelly, Gerry, 32–33
Song Bien Valley, 125–26, 128–29, 131, 134–35, 136–38, 140, 143, 144, 146, 153, 162, 164, 170, 171, 173, 176
Soui Run Valley, 109, 117–21, 125, 176
Stephens, Lt. Rufus, 134, 207–8
Sugdinis, Capt. Joel E., 19–21, 23–24, 33–40, 64, 104, 162

Tactical Zones
  I Corps, 12, 29, 165
  II Corps, ix, 3, 12–13, 29, 85
Tay Nguyen (Western Highlands) Campaign, xiv
Tet Nguyen Dan (Vietnamese New Year), 3

United States Air Force (USAF):
  2nd Air Division, 26
  21st Tactical Air Support Squadron, 26, 184
  311th Air Commando Squadron, 192
  602nd Fighter Squadron, 26
U.S. Army (units):
  1st Cavalry Division (Airmobile), xii, xiv, xv, 5, 6, 205, 207
  1st Brigade, 84, 121–2, 156, 167–68, 173, 176, 185, 189
  2nd Brigade, 6, 13, 83, 84–89, 91–92, 122, 140, 151–53, 170, 173, 176, 177–78, 182–85
  3rd Brigade, 6–12, 17, 24–25, 27–29, 34, 42, 44, 46–47, 71–73, 81, 83–89, 92, 97, 99, 101, 105, 112–14, 121–22, 155–56, 167, 170, 189
  1st Battalion, 5th Cavalry Regiment, 72, 84, 87, 89–92, 127, 131, 139, 144, 146–47, 150–53, 171, 173, 174–75
  1st Battalion, 7th Cavalry Regiment, 6, 8–9, 17–18, 26–28, 34, 39, 47, 51–55, 59–62, 64–66, 73, 75–76, 80, 97, 101, 111, 121
  1st Battalion, 8th Cavalry Regiment, 22, 122, 167, 182–83, 185
  1st Battalion, 12th Cavalry Regiment, 8, 17, 47, 64, 71–73, 77–78, 84, 87, 97, 101–6, 109–10, 112, 122, 168–69, 171–73
  1st Battalion, 21st Artillery, 17, 118, 122
  1st Battalion, 30th Artillery, 85

1st Battalion, 77th Artillery, 139
2nd Battalion, 4th Marines Corps, 85
2nd Battalion, 5th Cavalry Regiment, 87, 89, 92, 127–29, 131, 133, 136–39, 143–44, 146–47, 150, 152–53, 173, 179–81, 183
2nd Battalion, 7th Cavalry Regiment, 9, 18–19, 21, 23, 25–26, 27–28, 31–32, 34, 38, 43–44, 46, 48–49, 53–54, 56, 65, 73, 75, 87, 97–98, 100–4, 111, 119, 121, 125, 162, 164
2nd Battalion, 8th Cavalry Regiment, 122, 171–73, 181–84, 185
2nd Battalion, 9th Marines Corps, 85, 87–88
2nd Battalion, 12th Cavalry Regiment, 43–44, 46–54, 65–73, 76–78, 81, 84–85, 87–88, 91–92, 112, 122, 129–31, 136–40, 143, 146–47, 150, 152–53, 171, 184
2nd Battalion, 17th Artillery Regiment, 99
2nd Battalion, 19th Artillery Regiment, 122
3rd Battalion, 18th Artillery Regiment, 98, 99
8th Engineers Battalion, 80, 139, 156
13th Signal Battalion, 125, 136, 156, 162, 164
15th Medical Battalion, 27
20th Artillery (ARA), 17, 24, 26, 28, 38, 47, 52, 59, 63, 66, 72, 77, 90–91, 98, 101–7, 113, 116, 118, 130, 135, 143–44, 148–49, 153, 170, 172, 174–75, 182–83
227th Assault Helicopter Battalion, 135, 136, 139, 143
228th Assault Support Helicopter Battalion, 39
229th Assault Helicopter Battalion, 26, 38
11th Pathfinder Company, 32, 179–80
1st Squadron, 9th Cavalry Regiment, 8–9, 17–18, 24, 26–29, 39, 47, 53, 60–61, 65–66, 78–80, 84–85, 87, 89–91, 97–98, 101–2, 104–5, 109, 113–14, 116–18, 121–22, 135, 138, 182, 184–85
see also Military Assistance Command, Vietnam; Project Delta

Viet Cong:
1st Viet Cong Main Force Regiment, 165
2nd Viet Cong Regiment, 4, 93, 114–16, 121, 125–26, 131, 139, 144, 146, 153–54, 168, 170–72, 176, 184, 188, 189
407th Viet Cong Main Force Battalion, 155, 158, 160, 163
Heavy Weapons Battalion, 139, *141*
D21 Viet Cong Local Force Company, 4, 27
2nd Main Force, 114, 126, 155, 158, 165
Viet Minh, 2, 19, 96, 147
Vietnamese Air Force (VNAF), xii
Vinh Thanh Mountains, 18, 96, 189
Vinh Thanh Valley, 18, 96

Wagner, PFC Jack, 22, 36–37
Westmoreland, Gen. William C., xii–xv, 1, 3–4, 11, 13, 86, 164, 187, 189–90
Wheeler, Gen. Earl G. "Bus," 86
Wright, Brig. Gen. John M., Jr., 165

Zeller, Al, 48, 50